BEFORE I SLEEP

A MEMOIR OF TRAVEL AND RECONCILIATION

We shall not cease from exploration
And the end of all our exploring
Will be to arrive where we started
And know the place for the first time.

—T.S. Eliot, *Four Quartets*

BEFORE I SLEEP

A MEMOIR OF TRAVEL AND RECONCILIATION

BY F. H. THURMOND

et alia press

LITTLE ROCK, ARKANSAS
2012

www.etaliapress.com

Published in the United States of America by
Et Alia Press
5001 Woodlawn Drive
Little Rock, AR 72205

ISBN: 978-0-982818-41-1
Library of Congress Control Number: 2012933909

Cover Design: Jesse Nickles
Interior text design: Angelia Northrip-Rivera

For Barbara and Russell Thurmond,
in gratitude for the journey.
And for being there.

CONTENTS

PART I—RITES OF PASSAGE

They fuck you up, your mum and dad.
They may not mean to, but they do.
They fill you with the faults they had,
And add some extra, just for you.

—Philip Larkin, "This Be The Verse"

THE CALL

After a dull grey morning of cold drizzle, the late afternoon sun had finally pierced the English clouds, revealing wisps of blue sky. A spring breeze scented with jasmine wafted through an open window, where sunlight transformed raindrops lining the panes into pearls of liquid silver. The light suffused my tiny student room with sudden warmth, and through the window across the desk I watched a moving grove of bright umbrellas transfigure into human faces along the street below.

I sat back in my chair and took a deep breath. The fresh air and sunlight seemed a welcome sign that a break from academic work was in order. The lowering clouds in the distance swirled above a row of red-bricked Victorian rooftops, reminding me of an engagement that evening: I was invited to a formal dinner and guest speaker reception following that night's debate at the student union. I laid out my dinner jacket on the bed. It badly needed pressing, but would do. The shirt was a different story, and I frowned upon seeing the red stain that had seeped over the fine fabric—an apt reprimand for taunting a closed door with a full glass of port. It was too late to have the shirt dry cleaned, so I'd have to keep my jacket buttoned and hope nobody noticed.

The phone suddenly rang like a herald. I absent-mindedly answered and felt pleased to hear my mother's voice, although surprised to hear it outside of our usual Sunday chat. But her voice revealed that something was not quite right. Something, in fact, that would completely transform my life.

After I hung up the phone, I sat back in a daze. On the walls of my room, the orange glimmer of sunset created a glowing patina of serrated light before fading with dusk to a dim, crimson glow. A drop of warm dampness upon my arm startled me. The tears in my eyes painted an impressionistic forest of blurry images.

When Brad found me at a table in the Gloucester Arms pub half an hour later, I was studying a shamrock drawn upon the creamy top of a cool thick pint of dark stout. He sat down across from me.

"You okay?"

I realized too late my face was streaked once more with tears, and my friend was taken aback. We'd known each other several years now, fellow Yanks at Oxford who had connected as being both from the South—with all its associated idiosyncrasies that few other compatriots seemed to appreciate.

"I just heard from my father." I hardly spoke the words before I found it difficult to go on. "I think I told you once that I never knew him."

Brad nodded thoughtfully. "Yes, I remember your mentioning that."

"Not since I was three years old at least, when he left." I paused again to regain composure. As I struggled to express my predicament, I felt a profound sense of gratitude just for having a friend there to listen. I drank a deep sip of beer, savoring its cool, bitter taste.

"My mother called to say she'd heard from him. Or from his family, rather. They said my father's on his death bed, dying of lung cancer. The doctor says he's got less than a week to live, and now he wants to speak with me before he dies."

I had told my mother that I would accept my father's call. She said they had asked about the time difference and when would be the best time for him to call me, and I asked her to set the time for three in the afternoon the next day.

"You have to go see him," Brad said.

"What?"

"You should get on the next flight home to the States and meet your father before he dies. You'll always regret it if you don't."

I told him I had already suggested this to my mother, but she was adamant that I should not do so. She wondered why I should fly across the ocean to meet a father who, as it turned out, had spent the last three decades just up the road from where I grew up without making any effort to contact me. That point so angered me that any desire to meet this permanently absent biological father—apart from a quick chat by phone for the sake of closure—felt completely removed.

Brad was insistent that I should meet my birth father. He explained that not doing so when I had this one chance would haunt me for the rest of my life. And he was speaking from experience, having lost his own father prematurely. He said the only way I could ever confront the lifelong sense of emptiness I had endured was to finally meet, just once before he died, the father I had never known. This was the only way I might achieve a true sense of closure.

What Brad said made sense. But why hadn't my mother seen it this way? And would my hitherto unknown birth father even care to meet *me*? After all, my mother had a point: He had never shown any interest in me whatsoever. (Not that I yet knew of, at least.) I also understood in my heart that if I suggested a meeting to him on the phone and he refused, the angst of rejection I'd felt my entire life might become unbearable.

That night we went to the college bar, where other students exhorted me to book the next flight home—including one young man who described once having a similar choice: He likewise had the opportunity to meet the birth father he'd never known, but failed to do so before it was too late. He was now consumed with regret that would last a lifetime. "Do not," he said to me, "make the same mistake." It occurred to me that meeting these kindred spirits on this fateful day, with the gift of their insightful advice based on hard experience, made my path clear. By the end of the evening I had made my decision. I would travel home to meet my father.

The next day remains a blur. I remember only the anxious minutes before the appointed hour of the call. It was a fine May afternoon, the kind of day that makes a whole year's worth of English weather worth the wait. I walked down the street to a small park in Wellington Square and sat in the grass beneath an enormous old oak.

I looked at my watch. Forty-five minutes. In forty-five minutes, the phone on my desk would be ringing, and on the other end of the line would be the voice of my father. A voice I had never known in my conscious life. What would it sound like? What would he say? What would *I* say? These were questions that must have been buried within me my whole lifetime up to that very moment—along with the ever-haunting question of his absence. Everything else that had preoccupied my mind only a day earlier, before my mother's call, had vanished. It was as if all my daily concerns, the day to day reality that normally seemed so damned important, had melted away in the mists of memory. Memories of earliest childhood, long forgotten, flooded my mind, as a lifetime of experiences flashed before my mind's eye like the fabled moment of death.

In the park, the summer roses were in full bloom. I walked over to a rose bush and inhaled, slowly, deeply and deliberately, its pungent sweetness. As I bent down and smelled each rose in turn, their redolence transported me to a place nearly forgotten outside of dreams.

1

BEGINNINGS

At first the infant,
Mewling and puking in the nurse's arms.

—Shakespeare, *As You Like It*

In Stamps the custom was to can everything that could possibly
be preserved. . .There were choices on the shelves that could set a
hungry child's mouth to watering. Green beans . . . collards, cabbage,
juicy red tomato preserves that came into their own on steaming
buttered biscuits, and sausage, beets, berries and every fruit grown
in Arkansas.

—Maya Angelou, *I Know Why The Caged Bird Sings*

Sunlight streamed through parting clouds after a heavy rain, and
the humid summer air hung thick beneath a sprawling old live
oak. From below, its leaves glistened like emerald stars illuminating a
green sky. The tree's gnarled roots seemed magical, grasping outward
from the trunk like tentacles, their crevices now filled with rainwater
that I imagined as tiny oceans filled with fish. And that reminded me
that my cousin had promised to take me fishing down at the pond as
soon as the storm broke.

The sound of clippers stirred me from my reverie, and I looked to
see my grandmother resuming her work in the garden. She was prun-
ing the rose bushes. I ran over to her, delighting in the flowers' radiant
colors after the rain: pink, white, yellow and scarlet red, all dripping
with the sunlit sparkle of rainwater. I pulled a rose toward me and in-

haled the sweet scent. From beneath her old wide-brimmed straw hat, my grandmother's eyes glanced quickly at me with a look of concern.

"Now you be careful of those thorns, they're sharper than they look."

"Yes, ma'am," I answered perfunctorily, carefully allowing my hand to move backward with the stem until it found a smooth place between two thorns. My grandmother hadn't missed a beat, remaining engrossed in her gardening. She had moved over to the next rose bush, oblivious to the iridescent halo of butterflies flitting among the flowers.

I watched her curiously, always fascinated by her solemn work ethic. "Where's Mama?"

"She'll be home directly, I reckon." My grandmother remained a study in concentration as she carefully trimmed another rose bush like a sculptor. It was clear that this was the best answer I was going to get today, so I ran to the swing in the front yard. A window air-conditioning unit whirred to life, and I knew my grandfather must be up from his nap. I excitedly jumped from the swing and ran across the yard as fast as my three year old legs would carry me, up the wooden front steps and into the front hall of the old house. The living room door was closed to seal in the precious cool air, and I could already hear my grandfather inside tapping his pipe on the glass ashtray. I opened the door and enjoyed the sensation of feeling the stuffy heat of the hall mix with the frigid cold air streaming from the air conditioner. In the living room, my grandfather had just settled into his new reclining chair by the window, and as usual focused immediately on filling his pipe from a small red tin of Prince Albert tobacco.

In the thin sliver of natural light slanting through the window, a galaxy of dust motes orbited my grandfather's face. They vanished suddenly as he switched on the lamp.

"Hey, buddy!" he mumbled affably upon seeing me, holding the pipe stem to his mouth with one hand while lighting a wooden match with the other. After a few puffs the tobacco in his pipe glowed crimson, as several sparks flew off in various directions—the sort of sparks that had, to my grandmother's chagrin, left burn marks on the furniture and floors, and that would one day set the whole house ablaze, burning it completely to the ground along with everything in it.

I sat contentedly on the old red couch next to my grandfather in his chair, savoring the smell of his tobacco and the gentle hum of the air conditioner. I still wasn't sure where my mother was, but here inside with my grandfather, I felt safe.

In my earliest memory, I am sitting on the floor playing with toys while my mother and father talk on the couch. I cannot recall their faces. I'm dimly aware that they are speaking about me, although I don't understand what they are saying. There is a perceptible tension between them. My father gets up, hands me a toy, and leaves. I've tried ever since to recall his face. (Despite an extensive photo album chronicling these first years, my mother at some point removed every photograph depicting my father—or had otherwise ripped his image out of the picture.)

Another irrepressible image is that of a window, through which I am looking out at city lights twinkling amid darkness. The memory comes with a hint of fear, as if I'm aware of circumstances that are unsettled, changing. I am confined in the crib, feeling trapped within its wooden bars, crying desperately for help that does not come. I have ever since found myself staring through similar windows, dreaming of some other place where happiness might exist if I could only escape there.

These early memories are from Paragould, Arkansas, where I was born on a rainy 23rd of April, the significance of which date I would later appreciate as a student of literature. The year was 1967, the so-called "Summer of Love." My newborn ears would have picked up from the airwaves some of the innovative music of the period, including the unique rhythms and magical harmonies of an album released that June called *Sergeant Pepper's Lonely Hearts Club Band*. I remember the impression made upon me several years later on the day my mother commented that "The Beatles have just broken up." And I recall that despite her attempt to explain the meaning of this momentous occasion, I pictured instead a group of coleopterans scurrying madly away in every direction, in contrast to the group of young Liverpudlians for whom my appreciation would one day, many years hence, prove redemptive.

Paragould is a small northeast Arkansas town near the Mississippi River delta, not very far from Memphis, and named after two rival 19th century railroad tycoons, Colonel J.W. Paramore and notorious robber baron Jay Gould. It is near Piggott, Arkansas, which I later discovered was the occasional home of Ernest Hemingway where he often stayed with second wife Pauline Pfeiffer and her family. Here, Hemingway drafted much of *A Farewell to Arms*, along with numerous short stories. The beautiful antebellum house has now been converted into a museum, including the backyard barn converted by the Pfeiffers into a studio for Hemingway, with some of his possessions—including his writing desk—still in place. Hemingway enjoyed the many woods and streams in the Ozark Mountain foothills, traveling throughout the region on hunting and fishing excursions. The locals were, however, rather unimpressed with (and even frightened of) him, with old-timers recalling Hemingway as being particularly unkempt, irascible and intoxicated.

Paragould was the main commercial and banking center in the area, and Hemingway's mother-in-law, a devout German Catholic, traveled there by train to attend Mass. (I would later learn that my paternal grandfather, Cecil Mitchell, was a prominent Paragould banker who became president of the region's main bank.)

My own sojourn in Paragould, however, would be quite brief. But I always recalled, particularly in a recurrent dream throughout childhood, the distinctive architecture of our house there with its white stucco exterior and red clay tile roof. It would be decades before I ever saw this town and house again. By the time I was three, my parents had split. Exactly why would remain a haunting question until that fateful phone call years later. But for then, life was taking what would prove to be only the first of many twists and turns.

After her separation, my mother returned with me to her parents' home in southeast Arkansas, where they lived on a rural farm close to the Louisiana line. The farm, set amidst the flat pastures and cotton fields of the southern Delta, was near the small town of Crossett, founded in the 1890s by lumbermen investors from Iowa (including the town's namesake, Edward Crossett) seeking to exploit the vast forests of the lower Mississippi River valley. The town was built around the new Crossett Lumber Company's sawmill, and has remained a regional forestry center ever since. My mother's ancestors had farmed the arable land of this region, and throughout the South, for generations.

Like her father before her, my mother attended Crossett High School, which, thanks to the support of the paper company, was well-endowed (exceptionally for the region) with quality teachers, facilities and educational opportunities, and where she made a number of life-long friends. One of her schoolmates and friends—and an occasional visitor to the Hancock house—was a young man named Barry Switzer, the son of a local bootlegger. (Ashley County was then and remains today a "dry" county.) Barry was a Crossett High football star who would go on to become a national figure as a college football Hall of Famer and Superbowl-winning NFL coach.

Now, as a single mother with no other place to go, my mother's parents welcomed the two of us on their farm, where my earliest memories and experiences would be forged in the pastures, woods and bayous in this sleepy corner of the rural South.

As I recollect life on my grandparents' farm at the start of the 1970s, I realize I experienced an almost frontier way of life, with my grandparents living off the land in the same way their ancestors had done for generations. The old, white wooden house itself was over a hundred years old, of the type described by Switzer—in his memoir *Bootlegger's Boy* (1990)—as a "shotgun house," so called because its rooms were on two sides of a large middle hallway, through which one could shoot a shotgun straight through from front to back without hitting anything (or hopefully anyone) inside.

Childhood in Crossett would prove a magical place, not just in those earliest years but throughout school and even college. I was very fortunate that my grandparents, though already elderly when I was born, were blessed with exceptionally long lives. My grandfather in particular retained a strong mind and clear memory to the end of his 97 years. Long after leaving, Crossett always remained a place of refuge, a place to reconnect with nature and self, and to reflect.

There was a small pond at the edge of the pasture, and I would take one of my grandfather's cane fishing poles there, along with a jar full of worms painstakingly unearthed from the moist soil under the bricks lining my grandmother's garden. When I had cast the line out as far into the deep center of the pond as possible, I'd watch the plastic bobber float on the murky brown water, hoping for a bite while listening to the orchestra of nature conjure up a symphony of birdsong, bullfrogs and cicadas; curious dragonflies always buzzed around the tip of my pole until one finally landed there and stared towards me with unearthly eyes.

I'd often forget the fish for a while and slip into some daydream as I stared into the water reflecting trees and blue sky, listening to the sough of leaves in the branches above. Gusts of wind created flotillas of ripples across the pond. Then, with a telltale *plop*, the bobber would plunge beneath the surface, as I scrambled to grab the pole before some monster of the depths dragged it out of reach into the water.

The taut line would pull the pole into a desperate arch as I drew it back high into the air to drag out the fish. I knew too well the line could snap if I pulled back too abruptly. I never forgot "the one that got away," when for days I could only stand on the bank and watch in despair as the bobber on its severed line surfaced and submerged all around the pond. I knew this must have been a catfish or even an alligator gar, because only they fought with the fierce voracity I could feel in the tug that pulsed through the cane. The trick was to let it fight itself out, until I could safely pull it into the shallows and finally haul it ashore to admire the sleek, slimy, body beyond its gaping mouth. I could already smell it cooking that evening in my grandmother's sizzling skillet.

Sometimes in my scramble to pull in a large fish I would forget to watch my step. The pond could be a dangerous place, especially in the summer months when birds and bullfrogs weren't the only creatures enjoying the local ecosystem. The place was often seething with water moccasins, a particularly poisonous type of pit viper indigenous to southern swampland. They are as lethal as their rattlesnake cousin (also a local resident), though without the courtesy of a warning rattle before striking. They can be difficult to see, too, with their pale grey skin camouflaged with dark spots, the slough of which often hung from nearby branches as a reminder that you needed to watch your head as well as your feet. Once, when I was sitting on the bank fishing, I heard a branch snap and looked up just in time to see a snake dangling above me and preparing to drop right on my head! At other times, one occasionally slithered across the water in my direction while I was fishing, looking like a moving letter **S** gliding across the pond's surface.

One day when I was around seven, however, I came prepared for battle, toting my grandmother's sharp-edged garden hoe with me to the pond. I later gave my family a terrible fright when I proudly returned with the longest serpent I'd ever encountered draped across the outstretched hoe, its mangled body oozing bloody slime. My grandmother ran out in shock, and it didn't help when I narrated my close call with the snake—which I'd only noticed after nearly stepping on it, managing to nail it across the neck with the blade just as it was poised to strike.

With such backyard perils it's not surprising that my grandmother worried unceasingly about my whereabouts, or that she especially loathed the pond and feared for my safety there. My private natural paradise was for my grandmother an infernal den of vipers. Whenever she knew I was there, it wouldn't be long before I would hear echoing across the fields the back porch screen door slamming shut, and my grandmother's voice calling with such volume as to belie her small frame.

"Fraaaank!"

"Whaaat?"

"C'mon!"

I would try to shout back a request for more time, but invariably the door would slam shut again and I knew I'd better head back. De-

spite her benign grandmotherly nature, Mama Doris had on occasion
been known to create a switch out of a small bush or vine and threaten
to give me a *whippin'*. This had never actually happened, as I'd always
managed to escape inside before incurring the threatened corporal
punishment. Still, I was never certain whether or not she was bluffing,
and fortunately always thought better of pushing my luck with this
gentle but hardy daughter of pioneers.

I often found myself put to work with garden and farm chores. This
included helping gather freshly fallen apples, pears and plums in the
orchard before the worms got them, or standing precariously on a ladder picking peaches. From these Mama Doris would make delicious
cobblers, before canning others with a little sugar and freezing them,
providing a wonderful treat each hot summer when I could thaw them
out as a cold sweet snack. Then there were the crabapple trees, whose
pink spring blossoms inevitably gave way to bushels of small round
bitter fruit which Mama Doris would turn into a sweet jelly that would
make breakfast toast and her homemade biscuits a year-round sump-
tuous delicacy. In the garden I helped pick the bright red strawberries
in summer, which she likewise turned into exquisite preserves.

I also helped pick the tomatoes, peas, beans and corn my grandparents painstakingly planted and tended. And I was always extra wary
after once, in the cornfield, nearly setting my hand directly on top of a
small but sinister-looking spider, pitch-black apart from the gleaming
scarlet hourglass on its belly that put the fear in me. But after the picking was done, I knew the real work would begin: sitting on the back
porch for hours shucking the corn and shelling the peas, a seemingly
Sisyphean task as each filled tub of purple hull peas, string beans or
butterbeans would be replenished with yet another. It would be worth
all the work later when I was sopping up my supper plate with homemade corn bread.

My favorite task was helping with the livestock. This included
walking with Mama Doris each afternoon to the chicken yard to feed
the chickens and gather the eggs, when the hens and roosters, clucking
excitedly, would come scurrying from around the yard and out of the
large wooden henhouse as Mama Doris scattered leftover vegetables
and cornbread over the ground. Inside the henhouse, she held an old
metal pail as I reached into each nest and gently gathered the eggs. I
always felt a sense of awe at the way each day these eggs would somehow magically appear. Occasionally, one would break in my excitement
to fill the pail, bringing an instant sense of guilt with the perception

that here on their farm even a simple egg was of precious value to my grandparents.

I always found the whole process with the chickens a mystifying cycle: One day a new generation of just-hatched Leghorn chicks would arrive, their soft peeping converting the incubator into a yellow-feathered music box. Then in a matter of months these pullets ("leg-guns," as my grandparents called them) would be running carefree in their yard, soon as hens laying a steady supply of tasty eggs. Yet I knew in time that it would be the fate of each chicken to wind up at the chopping block in the barn, where Daddy Frank would—like some medieval executioner—bring his axe down upon the neck of the poor creature, whose body I would watch with intrigued horror as it ran headless away across the yard.

My greatest pleasure came late in the afternoon after Daddy Frank's nap, when I would accompany him to the barn. The moment he unbolted the latch of the barnyard gate, a loud burst of porcine grunts would break out from around the barn shed. There in the pigpen the hogs sensed it was feeding time, and as we slopped them with a hodgepodge mush of discarded leftovers, they clamored around us with frenzied zeal, squealing indifferently despite Daddy Frank's invective-laden shouting and attempts to shoo them off with his cane. In my young imagination their pointed snouts seemed twisted into perpetual grins, as if mocking their pork chop destinies.

After he filled the rusty troughs with fresh water, we would feed the cows and goats, the latter seeming to realize that good things always happened whenever I was present. I joyfully fed them by hand, delighting as they swarmed around braying for a chance to snatch a few pellets from my outstretched palm. Finally, at sundown, I would join Daddy Frank in the chicken yard, where our task was to coax the chickens down from the trees and onto their roosts in the henhouse for the night—safe from the villainous polecats.

Summer's best activity by far was going with Daddy Frank to the watermelon patch and thumping the largest melons until he determined the most ripe. I and various cousins would then gather ritually around a table under the backyard oak, where Daddy Frank would carve up each day's sacrificial melon as a cool treat on sultry July afternoons.

Each season brought striking changes, each with its own beauty—and peril—for denizens of the Delta landscape. In addition to the ever-present threat of flooding, conversely (and equally devastating) were the summer droughts. Prolonged stints of intense, mosquito-laden heat and no rain wreaked havoc on my grandfather's crops, and I

often watched with helplessness the growing anxiety in my grandparents' eyes as they surveyed wilting stalks of corn or dry, worm-ravaged
tomatoes. Winters could be equally harsh. Despite the beauty of crisp,
bright mornings sparkling with silver frost, temperatures might suddenly drop well below freezing on dark nights full of sleet, covering
the landscape in thick layers of ice. The land became eerily quiet, with
every flower, tree branch and even blade of grass encased in a shell of
ice, rendered so brittle that a large branch might snap and fall without
warning. Icicles hung like daggers from the roof of the house. And
sometimes an entire tree might suddenly fall in a gust of wind, hitting a house or a car or bringing down a power line and knocking out
electricity for days.

Warmth came from the fireplace in the living room, and I would
help Daddy Frank bring in the firewood that he had carefully chopped
and piled by the well. Often the wet wood was slow to start, as I stood
shivering in the living room watching my breath fog up the frosted
windows. At night I would shiver under the eloquent handmade quilts
painstakingly woven by Mama Doris on her antique, pedal-operated
Singer sewing machine in the hall. But each morning she would slip
quietly into the bedroom and light the old gas heater, whose flames lit
up the room with a warm, bluish light. The sound of the gas quietly
sighing through the pipes was relaxing as I waited for the room to
warm up enough to slip out of bed; then I'd rush through the cold hall
to try to beat Daddy Frank to the house's sole bathroom. From the
kitchen always came the scent of bacon and eggs sizzling in Mama
Doris' skillet atop the old gas stove. Over breakfast, the way Daddy
Frank drank his coffee intrigued me: He'd pour it into his saucer and
swirl it around a few times to cool the coffee before sipping it straight
from the saucer. I later learned this was a habit he picked up in the
World War I trenches, where doughboys had little time to get their
morning coffee down before battle.

Finally the harshness of winter would give way to a glorious
spring, when my grandmother's tulips appeared like magic around the
yard. And all around the old white house the bare branches of trees
erupted into flowering cascades of white dogwood, pungent magnolia,
pink crape myrtle and the sweet perfume of crabapple blossoms. At
sunset I'd sit on the front porch, listening to the cicadas' song rise from
quiet hum to fever pitch before, like the dying oscillations of some
unseen engine, softly fade to silence before repeating the cycle. As sunlight faded to twilight the stars appeared through high oak branches,
and on the darkest nights they would illuminate the sky so densely I
imagined they were clumps of low-hanging diamonds a giant might

scoop up into the palm of his hand. Or else they were pinpricks in some black cosmic canvas spread over the sky, through which a radiant light shone from the heavens beyond.

On bright mornings sparkling with dew I'd help Daddy Frank till the fields, sitting atop the old mare, Ginger, and guiding her with the reins as she pulled the rusty iron plow across the ground. Meanwhile

Crossett, Arkansas, Summer 1970

Mama Doris would arrive with packets of seed, which I'd help her plant in the garden in anticipation of summer flowers.

Autumn was my favorite season, best expressed by John Keats as the "Season of mists and mellow fruitfulness." Keats evocatively describes the season in his poem "To Autumn," in words that capture very pertinently the autumnal atmosphere of south Arkansas:

> Where are the songs of spring? Ay, where are they?
> Think not of them, thou hast thy music too—
> While barréd clouds bloom the soft-dying day,
> And touch the stubble-plains with rosy hue;
> Then in a wailful choir the small gnats mourn

Among the river sallows, borne aloft
Or sinking as the light wind lives or dies;
And full grown lambs loud bleat from hilly bourn;
Hedge crickets sing; and now with treble soft
The redbreast whistles from a garden-croft;
And gathering swallows twitter in the skies.

A crowing rooster heralded each new day's resurrection with golden mornings of amber-tinted light. Something within my young soul responded to the season's restless melancholy, a feeling that in later years transformed to almost unbearable nostalgia whenever I caught a taste of that same autumn air, calling me home to those dusty country roads roofed with yellow boughs.

Then one day my mother, now living in the old back room of her youth, said we would soon be moving far away to a place called "Little Rock." I wondered why in the world we'd want to leave the farm behind for some strange place with only a rock. I panicked, begging Mama Doris to let me stay with her and Daddy Frank in Crossett. Despite my protests and attempts to hide from my mother, she, I and our new poodle dog (aptly named "Trouble") climbed one day into Mom's old green Chevrolet and headed north.

Before we left, Daddy Frank gave me a parting gift: a real Stetson hat. I put it on and felt like a true cowboy as we headed into the unknown.

With Daddy Frank, May 1969

2

La Petite Roche

It was late 1970 when we moved to Little Rock and settled at the Rivercliff Apartments, so named because their hilltop setting gave a sweeping view of the Arkansas River valley winding ribbon-like past the city's downtown. We lived right at the point of the river where the landscape began its gradual shift from the flat landscape and cotton fields of the Arkansas Delta region into the foothills and forests of the Ozark Mountains that roll across northern Arkansas and southern Missouri. It was at this point on the river that early French pioneers found the river shallow enough to ford the river with horses and supplies as they colonized the region in the 18th century. The way these explorers mapped the spot was by noting two distinct bluffs that rose above the river as it wound northwards into the hills. The further bluff, a large granite cliff which rose high above the water as the first significant feature of the changing landscape and beyond which the river was too deep to ford, they dubbed "La Grande Roche" ("The Big Rock"). The lower bluff, marking the best point to cross the river, was hence named "La Petite Roche." It was here that they founded a permanent settlement by the river, later Anglicized as "Little Rock" for what would eventually become the state's capital city. (The name "Arkansas" comes from a French phonetic approximation of the name of an indigenous Native American tribe originally inhabiting the territory, meaning "the downstream people.")

Here my mother hoped her training and experience as an English teacher might land her a job at a local high school, but in the meantime she had just enough money from alimony payments to pay the rent for our tiny apartment and cover basic living expenses. She also managed to enroll me as a pre-schooler in the new Little Rock Montessori

School. The Montessori system, with its focus on imaginative visual and kinetic learning techniques, has since become a highly successful institution worldwide, but at that time it was clearly a daring move on the part of my mother—not to mention the financial sacrifice this meant—and her faith in the program allowed me to get an early educational experience that would prove seminal in ways that she could not then have guessed.

From a purely social viewpoint, the opportunity to learn and play with a truly diverse group of children was probably one of the most important experiences of my life, particularly given that the time and place in which I lived—Little Rock only thirteen years past the Central High "Little Rock Nine" integration crisis of 1957—was an otherwise unlikely locale for experiencing racial harmony. Yet from my earliest memories I counted among my best friends not only children who were black but also international kids—including a boy named Althoff whose family had moved to Little Rock from India at a time when there were few "outsiders" to be found in the area. At the same time, my first teacher, Miss Francis—a large and buoyantly enthusiastic woman whom I still remember fondly as a truly positive influence during my pre-school and kindergarten years—was a Native American, in a place where sadly very few of our original residents still lived in their native environs. And my friendship with a little girl named Sarah during those early years has stood the test of time, as both she and her beloved father, Sam, became lifelong friends.

Along with this unique diversity at school, my chief entertainment at home was provided by the new children's program on public broadcasting called *Sesame Street*. This was a groundbreaking series, especially in the way it brought together for the first time a multiracial cast and group of children that in their diversity represented the melting pot of contemporary America—not to mention throwing into the mix a lively bunch of Muppets of every size, shape and color imaginable, who created real magic in their interactions and teachable moments featuring people as wonderful as the young Bill Cosby (whom I recall clearly as a favorite guest on both *Sesame Street* and *The Electric Company*—not to mention the cartoon *Fat Albert*). It was without a doubt that through this parallel experience of diversity, both at school and at home, I was instilled as a child with the gift of 'color blindness'. This foundation was strong enough to outlast the gross realities of racial prejudice and hatred of *the other* that I would be forced to learn about the hard way, when various friends and family members eventually revealed their own true colors and I had to confront headlong the reality of bigotry, with all its undercurrents of fear, ignorance and petty self-righteousness. I'd also have the opportunity later to benefit from extensive travel abroad, the enormous benefits of which were expressed so well by Mark Twain: "Travel is fatal to prejudice, bigotry, and narrow-mindedness. Broad, wholesome, charitable views cannot be acquired by vegetating in one little corner of the earth all one's lifetime."

While our new life in Little Rock proved a delightful time for me, I was oblivious to what must have been a truly difficult time for my mother: Her resources were stretched as thin as they could go to support us, and she must have felt lonely and isolated as a single mother in that tiny apartment with only a young child and a poodle dog named Trouble for company. Eventually, however, she befriended a woman who shared the same floor and who happened to know of an eligible bachelor. This neighbor succeeded in making the match, and soon my mother was dating the gentleman whom she would ultimately marry.

Russell Thurmond was the son of local businessman Frank Thurmond, a scion of the East Coast family of the same surname best known for a rather long-lived (and somewhat notorious) United States senator. Frank Thurmond helped establish what would become one of the leading investment firms in the region, and he and his wife, Francis, lived in a fashionable area of town in an impressive house on Sunset Drive overlooking the river. It was certainly a welcome step for my mother from obscurity to local society, and we moved from the apartment to a small rented house on Deerbrook Road in what was then an area of suburban development to the west of downtown Little Rock.

Russell immediately made an heroic effort to put on a father's hat and treat me every bit as his own son, and I thus had the good fortune to experience the things a young boy needs from a father—everything from my first bike (and lessons for riding it) to my first baseball mitt and the chance to play on a "tee ball" team following backyard practice sessions learning to swing a bat. One morning my mother approached me as I was playing on the patio and suggested that, instead of "Russell," I start calling him "Dad." She explained that he wanted to adopt me as his own son, if I would be willing to consider him as my father. I can't recall how I responded, or if I even pointed out that I vaguely remembered some other guy having previously answered to that title. But I do know that I soon willingly and naturally called Russell "Dad." Not long afterward, my surname was changed from "Frank Reiff Mitchell" to "Frank Hancock Thurmond," thus by chance letting me share a name with my new grandfather Frank Thurmond ("Pop") as well as "Daddy Frank" Hancock. Half of my identity was now in effect suddenly erased with the stroke of a pen, and for much of my life I even forgot altogether that I'd ever been fathered by someone else.

Someone who was living, as I much later discovered, only a few miles up the road.

Life on Deerbrook Road remains a special place in childhood memory and a time of discovery. There were a number of other children of similar age in the neighborhood, so for the first time I now had companionship with other kids outside of school. My first true cultural "adventure" occurred here as well: Althoff and his family lived down the street, and entering their house was like crossing the threshold into another world—one filled with the pungent aroma of spicy curry and incense, and decorated with the symbolic art of Hinduism. Despite my mother's general open-mindedness, I'll never forget her face when she came looking for me and found me seated cross-legged on the floor enjoying curried rice with Althoff and his family. Something about this scene was beyond her experience and clearly frightened her, and after scolding me for being there, she marched me home in anger. But perhaps this early experience lends explanation to my keen fascination later in life with Eastern cultures and religions.

My imagination was particularly fired at that time by the spectacular Apollo rocket launches. There could be few spectacles more exciting for a young boy than to watch a live countdown as the count wound down to zero and, its giant thrusters igniting in a swirl of fire and smoke, the manned Saturn rocket slowly lifted miraculously from the ground as the announcer shouted "We have liftoff!" Then I would munch my breakfast Fruit Loops cereal anxiously as the rocket hurtled into the deep blue Florida sky, until vanishing beyond sight on its way to the moon. Like so many children of my generation, I had decided that I would be an astronaut when I grew up, a desire fed further when, during a trip to Disney World in Florida, we visited the Kennedy Space Center and I was able to see the spent parts of actual rockets and lunar landing modules, along with moon rocks recently returned to earth by Apollo astronauts.

I would have been heartbroken to learn that I was seeing the space program at its best, and that manned missions beyond our planet's immediate low orbit would cease and forty years later we would still be trying to get back.

Our time at Deerbrook came to an abrupt end when my mother explained one day that we would be moving to a place called Garfield Street across town. I could not at first understand why and recall getting terribly distressed over leaving what had become a beloved neighborhood full of new friends. But the moving truck arrived, and though I never saw any of my friends there again, I would soon be surprised with an even bigger change.

Our new house was on a dead-end street bordered by woods, through which a creek trickled. Under every creek rock seemed to lurk a pincer-wielding crawdad. (A more threatening discovery under land-based rocks in the woods might be a large, hairy tarantula, or even a scorpion, its back covered with crawling young beneath the guard of their mother's arched tail with its deadly sting.) Sometimes other creatures from the woods, such as raccoons or possums, would pay unwelcome nocturnal visits, rummaging around outside and some nights peering through the window with eyes gleaming in the dark.

The backyard of the house proved a wonderful place to play, including a large patio surrounded by a wooden fence covered with sweet-scented wisteria. I was especially fond of the large knotted pine tree in the backyard, with its high branches for climbing. This came with its own set of perils too, including a surly blue jay which once, after I inadvertently approached her nest, attacked me so fiercely I had to jump for my life and run inside with a bleeding scalp where she had pecked me. There was also a fig tree there, which allowed my parents to instill within me an entrepreneurial spirit by encouraging me to pick the ripest figs and sell them to a local market. I did the work with joy, and was overwhelmed when the proprietor of Terry's Market handed me a twenty dollar bill for the basket of fruit I'd brought.

The house was noticeably larger with three bedrooms, although I still had no idea why we'd moved there. In time, my mother explained that I would soon have a sibling, and as her pregnancy progressed I was mystified to feel a child kicking inside her belly. I also noticed with some degree of trepidation all the preparations now being made in advance of the baby's arrival: The middle room was being specially decorated, a baby crib was brought in, and baby toys were assembled. So it was with a sense of relief that I found myself sent to Crossett for an extended visit alone with my grandparents. But when I returned to Little Rock, everything had changed.

Upon entering my room, I was delighted to find a large and beautifully wrapped present waiting for me—though perplexed too, given it was neither Christmas nor my birthday. I eagerly unwrapped it to find my dream gift inside: a toy race car set, complete with a track and an assortment of cool race cars. Perhaps, I thought, it's all still about me after all!

But it wasn't. I had a new little sister. The middle room became the center of attention, and—as with any first-born—this would take some getting used to. And yet, looking back, I'm all the more appreciative for the way Dad continued his fatherly devotion toward me as well. I was reminded of this when I recently returned to the house on Garfield and found, still thriving there in the front yard, the same colorful little tree—a Japanese dwarf maple—that he helped me plant all those years ago to fulfill a Cub Scout project. One incident in particular won my undivided respect. One day I went out to find a man with a large net chasing Trouble in the front yard. The white truck idling in front of our yard indicated he was from the animal shelter, and this professional dogcatcher was running through our own front yard attempting to catch our dog. I shouted at him to no avail, telling him to leave Trouble alone, when Dad came out and gave the man hell. I had never felt more relieved or happier than when Dad chased the man away, and I had my little dog safe in my arms again. For some time afterwards, I would have a recurring nightmare involving "mean men" coming after both me and my dog.

Despite his father's own success, life for Dad had not been easy. Before meeting my mother, he held a string of odd jobs, including as a substitute math teacher at a local junior high school. He also struggled with alcoholism, until my mother finally convinced him to get help and quit, and he managed to stay completely sober for twenty-five years. She also encouraged him to study for a state real estate license, which allowed him eventually to move into a managerial position with a local company. In the meantime, both he and my mother continued to teach part-time in the effort to keep food on the table and provide me and my sister Kate with a comfortable home and decent education.

And education suddenly became a key issue. One of my teachers at Montessori must have noticed something anomalous in my schoolwork, because I found myself undergoing an extensive series of tests that I still recall as quite an intimidating affair. The end result was that I was diagnosed with the learning disorder known as dyslexia. What this meant, according to the specialist who explained the diagnosis to my parents, was that my chance of ever being able to read and write properly was minimal at best.

3

INNOCENCE LOST

Then the whining schoolboy with his satchel
And shining morning face, creeping like snail
Unwillingly to school.

—Shakespeare, *As You Like It*

My parents were referred to a special school at the University of
Arkansas for Medical Sciences (UAMS) called the Child Study
Center. In the early 1970s, new research on dyslexia linked the disorder with defects in phonological processing, and clinics such as the
Child Study Center utilized these findings with experimental peda-
gogical techniques for teaching reading to primary school children.
The program also incorporated psychiatric counseling to assist children through the often painful frustrations associated with their struggle to read and spell at even a basic level. We were at the same time
test subjects of the clinic's research, occasionally vaguely aware of being
observed through the long two-way mirror along the back wall as we
worked—like complacent mice in an ongoing lab experiment in quest
of little Algernons.

It was at this time that my mother began reading extensively to
me in the evenings, encouraging me to read along with her and to visualize imaginatively the stories behind the words. And it wasn't simple
elementary fare that she chose either, as the first book I recall reading with her was *Huckleberry Finn*. Perhaps she knew my early life on
the Mississippi Delta might provide a personal connection with the
troubled and adventurous Huck, a young boy faced with a wayward

father and some rather serious spelling issues of his own. A boy who nevertheless found happiness and freedom in his adventure along the mighty river dotted with grand steamboats, just like the very one from which my mother said my great grandfather—a steamboat captain— would have once shouted "mark, twain!" when approaching a shallow bend in the river (the phrase which gave Samuel Clemens his famous pen name).

The local woods and streams allowed ample freedom for adventures of my own. And like most boys of the time, I became obsessed with the phenomenon of celebrity stuntman Evel Kneivel, who began appearing regularly on television soaring with his star-studded Harley over increasing numbers of cars. Evel was a legend for having "broken every bone in his body" in his quest for daredevil perfection, and there was something refreshing in the naïve American optimism he represented at a time when the airwaves were otherwise dominated with a boring program that annoyingly kept interrupting my favorite Saturday morning cartoons—something the adults called "Watergate."

Evel finally outdid himself with a highly publicized stunt in which he planned to leap over the Snake River Canyon in a rocket-propelled cycle. My friends and I anticipated the event for months, and finally on live national television we saw Evel and his rocket shoot about halfway across the canyon before his "panic button" activated a cluster of parachutes and the contraption drifted anticlimactically down into the canyon below. I can hardly recall ever feeling so disillusioned as I did on that day.

Yet one of my favorite toys was an Evel Kneivel action figure, complete with a battery-powered motorcycle and a set of ramps and toy cars to boot. (I would also try my hand at building and launching model rockets, with about the same success as Kneivel.) Not content with mere daredevil simulation, my friends and I took things one step further. There was a new parking lot across the street which provided the perfect setting for building ramps and making daring bicycle jumps of our own. I still recall the awesome sense of freedom experienced when, after launching from a distance and building momentum towards the ramp, I saw it approach like a raised drawbridge until my front wheel abruptly shifted upwards taking bike and boy over the edge and momentarily airborne over the blurry sea of asphalt below— reaching in a moment a brief apex before, with butterflies of adrenaline excitement fluttering in my belly, I crashed back to earth with the screech of skidding wheels. One such stunt ended with a crash and a scar that remains on my knee today.

The year 1975 rolled in with the opening of a new roller skating rink called *Eight Wheels*, where I learned to fast break on four wheels as a DJ spun the latest hits at full volume—including the new music coming from England that would rock every generation to the present day, especially Queen's stately "We Are The Champions" with its iconic opening beat destined to become the standard stomp of ages at sports events around the world. There was also the band's innovative "Bohemian Rhapsody"—sung by Freddie Mercury in his inimitable voice (and unlike anything heard before or since).

Closer to home, another group topping the charts was The Jackson Five, with their prodigal young star Michael. There was something about this child sensation, not much older than myself, that I really connected with and felt inspired by. There was even a "Jackson Five" cartoon, featuring little Michael and his (even then) preoccupation with strange pets. He and his brothers became the first celebrities I ever saw in person when they came to town and appeared in the Little Rock Christmas Parade of 1972. When I saw on television they would be in the parade, I begged my parents to take me, and still remember the excitement of seeing the 14-year-old Michael and his brothers waving to an ecstatic crowd lining both sides of the avenue as they passed.

At the same time, I finally discovered that "The Beatles" were indeed more than some adult obsession with a group of insects. It was oddly enough during a visit to Crossett that I first recall hearing them. My grandparents had an old transistor radio in the kitchen that picked up the one local station, which in turn tried to please all listeners by playing everything from Johnny Cash to the Bee Gees. But when I heard "I Want To Hold Your Hand" I was hooked, and begged my parents for various Beatles' singles to play on my toy turntable.

This was when I also felt the first pangs of puppy love. A new family moved into the neighborhood, Mormons from Salt Lake City including a freckled red-haired girl named Danielle. She gave me every bit as much grief as my favorite cartoon character Charlie Brown's "little red-haired girl" caused him. Like him, I deliberated hours on end trying to muster the nerve to speak to Danielle, envisioning her delighted response. (I had just as much luck as Charlie.)

By the end of my second grade year, my teachers felt that I had made enough progress with reading and writing that I might be ready to make the transition to a standard public elementary school. Surprisingly, I had developed a deep love of reading, despite the time it took to read even an average-length children's book. But once having reached the ability (after so much pain-staking work at both school and home) to keep letters and ultimately words in proper order as I read, I began to savor the thoughts and images they produced in my mind, and the sounds they made when I read them out loud—whereas my ability to visualize in my head the images described was no doubt greatly enhanced through my mother's reading sessions of classic literature at home. In the autumn of '75, I found myself starting third grade at Williams Public Elementary School, within walking distance from home.

That summer, my mother gave birth to her third child, a baby boy named William Russell. (I helped choose the name in honor of my new school.) I also escaped back to the country, which would become an increasingly crucial place of refuge in the coming years. Summers in Crossett became an annual tradition of reuniting with all my favorite cousins, including Becky and her husband Jim Bob and their family, and Marilyn and her family, Michael and Mark from Savannah, Georgia—sons of my uncle, Frank Arnold Hancock—and Jon David Cash, a cousin of the singer Johnny Cash. (Cash himself was born a few miles up the road in Kingsland, Arkansas, and my Aunt Hazel Hancock often recalled meeting him at her father-in-law's house in Rison, when the teen-aged Cash had hitchhiked to visit his Uncle Russell.) Aunt Hazel was married to David Cash, who was also born in Kingsland and first cousins with Johnny Cash. (Uncle David, a World War II veteran, was famous for his exquisite homemade barbecue sauce that made each 4ᵗʰ of July cookout an occasion to savor.) One of my mother's favorite anecdotes concerns the time she organized a concert for Johnny and June Carter Cash in Little Rock; after the show, she told the singer: "Johnny, my sister Hazel is married to your cousin David Cash." Johnny, in his booming bass of a voice, replied—"Well, I guess that makes us kissin' cousins then!" And to everyone's surprise, including Dad and June, he pulled my mother into an embrace and gave her a proper kiss on the lips.

Michael, Mark, and Jon were all several years older than I, and it pleased me no end to hang out with these fun-loving older boys. Both Michael and Mark were avid collectors of baseball cards and always carried around cases of them, laying them out on the floor as we watched the St. Louis Cardinals play on long summer afternoons. (Jon would one day write his doctoral dissertation on the early history of St. Louis baseball, now published as a book entitled *Before They Were Cardinals* by the University of Missouri Press.) In the summer of '75, Jon had a 1967 Pontiac Grand Prix with an 8-track tape player, and we'd all cruise to town on hot afternoons and pick up iced cherry Sprites at the "Sonic" drive-in; then we'd cruise the streets of Crossett, singing carefree along with Lynyrd Skynyrd as the speakers blared "Sweet

Home Alabama." Afterwards, we'd return to spend an afternoon playing kickball in the backyard, frequently incurring Mama Doris's wrath
for converting her prized plants into bases.

Daddy Frank (front and center) with his five grandsons.
Clockwise from back left: Michael Hancock; Jon David Cash;
Me (with Will Thurmond in my lap); and Mark Hancock.
Crossett, Arkansas, Summer 1975.

Back in Little Rock I now had a little brother as well as a sister, and
this also meant yet another move to a larger house. Fortunately my
parents found a house on North Cleveland Street in the same general
neighborhood. Our new house was even closer to the school, still a
good mile's walk each way. It was nonetheless a major change and the
start of a new phase of life.

Vivid impressions from that time include a movie whose
soundtrack's opening measures would become as universally well-
known as the beginning of Beethoven's Fifth: The ominous bass pattern, starting with a single note before building momentum in a syn-
copated rhythm, will forever be synonymous with a monstrous evil
lurking just beneath a misleadingly calm surface. To my surprise, Dad
took me to see Steven Spielberg's *Jaws* despite its "R" rating. I vividly
remember it too, including the first experience of being made by a
movie to jump out of my seat. I also recall people walking out when
the sailing got rough—although the film was, in retrospect, quite tame

relative to contemporary fare. But to Dad's credit (I think, at least), we survived until the final frame. I've been wary of the water ever since.

Popular entertainers had immediate fun parodying both the film and John Williams' distinctive score. This was particularly the case with the young cast of a new television series that year called *Saturday Night Live*. The so-called "Not Ready For Prime Time Players"—Dan Aykroyd, John Belushi, Jane Curtain, Chevy Chase, Garrett Morris, Loraine Newman and Gilda Radner (not to mention future US Senator Al Franken)—really came into their own with a hilarious skit in which no single young woman was safe from a marauding "land shark" on the loose in Manhattan. The doorbell would ring with a pleasant voice identifying himself variously as a plumber, telephone guy or "candygram" courier, while the inevitable bass notes would intone until the door opened to reveal a wicked set of jaws.

That year my mother started a tradition that raised my cultural awareness to a new level. Just before the Christmas vacation, the Arkansas Ballet presented a production of *The Nutcracker*, including a girl from my class as one of the Sugarplum Fairies. Mom said she had been a sugarplum fairy in a performance of the same ballet as a schoolgirl, and had loved it and its enchanting music ever since. This was my first experience of classical ballet and live orchestral music, and it made an indelible print that continues to enrich my life.

Third grade, in addition to clear memories of the effusion of American bicentennial celebration events, was when I also forged a couple of lifelong friendships. One was with a boy named Brian whose mother hosted the local Cub Scout "den," which provided the opportunity to experience the sense of accomplishment that came from earning, after hard work, each new "badge" based on an increasingly difficult set of activities (such as planting the tree that would take root and live to greet me upon my return as an adult almost four decades later). Another friendship developed out of unlikely circumstances. One day at school I wrangled with a kid named Tyler, and then agreed to come by his house after school to settle the matter. I arrived on schedule and rang his doorbell with a sense of dread; I'd never been in a fight and wasn't sure what to do, but I knew instinctively that backing down would ruin any reputation I could ever hope to have at my new school.

Tyler answered the door, and to my surprise he began the proceedings not with a fist in the nose but instead with a polite question.

"Would you like a bowl of ice cream?" he asked.

"Um, sure," I replied, and hence the start of a great friendship that has lasted to this day.

The next few years remain something of a jumbled blur, punctuated by recollections of several major milestones of popular culture. Meanwhile, since Williams Elementary stopped at third grade, I found myself catching a bright yellow school bus downtown to attend Gibbs Elementary School for the fourth and fifth grades. I recollect very little from the fourth grade, apart from an emotionally painful early childhood experience. One day not long after Halloween, our dog disappeared. Mom said not to worry, that he was probably just lost and would be back soon. But he never did return, and finally Mom explained that he had not been found and was probably lost forever. I felt heartbroken that the little dog, who during the course of my short life since leaving Paragould had so often seemed my only constant friend, was gone.

Fifth grade brought happier times, not least thanks to a movie fronted by yet another John Williams soundtrack now permanently stamped into today's collective consciousness as the fanfare beacon to a galaxy far, far away. All year long, the movie trailer had promised something truly spectacular, and when George Lucas' *Star Wars* finally opened that summer of '77 and I convinced Mom to take me to see it, the amazing adventure that filled the big screen took into hyperspace my young imagination along with it. For a ten-year-old boy who missed the real-life launches of manned space missions that had so abruptly ended, the discovery of science fiction helped fill that longing. That year at school I started mining the library for books and stories in the genre. This would ultimately lead to the discovery of such writers as Jules Verne, Ray Bradbury, Arthur C. Clarke and H. G. Wells. But for now there were plenty of good children's titles available, including books by authors like Judy Blume and Beverly Cleary.

That year brought another extraterrestrial adventure, with Spielberg leaving the perils of the deep to invite audiences to ponder whether "We Are Not Alone," as the tagline went for *Close Encounters of the Third Kind*. Another movie released later that summer further sparked my interest in all things adventurous. When my two cousins from Georgia, Michael and Mark Hancock, came to visit, Dad took us all to see *The Spy Who Loved Me*. This featured Roger Moore in his third appearance as James Bond, paired with the lovely Barbara Bach as a Russian KGB *femme fatale*—providing, no doubt, my first awareness of truly seductive feminine beauty (and its potential perils, as in time I would appreciate). The film featured an equally seductive title song by Marvin Hamlisch and sung by Carly Simon, "Nobody Does It Better," that dominated the airwaves and fit the stylish, innovative feel of the movie like few Bond themes since. I left the theater that day firmly hooked on Bond and eager for more. Thankfully there would be plenty to come.

One event at school that year is particularly memorable. The Harlem Globetrotters were in Little Rock, with a classic lineup of phenomenal hoopsters including Meadowlark Lemon, Curly Neal and Hubert "Geese" Ausbie. I knew them primarily from their own cartoon series in the early seventies, along with several animated appearances on my favorite cartoon series of the time, *Scooby-Doo*. I even had the single of the Harlem Globetrotters' whistling theme song, "Sweet Georgia Brown." Dad took me to see them play, and on top of this our teacher informed us that "Geese" Ausbie would be visiting our school in person to speak to us. (Ausbie had played basketball at Philander Smith College, an historically black college in Little Rock, and seems to have had a connection with someone at school.) I vividly recall "Geese" working his magic on the playground hoops in an exhibition just for us, and then all the kids gathering around him as he told us his personal story.

As long ago as it was, I still remember my fifth grade teacher, Miss Thompson, as being in the top tier of influential teachers. This was primarily because she supervised the school newspaper, for which she asked me to report on various school activities and to interview the principal about key issues of concern. I recall the satisfaction that came from seeing my articles in print and disseminated around the school to hundreds of schoolmates. One day, after reading a composition out loud in class, Miss Thompson looked across the room and smiled. "You're going to be a writer some day," she said. I wasn't entirely sure what she meant, but it sounded good all the same.

Gibbs Elementary stopped at fifth grade, so I was bussed still further away from home for sixth grade at Carver Elementary School on the edge of town in the shadow of the airport, a place where clucking chickens seemed to own the local neighborhood streets. This was the beginning of a long series of especially strong English teachers with whom I would be blessed.

We had a regular reading group which involved students sitting in a circle and taking turns reading passages from a textbook. For the first time, I felt comfortable reading passages aloud in front of my classmates. I don't suppose the significance of my doing that—in light of the progress I'd made since first grade at the Child Study Center, when for all anyone knew I might never be able to read properly even in silence—was apparent to me then, but this must have been a major breakthrough for me. (It also demonstrates the way one teacher, especially at such a crucial time for a kid with precarious abilities and motivation, can truly make or break an individual's lifetime aptitude for a particular subject.)

I remember an excerpt from *The Lion, the Witch and the Wardrobe* by C.S. Lewis; this had only the opening chapters of the book, describing Lucy's adventure through the wardrobe and her accidental discovery of the enchanted land of Narnia, but after we finished reading of Lucy's encounter with Mr. Tumnus the Faun and her narrow escape from the White Witch, I was hooked and had to read more. So I consulted the school librarian, who pointed out the seven volume *Chronicles of Narnia* series on a shelf. (I also discovered at this time a love of classical mythology and the tales of Edgar Allen Poe and Sherlock Holmes.) Thus began a long and magical literary journey—and a lifelong love of literature.

Math was another matter. I had progressed well with it thus far, but when letters suddenly started appearing next to the numbers, I was flummoxed. Years later I would finally learn that this is a natural difficulty for dyslexics, but throughout the rest of grade school, math became a subject of fear and trembling (as well as embarrassment). At first Dad, with his experience as a math teacher, was able to help me with homework and test preparation, but eventually it would take hours of outside tutors to help me stumble through with passing grades. (Unlike today, when 'special needs' kids at school and even college may receive a variety of benefits including extra help at school, lenient grading, and extra test-taking time, in those days you had to go the extra mile to keep up and avoid failure.)

My sixth grade math teacher wasn't of much help—nor was the school environment particularly conducive for learning a difficult subject. The teacher was an avid adherent of corporal punishment (then still allowed in public schools), and this gave him the means with which to instill a fear in pupils that could be distracting in the classroom. His favorite method of expressing disapproval was to have the student hold out his hand, upon which the teacher would administer a brutal walloping with his long wooden ruler. This had the short term effect of a seriously blistered hand, along with an apparent mental aversion not only to rulers but to any math application associated with them.

The principal of the school was likewise happy to inflict physical pain upon the smallest provocation, his favorite method being the fervent application of a firm ping pong paddle upon the offending student's derrière. This threat of violence from teachers and administrators was not, however, sufficient to stymie violence among students. One day while attempting to work problems in math class, there was a horrible shriek from the hall just outside the classroom. The teacher ran outside, and the class instinctively followed. What we saw was a terrifying sight. Two girls were running down the hall, one in a panic just ahead of another brandishing a butcher knife. We stopped short outside the classroom, terrified by a sight I would never forget: a pool of blood glistening dark red against the polished green paint of the floor. More blood led from it in large drops all along the hall down which the young victim had fled. Soon afterwards we watched in fear as police and medics arrived with loud sirens in front of our school.

I wasn't twelve years old, and the hallway of my school was stained with blood. Perhaps it's no wonder that the gas lamp outside my window at home, its warm yellow flame illuminating drifts of snow on dark winter nights, became for me a beacon to another world—the magical land of Narnia which, despite its fairyland perils, seemed a far better place to be than the all too real world of my elementary school.

I looked forward to starting seventh grade at yet another school, Forest Heights Junior High, back within walking distance from home. But before the summer was over, I'd made a new friend—one whose acquaintance and friendship over the coming years would make an invaluable contribution to my life.

There was considerable neighborhood curiosity (and perhaps even concern) about the new family that had just moved into a vacant house on the block. Had it been a few years earlier in the decade, the arrival of an African-American family in the midst of an otherwise middle-class white Little Rock neighborhood might have evoked a scene worthy of Lorraine Hansberry's depiction of segregated Chicago. Yet while nothing negative immediately transpired, there was no rush on the part of neighbors to roll out the welcome mat either. But then something happened that drew the neighborhood children to the new family's house in droves.

Whether by chance or design I don't know, but what the new family did soon after settling in was a stroke of genius in terms of gaining instant popularity for their children with local youth. One day two boys could be seen in the yard, in full view of the street, engaged in an activity which proved an irresistible magnet to every child within biking distance. There was a large trampoline in the yard, upon which the two brothers appeared from a distance to be floating in the air like orbiting astronauts. A trampoline such as theirs was quite a novelty in those days—I had certainly never seen one, and there were no others in the neighborhood—and eventually the first local kids turned up at the margins of the yard, watching tentatively from a distance until the boys gestured in welcome from the trampoline. In time this blur of bouncing boys grew to a throng of kids (including myself) standing around the trampoline all waiting their turn to jump. The older brother, Darryl, was close to my age and would be attending the same school for ninth grade, and he quickly became my best friend as well as a key influence through those difficult years of early adolescence.

There was a mall within walking distance that had two places Darryl and I began to frequent as the summer drew to a close: a bowling alley and a pinball arcade. Visits to the arcade increased with the advent of hit new games for which kids lined up in droves—games like *Pac Man*, *Space Invaders* and *Asteroids*.

Darryl and I must have seemed an unlikely pair to passersby as we walked along the busy University Avenue to the mall: I being rather tall and lanky for my age with a head of thick, blonde curls, striding next to the shorter (and rather heavy-set) Darryl sporting a thick "afro" beneath a floppy white hat. We would follow the arcade with long afternoons of bowling, where there was a juke box which brought out the striking divide between our musical tastes. Whereas I insisted on spinning the latest singles by bands like Boston, Journey, Styx, Supertramp, The Cars and Fleetwood Mac, Darryl insisted on Diana Ross, Chic or Cameo. I once naïvely insisted Darryl give Jimi Hendrix a chance, assuming of course he'd like Hendrix simply because he was black, but Darryl would have none of it. We did, however, find common ground with Michael Jackson, whose new album *Off the Wall* had just been released; and to my surprise Darryl bought the new Queen album later that year, featuring their funky tune "Another One Bites The Dust." We were also both fascinated with the album released that year by the Sugarhill Gang called "Rapper's Delight," introducing the new genre of rap music.

Our bowling quickly improved to the point that we were invited to join a local bowling league, which provided a constructive activity—along with Boy Scouts—to keep us occupied on weekends and during free time all that year. A good thing too, as many of my peers found an altogether different direction which would ultimately lead some of them to disaster.

Day one of seventh grade arrived, and I met up with Darryl at his house to begin a tradition of walking to and from school together. When we arrived daily at the back wall of the school after climbing the high hill from University Avenue, if the sun was out Darryl would stop in front of the brick wall, remove the "pick" held firmly in place by his hair, and then remarkably manage to smooth his afro in place guided by the shadow it cast against the wall. (I tried this myself to no avail.) Then we would part for the day, he to the ninth grade hall of the school and I to the lowly seventh.

The year got off to a good enough start, and I even went so far—with Darryl's encouragement—to try out for the football team. I told the coach I reckoned that, with my running speed, I'd make a fine receiver. The first tryout proved a rather humbling experience, as despite being taller than most kids my age, I was lanky as a loon and the coach clearly perceived that one tackle by a burly linebacker would most probably be sufficient to sideline me interminably.

After that setback, it wasn't long before my build—combined with a growing and perceptible sense of insecurity—made me a prime target for bullying. The bullies were invariably white boys my own age who, while more muscular, were nevertheless significantly shorter than I—and who must have derived some thrill from picking on a taller boy. But to the bullies' chagrin, I benefitted from being well-liked by more popular students, including the most popular boy at school: a star football player named Barry. While I was certainly never part of Barry's "inner circle," feeling accepted even on superficial terms helped get me through that year. (One day almost thirty years later, after moving to Los Angeles and knowing hardly a soul there, I would miraculously bump into—and recognize—Barry at a gym in Los Angeles. I had requested a session with a professional trainer, and upon arrival for my appointment the trainer was Barry! This led to a lasting friendship, as well as deep reflection upon the capacity life has of coming full circle.)

I experienced a growing dread of school, where my number one nemesis, a short, stringy-haired kid named Kyle, made biology class hell. It was a class that involved lab work, and Kyle found countless opportunities to inflict pain (emotionally more than physically) at every possible occasion. But along with the fear of bullying, I also experienced my first true romantic crush. And this naturally had to be upon the most beautiful and popular girl at the school—excepting Barry's girlfriend, who was of course without peer and unapproachable. But the girl of my fancy (and fantasy) was equally out of my league, being a year older in the eighth grade and a popular cheerleader to boot. At football games I would see Kathy cheer and dance, for the first time aware of the meaning of "sexy" and pining for a reason to speak to her—then pained all the more to realize she hadn't even the slightest idea I existed. What's more, I feared the worst possible torment of all—beyond the humiliation of failure to make the football team or the dread of Kyle's fist: the torment of being laughed at. I began to see this in my dreams, along with my fantasies of being stronger, popular like Barry, and possessed of a girlfriend like Kathy.

In our daily commute to school Darryl was full of advice on how to talk to the *ladies*, and he said he was quite the "player" even though I saw no evidence at the school to support this claim. But as the year progressed I began to turn more and more inward, finding solace through reading and music. There was a new radio station called Magic 105, featuring two dynamic DJs named Tom Wood and Tommy Smith, who still preside over Little Rock airwaves to this day. They played "album rock" and opened up a new world of music both past and present—where new hits from Pink Floyd's *The Wall* would play back to back with The Who's "My Generation" (a perfect power-chord driven expression of preadolescent schoolboy angst).

English continued as my favorite (and strongest) subject, and became even more interesting as we began my first formal survey of American literature, including stories by Steinbeck and Melville, with whose character Bartleby and his oft-repeated personal preferences I could easily empathize. Meanwhile my hippie math teacher had an unlikely penchant for quoting Shakespeare to illustrate algebraic points. This, along with his classroom radio set nonstop to Magic 105, finally made math class tolerable for me, if even less intelligible than before.

One day I went to the school library in hopes there might be something more by C.S. Lewis about the world of Narnia. I had finished the "Chronicles" and felt an insatiable longing for more enchantment of the kind those books had brought. The librarian delivered the disappointing news that there were in fact no further books about Narnia, but she offered to recommend another story that I might enjoy. I followed her curiously to a bookshelf, and eagerly accepted the book she handed me. It was called *The Hobbit*. And if I wanted to judge the book by its cover, the intriguing painting on the front of the book, with its odd depiction of a string of barrels floating down a river towards a distant mountain, piqued my interest sufficiently to check out the book and take it home. That night when I began reading about the comfortable hole in the ground in which there lived a hobbit, I was hooked. This tale of the unlikely (and unwilling) little hero finding himself in a band of dwarves led by a wizard on a quest for dragon's gold was beyond anything I'd ever hoped to find.

Despite the growing bubble of frustrated energy, I felt welling up inside, pent up without yet any means for creative expression, I managed for the most part to stay out of trouble—apart from one episode involving a novelty toy I'd seen advertised in a *Spiderman* comic book. This was a small device called a "Bullshit Detector," being simply a plastic brown box with a single button and a speaker. If you pushed the button, a loud voice shouted "Bullshit!" and then laughed hysterically. So I brought it to school one day to show it off, and it proceeded to generate the desired attention from classmates. But later that day, right in the middle of history class, the teacher had just finished making a point when in reply came the loud answer of "Bullshit!" followed by hysterical laughter.

"Who said that?" demanded the teacher.

"Bullshit!" again came the reply, and all eyes turned in my direction. I turned back to see Kyle sitting behind me, and realized to my horror that the Bullshit Detector in the bag beneath my desk had been within his reach. He pointed at it and then to me, exclaiming: "Frank did it!" The teacher promptly confiscated the device with instructions to report to the Teacher's Lounge immediately after school.

I spent the rest of the day dreading the final bell. But when it came I duly knocked on the door of the office and asked for the teacher. To my surprise, she handed me the toy and said it had brought all the other teachers to tears of laughter. However, the Bullshit Detector was no longer welcome in the classroom.

When that year finally ended, I headed off to summer camp for a highly anticipated respite in the country. On the way out of town, I asked Mom to take me by our local bookseller Rod Lorenzen's small bookshop called The Paperback Writer. Having finished *The Hobbit*, I was excited to begin reading its sequel. What I expected was of course another modest-length children's book depicting Mr. Bilbo Baggins in a further succinct adventure; what I found instead was a package of three enormous paperbacks purporting to tell an epic story in one grand adventure called *The Lord of the Rings*. Undaunted, I bought the entire set, aware that I'd probably need more than the entire summer (and then some) to read through it all. But what an adventure it would ultimately prove!

Summer camp was in the beautiful countryside outside Hot Springs, Arkansas, a town famous for its spas as well as its horse track— not to mention its earlier reputation as the "Vegas of the South," when gangsters the likes of Al Capone ruled city streets tinted red by both lights and blood. (Until finally in the 60s Governor Winthrop Rockefeller cleaned out the casinos and the brothels, restoring the area's tourist credentials.)

The camp was directed by a vivacious lady named Bettie Sue, who had a much deeper mission behind what on the surface was a standard summer camp focused on outdoor activities. Interspersed with horseback riding, go-cart and mini-bike racing, and fishing were long sermons featuring Bettie Sue's fiery preaching on the imminent coming of Jesus. Her evangelical mission of the camp was that not one of us would leave before being truly born again, ready to traverse the world as missionary soldiers to preach the Good News gospel of Christ. From Bettie Sue, I learned that pretty much everything that sounded fun in life, including the joy of feminine companionship about which I had only dimly begun to fantasize, were all strictly prohibited. Everything fun, it seemed, constituted the kind of sin which would guarantee a hot place in Hell—which, from Bettie Sue's vivid description, made Dante's *Inferno* sound like a family picnic. But if I found myself wondering how, if all this was the "good news," there could nevertheless still be any "bad news" to spare, I came home from camp utterly converted and determined to devote every minute of each day to the love of Jesus. To this end, the first order of business was to toss out all my KISS records, because Bettie Sue had insisted that that popular rock band's name was an acronym for "Knights in Satan's Service." I had now taken the first crucial step along the path to redemption and eternal salvation. Bettie Sue would be proud.

I remained "born again" for about a week. Then I began to regret the loss of all my Kiss records—all the more so years later when they became very collectible. But I wish now my piety had lasted the summer in light of a behavior I still regret.

A new boy around my age moved into the neighborhood, and when a few other local kids and I invited him out to play, we immediately noticed something different about him. Russell had a type of hyperactivity disorder, and at the slightest provocation he would go absolutely berserk. Although we were at first alarmed and then briefly sympathetic, the evil side of schoolboy nature finally gained the upper hand, and we took advantage of the boy's condition for our own devious entertainment. I have always been disturbed that, despite (or perhaps because of) what I had experienced myself in the form of bullying, I would participate in such cruelty against a helpless human being. But as I recalled years later in college when writing the following narrative poem about the experience—my first publication—Russell taught me a tough lesson about the danger of taking for granted the apparent weakness of others:

THE LESSON

The hyperactive kid on the block always intrigued us,
the way you could stir him up, sever the delicate
thread of his sanity. So we coerced him from his
mother by feigning friendship (the thing he needed),
let him join the group and feel wanted.

We always had a scheme. A loud word, an insult maybe,
a thrown rock . . . the slightest provocation and he'd
go nuts. Then we would test how spastic he could get,
his mind like a busted engine sending lunatic signals
to a body out of control, fixed on a collision course.

Those were the days when we would throw rocks at
wasps' nests from a distance, watching them panic over
the smashed larvae. We would keep at it, pelting until their
stings found us, coloring our skin red like an angry face.

Sometimes I wonder what he felt, our human wasp, in that
state of neurotic nirvana he had reached by the time we were
running from him, dodging bottles, sticks, whatever he
could find to use against us. His scrawny body seemed to
transcend consciousness, then strengthen with rage like The Hulk.

What was he thinking that time he chased us with a thick
branch he had found, when I had tripped, fallen, and felt
in the next moment his wrath, beating me into the dirt?
Maybe to him I was the mad one, and he was just giving
the good stinging that I needed, teaching my insolence

with welts. Yet sometimes that isn't enough. The instinct
To stretch and entangle the threads of our sanity
outlives experience, driven by the insane pace we live. Maybe
it's the insane who truly see, and in reality itself is the madness.

By the end of that summer I would learn another hard lesson about
reality. When I went down to Crossett, I planned to ask my grandparents if I could invite Darryl down for a visit. I was quite excited about
the idea too, as I'd told him so much about the place and how I wanted
him to come down and fish with me at the pond. Soon after my arrival with my young siblings, Kate and Will, for a brief family visit, a
respected family member called me aside and said she needed to talk
with me.

"I hear you have some colored friends up yonder," she said.

"Yes ma'am," I answered, assuming she must mean Darryl and his
family.

"Well now, you keep 'em away from them young'uns, you hear?"

I hesitated. "Yes, ma'am," I finally answered. She went on to say
something about how "they" were different than we were, and the negative influence this could have on my young brother and sister. But I
was too shocked to listen closely. I was, in fact, devastated.

From that moment on I would have mixed feelings about my heritage. I was (and remain) proud of my pioneer ancestors, including my forefathers who fought so bravely in the Civil War—which I knew had been about so much more for those who fought and died in it on both sides than the simplified good vs. evil fight over slavery. Still, there it was: Whether they individually believed in it or not, the fact was that human beings had been possessed as slaves, and would have continued to be had the side from which I descended prevailed. This was a fact that had been convenient to sweep under the rug and ignore when celebrating the myth of the "grand old South" and its traditions of which Arkansas—or at least the state's more "Southern" Delta region—claims a part. (When speaking of the "Civil War" for example, I was always corrected to call it "The War Between The States"; I've never known whether this is a disclaimer of any "civil" concern over slavery or a denial that this was a motive for the war.) Here it was being rubbed into me that by so much as daring to cultivate "colored" friends, I was somehow a traitor to both God and Dixie. This was not the first time the hideous specter of racism would raise its head from within my own family to threaten my choice of friendships and, ultimately, relationships.

The question of my Southern identity has continued as a source of sometimes painful conflict—inwardly as well as socially—ever since this initial disillusionment.

Autumn 1980 found me in still another new school. My mother was unhappy with the methods of various Forest Heights teachers, and when she heard about the new Lutheran parochial school, she enrolled me there right away. I didn't mind the change; my closest friend at Forest Heights, Darryl, was now starting 10th grade at nearby Hall High School anyway, and it provided a convenient escape from the dreaded den of bullies like Kyle. But upon arrival for my first day of 8th grade, I was in for a shock.

There to greet me in homeroom class stood Kyle himself. It seemed that his parents had had the same idea as mine. I immediately felt painfully dismayed to observe that here at this tiny new school every class (and each activity) would involve working in close proximity to Kyle. My worst nightmare!

On that first day of school I also noticed a quiet boy sitting in the back of the room. He had deep, dark eyes and raven hair and clearly knew no one in the class. I eventually summoned up the courage to speak to him, wondering if he might prove an even worse monster than Kyle. Fortunately it proved quite the opposite. His name was Donny, and he had recently moved with his mother to Little Rock from a small town in southwest Arkansas called Arkadelphia, just a short distance away from Hope. We struck up a friendship almost immediately. Yet beneath his quiet surface, I could perceive there was something he was hiding inside. Something painful, even.

It wasn't long before we were recruited by the basketball coach for the new team. At first it appeared I was chosen because of my height; upon arrival at the first practice, it became clear the coach was just desperate for enough boys to form a team. Even the shortest kids were there (including, of course, Kyle). But being part of a team was a new experience, and it brought a sense of camaraderie that I'd seldom felt. I still kept my distance from Kyle, who had thankfully become less of a threat thanks to the stout presence of Donny by my side. Until, that is, the day Kyle confronted me in the hall in front of all my new friends.

He approached me with the usual barrage of insults and attempted to pin me down. But then something happened: Something inside me, a deep sense of unrealized pride perhaps, suddenly found its expression in the fierce anger that now overwhelmed me. I stood up tall to my full height and stared down into Kyle's eyes with what must have seemed to him an expression full of pent up resentment and even hatred. Then with clenched fists I said: "Don't you ever mess with me again, or I'll kick your ass to kingdom come!"

Immediately after saying this, the old fear enveloped me again and I found myself shaking in my certainty that it was in fact I who was in for the real ass-kicking. Then to my amazement there was a sudden look of fear in Kyle's eyes, as he immediately backed off with his palms outward in a gesture of defense.

"OK, sorry, man!" he said, and walked quickly away.

It was then that I realized for the first time the importance—and the power—of standing up for yourself, and of the capacity for summoning hidden strength in the face of adversity. Or of simply having faith in yourself and refusing to give in, despite the evident odds stacked up against you. I knew even then that this was a lesson worth remembering, and that I'd meet plenty more Kyles as my life progressed. Kyles who were bigger and smarter and significantly more dangerous.

Meanwhile, I assumed my victory to be short-lived and dreaded returning to school the next day for fear Kyle would be back with a vengeance to save face in front of our classmates. But to my surprise he approached me with an air of respect, and soon actually joined Donny and me to form our own little clique of friends, both at school and off campus. Kyle would, in fact, become a close friend, remaining even today as one of my oldest. Hence another early life-lesson: The strongest of adversities may lead ultimately to the greatest of friendships.

With my newfound confidence, I thought I might finally have a chance with the pretty girl I'd been infatuated with all year. But once again I'd fallen for the class babe, and, once again, my romantic stars seemed woefully crossed. My rival in love was Luke, the class jock (and unlikely son of a preacher)—basketball star, rock drummer, and all around jerk. It was the latter trait that I bitterly began to realize seemed to be the chief criterion for the hottest girls. I wondered if I would ever have it in me at least to feign sufficient "jerkness" so that I, too, might finally be able to impress the girls. But with my romantic fantasies once again thwarted, I again found solace in literature and in music.

Eighth grade English class was more interesting than ever, with a reading list that included *Animal Farm, The Prince and the Pauper, Fahrenheit 451* and *Beowulf.* The latter work rang a bell, and I remembered reading about its close association with the "Middle-earth" of J.R.R. Tolkien. Tolkien's magnum opus had proved a true delight, and after months of reading the three books all summer—over a thousand pages of continuous narrative—I had finally made it to the end of the third volume, *The Return of the King.* I could hardly bear the suspense of reaching the impending climax as hobbits Frodo and Sam trudged their way up the treacherous slopes of Mount Doom.

Donny chose this occasion to recount having seen a recent animated version of *The Return of the King* on television, and in so doing he deliberately gave away—just pages before I reached it—the climax of the whole story! I've still not forgiven him for it to this day. And I've particularly detested spoilers ever since.

In those days I had a paper route, which involved waking at 4 am and walking to the street corner where a bundle of *Arkansas-Gazette* newspapers would be waiting. I'd bring them back to our garage and fold and wrap the papers with rubber bands, no easy task in the frigid winter when a small space heater hardly sufficed to keep the blood pumping in my fingers; then I'd wheel the streets by bike before dawn, tossing papers like mad to finish my route before school. For company as I folded papers each morning, I had Kate's new little white cat, appropriately named Snow for the way she would completely vanish after a few steps out onto the snow-carpeted lawn.

In this way I kept up pretty well with the daily news, and relished knowing the day's headlines before anyone else had seen them, including the results of election day 1980 when Ronald Reagan won

in a landslide—along with the simultaneous release of the American
hostages being held in Iran, a crisis which had hammered the last nail
in the coffin of Jimmy Carter's presidency.

I was also the first at school to know of the tragic death of a rock
icon. There had been exciting rumors for some time that the legendary British rock band Led Zeppelin would be performing a concert in
Arkansas on their upcoming US tour (their first since 1977). I had not
yet attended a rock concert and resolved I would not miss seeing Led
Zeppelin no matter what. But this anticipation came to a cruel close
when I saw on the front page that the band's drummer, John Bonham,
had managed to die in classic rock star style by drowning in his own
vomit after ingesting an ungodly amount of alcohol.

Yet my desire to experience real live rock and roll was more than
fulfilled in the coming years, when Little Rock saw a string of some of
the top acts in the business perform at Barton Coliseum on the State
Fair grounds. My first concert was that of then-super group REO
Speedwagon (with Cheap Trick as the opening act), and the experience was thrilling as I experienced for the first time a packed coliseum
erupting into uproarious anticipation when the lights went out, the
sudden dark illuminated by the flicker of thousands of lighters held
high to greet the band. And when the first guitar chords filled the hall
like a bolt of summer lightning reverberating through the sky, I was
mesmerized.

Another concert we attended (and the best by far) was that of
the Canadian rock group RUSH, who performed in Little Rock that
spring of '81. They had a new album out called *Moving Pictures*, featuring a new, cutting edge sound on such songs as "Tom Sawyer," "Lime-
light" and "Red Barchetta." The moment the coliseum lights went out,
we knew we were in for something amazing as the ethereal opening
of their album "2112" filled the arena, and the silhouettes of three figures appeared through an iridescent light-soaked fog rolling across the
stage. Dressed like futuristic priests out of some Ayn Rand nightmare,
the three young musicians proceeded to dazzle with their unique combination of heavy rock and incandescent melody interwoven with some
of the most insightful and poetic lyrics in popular music. Most vividly
I recall the way their drummer, Neil Peart, could twirl his drumsticks
like miniature batons, sometimes tossing a stick halfway to the roof
and catching it without missing a beat.

The following year Donny, Kyle and I even managed to talk our
parents into letting us travel out of town for an Ozzy Osbourne concert
in Pine Bluff. My parents had mixed feelings about that one, especially
given Ozzy's notorious escapade at a recent concert—when he had

held up a live bat on stage and proceeded to bite off its head in front of the audience (resulting in his having to undergo a painful series of rabies shots). Quite the role model, Ozzy. But attend we did, and the concert proved especially memorable for its being one of the last appearances by legendary guitarist Randy Rhodes, whose flanger-filled solo was the finest rock guitar solo I've ever seen. They were on tour with their new album called *Diary of a Madman*, filled with incredible guitar work by Rhodes—every note of which I could play perfectly in my room with consummate skill on my air guitar.

Not long afterwards I would see in the paper that Randy Rhodes had died in a freak plane crash, involving a bizarre attempt to frighten Osbourne by nose diving towards him on the ground in their private airplane, then failing to level out in time to prevent a fatal crash right in front of Ozzy's eyes. Osbourne would soon profess to have "changed his ways" in light of the incident and its sobering intimation of mortality.

Donny and I particularly found a bond through shared musical tastes, and he had a record collection which expanded considerably my knowledge and appreciation of British rock. This included the fantasy-laced themes of the band Uriah Heep, and the darkly innovative rhythms and lyrics of early Pink Floyd. There was also the Australian band AC/DC and their new album *Back in Black*.

As the year progressed, I also discovered a more secretive, wild side of Donny. He was tall and lanky, although somewhat stouter and more confident in bearing than I. His straight, raven black hair was, he said, an inheritance from the Apache background on his mother's side. In time he finally opened up about what I had already perceived, from visits to the small apartment where he and his young brother lived with their single mother, was a difficult childhood. His father was a doctor who was a rather notorious figure for running the state's sole (lawfully, at least) abortion clinic. This naturally made him the target of frequent protests, hate mail, and even death threats. While I never learned what had led to Donny's parents' breakup, it had clearly been very bitter and remained acrimonious. His parents nevertheless had an arrangement whereby Donny and his brother spent frequent time with their father, and I found myself a regular guest at his luxurious condo on the grounds of a prestigious country club and golf course just outside Little Rock.

In Donny I found a friend to whom I could finally open up about my own paternal confusion. As the years passed, I sometimes all but wholly forgot about the mysterious silence of my own birth father, while becoming increasingly comfortable with seeing Dad as my *actual* father. And while Kate and Will were at least vaguely aware of our relationship as half-siblings, this never came up even once in conversation between us. There was, however, the occasional awkward moment when a family friend might inadvertently comment on the lack of physical resemblance between Dad and me. But at such times Dad would just give a knowing chuckle, and life would go on with a deep-felt yet unspoken subtext.

My acquaintance with Donny would lead later, especially in high school (and beyond), to some rather trenchant revelations about human nature and behavior; but in the meantime I was already in store for a deeply unsettling experience.

As Christmas vacation approached, during a visit to his apartment, Donny's mother explained that she was putting together a wonderful holiday trip for her boys. She planned to take them on a winter cruise in the Bahamas for a week of sun and surf just after Christmas and over the New Year. But in order to afford the travel package, she explained, she needed one other person to join the group. So she wanted to invite me to join them on the cruise, knowing what good friends I was with Donny and how much fun we would have. I was like family, she said, and having me with them on their trip would make it all the more special. I was of course delighted, and rushed home to beg my skeptical parents for permission to go. After speaking with Donny's mother, who repeated my praises and argued persuasively why this was such a fantastic—and uniquely affordable—opportunity, my parents reluctantly agreed to my going on the cruise.

Donny and I spent the rest of that semester eagerly anticipating all the fun we'd be having on the upcoming cruise, and the weeks before school let out for Christmas were almost unbearable as we looked longingly over the trip brochure. It depicted a majestic vessel sailing through sparkling emerald seas. But the Christmas vacation finally did arrive, and my mother took me shopping for clothes more suited to the warm, sunny paradise into which I'd soon be sailing.

The morning before the cruise, my mother called me to the kitchen table where she was reading the paper and pointed to a photo right on the front page.

"I think you should see this," she said, watching with concern as I took the paper. The picture was that of Donny's mother. And the article beneath it told of how she had just been arrested for attempting to hire a hit man to take out her estranged husband, the well-known abortion doctor. But the "hit man" she hired was in fact an undercover agent, and—the article continued—she had been taken into custody just before a planned flight to Mexico for a Caribbean cruise with her sons. Her presence on the cruise was to have been her alibi after the deed was done and her husband found dead. And I, as it turned out, was to have been her key witness.

I put down the paper in a daze and looked at my mother. It would be a long and cold winter after all.

4

Poetry & Music

If one advances confidently in the direction of his dreams, and endeavors to live the life which he has imagined, he will meet with a success unexpected in common hours.

—Henry David Thoreau, *Walden*

How am I to write about the High School? It is a subject so colossal as to strike any writer with despair. But write about it I must. [It is] a period of life when one year is the equal of at least five in the life of an adult . . . I learnt, or half-learnt, an enormous amount there, from books or otherwise; I made friends I still have, and I formed passionate friendships and blazing enmities with people who have drifted so far from me that I would not recognize them today if we met in the street. There were those, among both boys and masters, whom I feared and hated so much that to this day I cannot think of them without an accelerated heartbeat; and there were others for whom I conceived a love and respect which grows every time I look back. No matter how long I live, those years will never be an insignificant part of my life: but to describe them! It is like trying to write the history, mineralogy, entomology, and demography of a country I used to live in, but can never revisit, and on which there are no reference books.

—John Wain, *Sprightly Running*

I had nearly lost count of how many different schools I'd attended, but autumn 1981 would see me enrolled for 9th grade in the seventh different one since kindergarten. My new school, Catholic High, was considered the best high school in town, and admission (especially if one was from a non-Catholic family) involved sitting for a rigorous entrance exam. So that previous spring found me taking a PSAT-style standardized test in every subject imaginable, by the end of which I was fairly confident I had no need to fear spending my high school years in an all male prep school. When the results came back, however, I was surprised to find that I had done quite well. And soon I'd be exchanging the formidably Teutonic surnames of my Lutheran teachers for those of Irish, French, and Polish extraction.

Not only had I done sufficiently well on the entrance test to get in, but it seemed my overall score was strong enough to place me in the advanced academic track. I knew good and well there was no way in hell I should be in advanced algebra, but the curriculum didn't allow for exceptions: you were either in *all* honors courses or none. This naturally had disastrous results from day one, when advanced algebra became my worst nightmare.

I was blessed, however, with two of the best teachers I would ever have. Once again I had an English teacher who continued my lucky string of quality instruction in writing and literature, this time introducing the literary worlds both of ancient Greece and Elizabethan England in ways that would inspire me through the years to come. And World History was likewise a treat, with a young Harvard graduate named Mr. Marczuk shepherding us through the ages like an ecstatic tour guide able to transform the classroom into a veritable time machine through the power of his enthusiasm. What I learned (and how I learned it) that year alone would sustain my love of historical knowledge and research for a lifetime.

I'm also grateful, in retrospect, that Honors placement meant enrollment in Latin class, given that my study of what seemed at the time so dead a language inevitably contributed to my ability with Spanish and French later in life—not to mention the many subtle ways that having a little Latin (and even less Greek) can add to one's appreciation of innumerable disciplines. But the class itself was almost as tortuous as math, especially given the infamous *quinque*. The teacher, Mr. Moran, had a plastic container holding a pair of dice, which at the start of class he'd shake vigorously before reading out the result. If one die were a two and the other a three, for example, then the lucky boy sitting at the third desk of row two would be given a five point quiz on the spot. This might consist of historical facts associated with Caesar's *Gallic Wars*, or the declension of a word assigned for homework: *puella, puellae, puellarum, puellas, puellis*—to cite one noun which, for most of the boys at least, would stick. Invariably, when I *had* done my homework carefully, I'd be praying for the dice to roll my way so I could get much needed extra points for my grade, but it seemed the only times I ever did wind up in the hot seat I was ill-prepared and missed them all. "Zero for five," the teacher would smugly intone, before adding— "Congratulations, Mr. Thurmond." Given the frequency with which most of the class experienced this dilemma, we began to suspect that those dice were loaded—and that Mr. Moran instead picked his victims based on who looked frantic as a cat on skates when the dice were rolled. Matters only became worse when he introduced the *quinque's* vile cousin, the *decem*: a ten question pop quiz!

The head priest of Catholic High School for Boys was a local legend named Father Tribou. Tribou had run the school for many years, and generations of Little Rock men, including many business and political leaders, had passed through his halls. There were numerous formalities (students were addressed strictly by their surnames, for instance), along with rules of conduct—and grooming—that had to be carefully respected by every student; these included formal dress which included wearing a tie from first bell to last, and—most difficult of all at the dawn of the 80s—keeping one's hair cut short above the ears. The good father was especially strict concerning the latter, and randomly conducted hair checks—sometimes even entering another teacher's class in mid-lesson—to see who might benefit from an on-the-spot haircut by a barber (i.e. himself) most decidedly not serving the interests of current fashion. If you knew your hair was over the limit, you had to watch your back while walking around campus, as Father Tribou had a way of sneaking up and grabbing your excess bangs, which he'd then twist with his fingers as you were led, head akimbo with a face grimacing in pain, all the way to his office.

The simple garment of the tie proved an instrument of pain as well. Each morning every boy was to be seated at his desk in homeroom by the time the bell rang and the morning announcements began on closed-circuit television. Occasionally, a boy would have rushed to class without his tie completely on and then surreptitiously attempted to tie it when the teacher wasn't looking. The priest who ran my homeroom had a way of seeming not to notice this, then slipping up behind the student and making quite a scene. The other boys naturally found this amusing, until it happened to them. And one day it was my turn.

For some reason my carpool was late that day and I found myself rushing to class, only realizing just before entering that my tie wasn't on. The priest hadn't seemed to notice, and I padded quietly to my desk and waited for the lights to turn out for the announcements. I then slipped my tie around my neck and, after confirming the priest's back was turned as he watched the TV, looked down and quickly started to tie. Suddenly I felt the tie pull tight around my neck like a noose, and my head was jerked back as the priest began shouting at the top of his lungs: "Don't you *EVER* tie your tie during class again, young man, do you hear me?" I struggled to answer but could only choke as the noose tightened around my neck. The phosphorescent light on the ceiling above reminded me of the dentist's chair where, with gaping mouth, I'd sometimes felt the sting of a drill boring into my teeth. I could hear the other boys snicker, while I knew my face must be as red as those of the boys I too had laughed at previously.

"Do you hear me, I said?" repeated the priest. "Do you HEAR me, boy?" I forced a hoarse "yes" before feeling the tie abruptly go slack and the air return to my lungs. Later I faced, like young Stephen Dedalus, the quandary of whether to complain of the incident to the head priest. I wondered if Father Tribou knew already about this priest's "methods" (his approach to errant ties being only one example), and whether saying anything might only make matters worse. But unlike Dedalus, I gave in to doubt, finally resolving to mind my tie as much as my haircut.

I could hardly forget the class taught by Father Tribou himself: "Sex Education." Here I learned what exactly constituted the so-called "French Kiss," an expression about which I'd been curious but had found no elucidation until Father Tribou explained how it worked— along with the helpful fact that such a kiss was a sin. How, someone asked, could a kiss—no matter how involved—be a sin? It was a sin because, came the reply, "it leads on to other things." Very inappropriate things, as it turned out, which would be analyzed in more detail as the course progressed. We arrived one day to find a single word written on the board: "Masturbation." Father Tribou began the class by pointing at the word, and then scrutinizing the class while commenting: "I'll bet at least one of you boys in this classroom is guilty of this." Every last head immediately dropped towards its desk. We were then informed that this too was a sin. "It's a sin," the priest exhorted, with raised voice, "because it's a pleasure you have no right to!"

Though these lessons clearly set the stage for my meaningful progression towards the real world of manhood, there was still the question of math class. Early on, it was clear to my parents, based on initial grades, that I must be moved to a regular math class. So my mother went to Father Tribou and explained why this one class wasn't working out for me, and he replied with the same response my mother would get each time she went to see him about any given issue: "Mrs. Thurmond, the only concern you should have about your son is that he's a good-looking boy and he'll soon have girls chasing him." (This from a man who, during school dances, would thrust a ruler between dancing couples to ensure a properly measured distance.) It was hardly a satisfactory answer for my mother; and she would always send Dad back to the priest to sort out whatever the issue—including math class. It perhaps isn't any wonder that, at the end of 9th grade, my parents gave me the choice whether to switch schools the following year. I could remain at Catholic High or, alternatively, transfer to Hall High, the large public school just behind our house. I appreciated the way they made it *my* choice; but this was under the condition that whichever school I chose, I had to remain there the entire three years until graduation. As Dad explained, high school is a place where you can make lifelong connections, and after the disproportionate number of schools I'd attended, they wanted me finally to have that continuity through high school.

My mother took me for a visit and tour of the Hall campus, but for me the visit was a perfunctory one. I had made up my mind already: I would transfer to Hall. When I told Mom this, she breathed a sigh of relief. "Good," she said. "I'd just as soon have nothing more to do with those chauvinistic priests!" I couldn't have agreed more.

But an incident that summer would nearly make me a no-show for high school—or, indeed, for the rest of my life.

I had befriended a number of other kids in our neighborhood, including a boy named Joey who was one year ahead of me at Catholic, and with whom I'd carpooled to school that year. Joey shared my love of fishing, and we fished the local lakes and rivers at every opportunity. His uncle, Father Debosier, taught at the school, and his mother Enola was a warm (and rather eccentric) Cajun lady from Louisiana who often had me over for her famous homemade cuisine. (Rivaled only by my mother's own Southern cooking, which often found Joey, Darryl and other friends at our dinner table having arrived at the door—ostensibly by chance to say "hi"—just at our customary suppertime.) Two young girls had recently moved onto the street. Their dad had put up a basketball goal in the driveway which—like Darryl's trampoline coup earlier—now proved a magnet to all the boys in the neighborhood, and where most afternoons were spent with Joey, Darryl, and other local kids dividing into teams and shooting hoops. Even little Will, now seven, joined in and was delighted to play with the "big boys." (He would go on later to prove quite a talented basketball player in school.) When we got tired of basketball, we'd move on to tag football, somewhat dangerously playing mid-street despite the regular stream of traffic.

When the heat and humidity got to us, we'd retreat to my air-conditioned house where I had the new *Atari* home video game console, with which we could now play favorite arcade games like *Pacman*, *Asteroids*, *Pong* and *Space Invaders* right on the home TV. While the video entertainment played by kids today makes those first *Atari* games seem by comparison the Paleolithic scratchings of Cro-Magnon man, they were pure magic for us.

That year too, an older boy named Chad moved in with his mother and sister at a house on the far corner of the street, and he had a knowledge and love of what was then seen as "alternative" music—namely "New Wave," "Punk Rock," and "Heavy Metal." This drew me to his house regularly after school to rock out—made especially exciting by the drum set he owned (the first I'd ever seen up close), on which he played along to his spinning records of music by groups like The Sex Pistols, Black Flag, Adam Ant and Duran Duran. This experience coincided with a new cultural phenomenon: With the advent of cable television, a new channel suddenly appeared called "Music Television"—soon known universally by the abbreviation "MTV." This featured a group of young, hip hosts known for the first time as "VJs" for introducing the new genre of the commercial "music video." It was through this channel that a whole new British invasion took place, bringing bands like "Duran Duran," "The Pet Shop Boys" and "The Smiths" into the living room while completely changing the dynamic (and dissemination) of popular music. (It also had a considerable effect on 80's fashion, embraced immediately by Chad who sported what he called a "New Wave Punk" haircut.)

Chad was sixteen and had his driver's license, so in him I had a friend who could expand my horizons geographically as well as culturally. But he unfortunately was as wild behind the wheel as behind the drums. I never knew when he'd suddenly punch it, putting petal to metal to take us off like a roller coaster down one of the steep Little Rock hills. I sensed the inappropriateness—and danger—of his reckless driving, but nonetheless had faith in Chad's older, road-savvy wisdom. This I would soon regret.

One night we'd gone out for a burger, along with Chad's sister who sat in the back seat of their mother's Toyota Corolla. After dinner, Chad decided to go for a joy ride through the local neighborhoods. He put a favorite tape in the cassette deck, cranked up the music and took off. We wound through several dark neighborhood streets at a moderate speed before Chad suddenly punched it and took us skidding around a corner. Chad laughed and hollered with joyful abandon, but his sister must have sensed something alarming about his behavior and demanded he slow down. He sped up instead.

There were no streetlamps, and the dark street with its lines of neat, manicured lawns only revealed itself as far as the small car's headlights could reach. As we rounded the corner, a prescient fear took hold of me, and I realized I wasn't wearing the seatbelt. I hastily pulled the seatbelt over me and tried unsuccessfully to latch the buckle. Something told me to forget the seatbelt and hang on with all my might. I slid my hand through the rubber grip on my right side and grasped it tightly, pushing myself straight back into the seat. We appeared to be heading towards someone's front yard, and then the headlights bounced off something bright. Rocks! The entire front of the lawn was bordered with a row of large decorative rocks. An instant later the car went into a frontward flip; through the front windshield I saw the ground lit up in the flash of headlights now upon it, and then—after the hideous scrape of crunching metal mingled with a sound of shattering glass—everything stopped.

When the initial shock of the event passed after a few moments, I realized I was upside down, my head pinned in where the roof of the car had been pushed inwards. Something was in my right eye, a small fragment of glass perhaps. It's difficult to say exactly what happened next, apart from a dim recollection of yellow light appearing from open doors, people running towards us and asking if we were okay, the arrival of the ambulance with its flashing red lights.

Miraculously, each of us was more or less all right apart from minor injuries. It only occurred to me later how fatal this could easily have been for all of us, and especially for me in the passenger seat without my seatbelt fastened. I realized too that if I had not decided at that key moment to give up trying to fasten the seatbelt and concentrate on hanging on instead, I almost certainly would have flown headlong through the windshield as the car flipped over onto its back. It seemed miraculous that the strength of my (weaker) right arm was sufficient to hold me firmly in the seat during impact. I wondered if this had something to do with the purported inner strength that can manifest itself instinctively during life-threatening crises.

But I've worn my seatbelt ever since, a habit which has indeed saved my life on at least one further occasion in the years since. Yet that early intimation of mortality gave me a new perspective on life—and its precarious fragility—along with an early resolve to make the most of whatever opportunities might come my way.

One such opportunity presented itself shortly thereafter. My rock star fantasies had by this time reached a breaking point, and I'd resolved to do something about it. But unlike various friends who'd fulfilled similar dreams simply by acquiring an electric guitar or even a full drum set, my passion took a different—and unique—twist. For some reason, the instrument that struck my fancy was the electric bass guitar. This proved the perfect choice too, as it would (unlikely as this may have seemed) eventually set me apart from the crowd.

I'm not sure what drew me specifically to the bass, although it was probably the impression that had been made upon seeing bassist Geddy Lee in performance with Rush. Whereas the bass (and the musician playing it) is often confined to a background role, Lee transformed it into a veritable counterpart to the guitar, all the while remaining front and center as the band's singer. And unlike the often piercing scream of lead guitar, bass was the instrument you could *feel*, pulsating like the heartbeat of every song. My interest piqued, I began paying close attention to the bass lines in every song I heard. (A habit that, as my mother pointed out, would later prove advantageous on the dance floor.) Soon, especially with the chance now to *see* so many musicians in action courtesy of MTV, I discovered numerous other standout bassists such as The Who's John Entwhistle, Chris Squire from Yes, Sting of The Police, and of course Paul McCartney.

When the desire to actually acquire a bass of my own finally became overwhelming, I asked my parents about it, who said that if I really wanted it, I must save up and buy it with my own money. By *earning* a thing, they said, I'd truly appreciate it—as well as prove to myself I really wanted it and would use and value it. (I knew a number of kids whose parents gave them whatever they asked at the drop of a hat, only to see it quickly tossed aside and wasted once the thrill of possession was gone.)

So I saved up my paper route earnings, and when I thought I had enough money Mom took me to a local pawn shop to see if they had any basses. Sure enough, they had many, most of which had undoubtedly been pawned for next to nothing by hard luck musicians desperate for a quick fix. But one of them immediately struck my eye. It was the exact same model of bass, an early 70s era Rickenbacker, which I'd recently seen Geddy Lee himself play on stage. Chris Squire played one too. But despite Mom's savvy deal-making ability, the instrument still cost every penny that I'd managed to save up. This was the moment of decision: I knew if I made this investment, I *had* to make good use of it. I would be committed to learning to play the bass.

Word got around that I was in possession of a real Rickenbacker bass guitar, and before I could play a single note (not to mention buy an amp with which to hear it), I had boys from school who'd never previously have given me the time of day turning up at home to see the bass. As pleased as I was, one unfortunate incident nearly ended my musical aspirations just as soon as they'd begun. A popular boy named Howard, whom I was particularly pleased to see arrive at my house one day, suddenly held my bass along the neck for a better look. The ceiling fan was spinning at full blast. Howard stood directly beneath the fan as he inspected the instrument, and then to my horror abruptly thrust it vertically upwards for a better view of the neck and directly into the fan! The moment the spinning blades struck the elegant tip of my Rickenbacker's neck with a terrible CLACK, two tuning keys went flying across the room as their respective strings fell downwards like the slackened strands of just-scythed wheat.

I was flummoxed, but Howard assured me someone at the local music store, Boyd Music, would know what to do. He split before I considered the possible cost of repairs. Fortunately they were able to repair the instrument; however, no original Rickenbacker tuning keys were available and they had to replace the whole set with four new Gibson keys instead. My bass was no longer perfect, but at least it would play. Now all I had to do was learn to play it—a task which seemed daunting as I stared at the long neck with its mysterious frets, knowing their ability to bring forth infinite notes full of sound and musical color if I could only unlock the key.

During my 15th birthday party, after I blew out the candles on a homemade Red Velvet cake, Mom said she had a surprise gift. She had arranged for me to begin lessons with the bass teacher at Boyd Music.

By the time I started that fall at my new high school, I'd both recovered from the trauma of the car accident and made noticeable progress on the bass. (Fortunately, despite being a "leftie" I proved ambidextrous on the bass and thus avoided having to restring the instrument upside down à la McCartney or Hendrix.) My teacher used a series of Mel Bay instruction books, which took me from memorizing the names and values of notes in the bass clef to playing recognizable melodies within a matter of months. I threw myself into daily practice for my weekly lessons with a joy I'd previously only known from reading an exciting new book. I also got a small amplifier, which transformed the thick copper wires strung along the bass into the lush, warm sounds of my Rickenbacker guitar. I discovered I could even pick out the bass lines of many of my favorite songs; I'd play particular songs on my records, studying an individually challenging passage by lifting the needle and resetting it upon the appropriate grooves repeatedly until I could play it right. As I learned each new song, I would get carried away at times and crank up the amp full blast; but the little amp couldn't keep up with my stereo speakers, and I'd often wish the volume knob would go up higher—just one more notch, from "10" to "11".

Unfortunately my bedroom was just above the living room, where Dad perpetually sat in his comfy chair watching television. To his credit, he endured much of the noise emanating from above. But when I finally dwarfed my little amp by upgrading to a proper *Marshall* bass amplifier, the resulting house-shaking turbulence proved too much and I'd occasionally wheel around with my bass, completely lost in rhythmic ecstasy, to find Dad banging on the door and shouting to get my attention, demanding that I please TURN IT DOWN! We finally reached a reasonable compromise, which would keep the peace until the arrival of my garage band later that year.

After two years of rigid parochial school rules, combined with the re-lentless bombardment of religious dogma, the informal atmosphere of Hall High School and its wide diversity of student backgrounds proved refreshingly mind-opening. I'd also have over the coming three years my best teachers yet, especially in English and music, whose in-spiration would prove in many ways seminal even when compared to my finest college professors of later years.

This started from day one, when I first arrived in sophomore hon-ors English class and met its teacher, Sue Maddison. In addition to the passion with which she introduced the widest range of World Litera-ture I'd thus far read—including my first extensive study of both drama and *poetry*—she shared with us her interesting (and, for us, unique) background and stories, including her Jewish heritage and her mar-riage to a former London policeman she'd met while attending col-lege at the University of London. Her stories of studying literature in England immediately piqued my interest, inspiring a vague idea in my mind that would achieve fruition in later years.

Outside of school I continued to thrive with my bass lessons, and one day my teacher, Bob Lincoln, made an intriguing suggestion. By now I had great respect for Bob, a professional bassist with shoulder-length yellow hair beneath a worn baseball cap, as a person as well as a teacher. (Especially after hearing he played occasionally in Hot Springs with local girl Chrissie Hynde of The Pretenders.) Bob asked if my school might by chance have a jazz band, which it in fact did. He then proposed that I speak to the band director about joining. I immediately dismissed the idea, saying I'd never be able to play the kind of music I'd heard them play at the huge football assemblies held in the school's auditorium. Besides, they already had a bassist.

"Nevertheless, you should talk to the director," said Bob. "You might be better than you think."

I went home that day excited, yet also apprehensive. The jazz band had a great reputation already after a recent assembly when they'd played a moving rendition of The Beatles' "Penny Lane." Then something even more significant had happened: After the official jazz band cleared the stage, the drummer, guitarist and bass player remained on stage, all older boys I didn't recognize; then a girl joined them at the microphone and they burst into a rocking cover of the new Joan Jett and the Blackhearts song, "I Love Rock and Roll." The rest of the school was mesmerized; for my part, I couldn't believe my eyes and ears: Here I was at *school*, during a school day, watching students perform rock n' roll. But it of course went much further than that. Just hearing a live band perform at school wasn't enough. I wanted to *be* up there on stage, playing that bass in front of throngs of cheering kids—and, for once, admiring classmates.

And *girls*. After a year's hiatus at an all boy school, I was surrounded by girls. Girls who had somehow changed since 8th grade, not only physically but in another mysterious way that hinted at new depths of wisdom. They had suddenly become *seductive*. But one thing was now clear by the reaction I observed to the boys in the band: You didn't have to be a football jock to impress the ladies. With this revelation, my bass became a new symbol of hope and possibility, and my practice sessions imbued with a passionate sense of urgency.

Now that the idea was put in my head that I might actually be ready to play in a proper band, I waited anxiously for the opportunity to approach the band director. I finally gathered my nerves and entered the music room, a large space of tiered levels crowded with music stands, and knocked on the director's office door. I had expected a polite "thanks but no thanks" when I explained my interest, but what happened instead was—in retrospect—life changing. The band director, Lorenzo Smith, was a professional jazz musician and composer; and he was not only friendly but, as I'd soon appreciate, also possessed of a wickedly sick sense of humor. And he was immediately receptive to my interest. When I mentioned the other bass player, he answered: "I've wanted to put Tommy back on trombone anyway." He gave me some music to take home, which I found to my great surprise I could read with ease. Within a week, I was signed up for Jazz Band and rehearsing with the "big boys." It was the thrill of a lifetime.

Performing on stage, on bass next to the drums,
with the Hall High Jazz Band

Socially, my arrival at Hall High had not required starting from scratch. Most of my old friends from the Forest Heights Junior High days were there, as well as former enemy-turned-friend Kyle. So was Donny. And among the upper classmen, I felt privileged to count among my friends my neighbor Darryl, now a senior. He, however, made it clear that we could only hang out after school, as it would be considered uncool for him to be seen associating with a lowly sophomore—or, in the school vernacular, "slop dog" (or just "slop"). And although Darryl didn't say it, I was clearly further precluded from his group at school for being white (creating awkward moments whenever I did try to greet him on campus). But we remained close friends off campus, playing the latest *Atari* games and bowling (though no longer in a league) until he graduated and moved East for college. When we met again years later, he had established a successful career as chief accountant for the city of Atlanta. But my social life at school would now undergo a remarkable expansion, thanks to my music.

Playing in Mr. Smith's jazz band proved a transformative musical experience, one that expanded my narrow cultural horizons to new realms of artistic expression. I began to learn the names of various jazz greats, while mastering ever more challenging forms of rhythmic expression on the bass. I learned the importance of coordinating the bass line with the drums to form a tight rhythm section, requiring constant eye contact between bassist and drummer—almost a kind of musical telepathy, that at its best allows the two musicians to subtly communicate with each other how to coordinate beat and bass. I realized the power of the bass, despite its often overlooked status as a mere supporting instrument, to guide or—at its worst—even derail the band in mid-song. Unlike the guitar, you couldn't just stop and regroup if you lost your place. This was frighteningly illustrated for me when Mr. Smith got me my first professional gig.

A friend of his, David Rosen (from whose local music shop, Romco Drums, we bought band supplies) had a big band that often performed at local events. (I later learned that Rosen had once, as a band director at Hot Springs High School, directed the young Bill Clinton's jazz band.) They were to play at the upcoming Shriner's Circus, and they needed a bassist. I eagerly took the job, knowing little what it involved but by now smugly confident in my ability to play anything. But these fast, big band numbers had bass lines like I'd never seen, and I wasn't tested at sight-reading. So when I found myself seated with the band in the huge Barton Coliseum, suddenly hearing my bass notes echoing through the arena for thousands to hear, I nearly panicked. Most harrowing of all was when we performed for the tightrope walkers, and I became aware that they appeared to be following *my* bass rhythm as they walked the line. I was suddenly convinced that one missed beat on my part would result in an acrobat tumbling to a tragic death. Then I lost my place in the music all together. But I remembered Mr. Smith's advice just before the gig: *If you make a mistake, make it loud.* And so I did—I improvised, keeping the rhythm going despite the painfully audible discord with the band's horn section (and the resulting evil-eye or two from fellow musicians). Nonetheless the importance of improvising during a crisis—of boldly proceeding through a turbulent sea of treacherous mistakes—was a lesson to serve me well in future years.

A new opportunity soon presented itself, one which allowed me finally to try out the music on which I'd first cut my teeth as a bassist. My old friend Donny, now a classmate at Hall, told me he knew a couple of guys from Central High who played guitar and were looking for a bass player. I jumped at the opportunity and met up with these two young guitar prodigies, named Tyndall and Rob. I wasn't sure what to expect when I hauled my bass and amp over to Tyndall's house for my first proper jam session, but by the end of the evening I was amazed to be playing actual songs I'd heard on the radio for years. Within a few hours, we were playing complete renditions of Led Zeppelin and Rolling Stones songs including "Stairway to Heaven" and "Sympathy for the Devil"—as well as Lynyrd Skynyrd's iconic Southern anthem, "Free Bird." They also taught me exciting music I'd never before heard, such as "Statesboro Blues" by The Allman Brothers, requiring that I learn on the spot how to improvise an 8-bar blues progression. At the end of the session over five hours later, we made a recording of all the songs we'd learned. That night I listened to the tape over and over, amazed at the sound of this music I'd helped create.

Not long afterwards, Tyndall called to say he'd signed us up for a talent show at a downtown school. We'd have an actual opportunity to perform on stage in front of a large audience! But there was one small problem: We needed a drummer. I had a good friend named Jason at Hall who'd gained a reputation as a top-notch drummer, and soon we were a complete band—called "Loose Change"—and ready to rock n' roll. When the big night came, we performed the Stones' "Under My Thumb." We knew from the start that—being the only rock act on the talent list—our chances of winning the talent show were little to none, and we were right. But listening to the tape later, pleased with the vibrant sound of a live audience mingled with our music, I knew I'd crossed a major threshold: I was one step closer to fulfilling my dreams of musical accomplishment—and recognition.

First Gig: With Tyndall, Rob, and Jason as "Loose Change"' (Fall 1982)

At school, however, I was still in the backseat. Despite my success in replacing Tommy as bassist in the jazz band, he still got to play with the rock band, consisting of school rock legends Dan on drums and Sammy on guitar. I watched them practice with envy, along with the growing certainty that I could outplay Tommy if only given the chance—especially after my experience of performing live. But they were all older than I, and speaking my mind seemed out of the question. I resolved to show off my stuff at every opportunity during formal jazz band rehearsals, with the hope I might someday be noticed and given the chance to prove myself. I did not have to wait very long.

The car accident that summer had revealed to me the tenuous string upon which clings each individual life, a string which may be severed at any moment (if not inevitably by the passage of time). I had as a result begun to reflect on the precious gift of life, despite its evident ups and downs, and resolved to seek out experience and make the most of every opportunity given me. And I took to heart these words from *Julius Caesar* after reading them aloud in Mrs. Maddison's English class:

> There is a tide in the affairs of men
> Which, taken at the flood, leads on to fortune;
> Omitted, all the voyage of their life
> Is bound in shallows and in miseries.
> On such a full sea are we now afloat,
> And we must take the current when it serves,
> Or lose our ventures.

My own sails of ambition would soon be filled with the halcyon breeze of good fortune when, one day after a jazz band rehearsal, Dan the drummer said he'd like a word with me in private.

"There's another big pep rally coming up," said Dan, "and the cheerleaders want Excalibur to play." I nodded shyly. Excalibur was the name of Dan and Sammy's rock band, and the tone of Dan's voice ignited a spark of hope in my heart.

"We like how you play the bass," continued Dan. My heart nearly flew out of my mouth upon the wings of all the butterflies fluttering in my stomach. "We want you to play with us," he concluded.

"Sure," I stammered.

"Cool. We'll be practicing at my house. We're gonna play some Zeppelin and Van Halen. And maybe an Elvis song with that kid who impersonates the King."

Dan gazed at me thoughtfully for a moment. Then he nodded and started to turn away, but before exiting the music room added: "Oh, and don't worry about Tommy. I'll handle him."

"Okay."

I was now alone in the music room, and as I looked around at the rows of music stands and instrument cases, a sudden joy rose from deep within and filled every facet of my being. This was it. I'd made it. I was in the band, and I'd be performing rock n' roll on stage in front of the whole school. I packed up my bass and walked home on Cloud Nine.

When the day of the assembly finally arrived, I began to have second thoughts. Apart from the talent show, at which I'd performed briefly in front of a small group of strangers, I'd never performed on stage. And this would be in front of my entire school, *hundreds* of students, including all my teachers and classmates (friends and foes alike). And every girl from whom I'd ever craved the slightest notice. Even after weeks of band practice, I found myself wondering if—once I actually got up on stage where it counted—I'd really be able to play all my notes. These were my thoughts as I waited in the wings backstage for the band's turn to play.

We had worked out a pretty dramatic entrance too. Our first song was the Van Halen version of The Kinks' song "You Really Got Me." Van Halen prefaced the song on their debut album with a two minute guitar solo called "Eruption" (which introduced Eddie Van Halen to the rock world with his unique style of fast pull offs and hammers), and Sammy had learned the solo note for note on his Fender Strat, adding the Dixie battle call as a final flourish. So for our performance, Dan, Eric (our rhythm guitarist), and I waited behind the thick black stage curtain while Sammy appeared alone in the spotlight to a tumultuous applause. As I grasped the neck of my bass in anticipation, I suddenly wished Sammy's solo would never end! But end it did: And the moment he'd completed his Dixie flourish to the delighted crowd, after a low vibrato with his guitar's "whammy bar" he launched into the heavy distortion-filled power chords of "You Really Got Me." This was our cue, and at a signal from Dan I made a quick *glissando* down the neck of my bass to hit the first note on his initial beat. At that moment someone pushed a button to open the curtain, and I watched as it gradually parted to reveal the packed auditorium beyond the spotlight.

I nearly collapsed from fear, but refocused attention on my playing, finding it all I could do just to keep my fingers working the thick bass strings. I suddenly felt naked, standing there in front of all my peers—so many pairs of eyes—hoping I might be invisible next to the singer and Sammy's lead guitar and Dan's supportive drumming behind me. Yet I had the sensation of suddenly being stuck to the stage, my feet pinned firmly to the wooden floor as if confined in lead boots. Whereas during practice I'd loosened up to the point that I could sway in unison with Sammy as we played, just like I'd seen so many rock stars do on stage and MTV, now it was all I could do simply to play the notes. I couldn't move anything but my fingers, earning me a later (not unflattering) comparison to Who bassist John Entwhistle.

At the end of the first song Dan—twirling his drumsticks like Neil Peart himself—launched immediately into the John Bonham drum intro of Led Zeppelin's "Rock And Roll"; by this point it seemed I'd survive the ordeal, and we concluded the set with "Jailhouse Rock," featuring a kid who'd become famous for his Elvis antics. He entered dressed in a white jacket and matching suede shoes, like a young Vegas-era Elvis as he shimmered wildly across the stage.

Finally it was over. The curtain slowly closed again, and I sighed in relief as I hauled my equipment offstage. I had the sick feeling I'd blown it; I'd be the laughing stock of the school, and Tommy—who'd not hidden his resentment towards me—would be back in the band. But to my surprise, when Dan called after me as I was leaving the building, he said: "Hey Frank, great job man! See you at band practice after school." It seemed, as my bass teacher Bob Lincoln had predicted, that maybe I was better than I thought after all.

Thereafter my peers' opinion of me palpably improved: the lowly 'slop' made good, playing bass in the band with the big boys. From the moment that curtain had risen to reveal me on stage in the spotlight plucking the strings upon my Rickenbacker (frozen stiff with

On stage at school (from the Hall High School yearbook)

fear notwithstanding), I'd crossed a new threshold enveloping experience, society and ultimately personality itself. For the first time, I felt
truly accepted as part of the community in which I inhabited. I was
now known officially as the Excalibur bass player. Sammy gave me a
small sword pendant, part of an exclusive set for the band he'd "forged"
from lead during art class—which I proudly now displayed on the gold
chain around my neck. My new reputation led to new friendships, especially with fellow sophomores who played guitar and wanted to get
together and jam.

These included two boys named Robert and Joe, whom I met in
Physical Education class—where Joe, like me, escaped whenever possible from the gymnastic-oriented sports that hardly suited our awkward frames, preferring to lounge on the grass by the football field and
talk music.

It was also all I could do to keep from being recruited to the school
basketball team, the Hall High "Warriors" and soon-to-be state champions—led by future Arkansas Razorback Allie Freeman—on whose
team I knew I had no business. (But Coach Oliver Elders, a kind-
hearted gentleman whose wife Jocelyn would one day be Surgeon-
General of the United States, would often look me up and down from
head to toe, saying "You're so tall, you should play basketball for us!") I
did play briefly on my church basketball team, where my height earned
me the apt nickname of "The Tree" from Coach Jimmy Faulkner. Much
to Coach Faulkner's dismay, however, it turned out that I could block
shots far better than I could make them.

I got together one day with Robert and Joe at Joe's house and
spent the day playing along to all our favorite records, and this led
to a new group of school friends that would—just as my parents had
predicted—last a lifetime.

One day near the start of my junior year, as I walked home from
school up the long sidewalk across the middle of campus, I saw a girl
walking in the same direction on the perpendicular sidewalk along
the street. I didn't recognize her and thought she must be new; but
from the distance I could tell she was very pretty. I looked ahead and
realized that, if I slowed my pace slightly, I could time it so that we
reached the corner where the two sidewalks intersected at exactly the
same moment. I glanced carefully towards her, trying not to appear too
obvious, but felt certain she'd seemed to speed her own pace to match
mine. The distance between us quickly narrowed, and I pretended not
to notice her until we nearly collided.

"Hi," I finally said, shyly, realizing it'd still be easier to play a bass
solo nude onstage at the Playboy Mansion than to say the right thing to

a girl. But fortunately this girl was pretty direct, and I quickly learned the advantage of having a school rock star reputation to precede me. (An unlikely role rendered all the more awkward by my innate timidity.) Her name was Anna, and she'd recently transferred to Hall High. Her easygoing manner and friendly smile put me at ease, and we continued talking as we walked toward my street. As we prepared to part ways, I invited her to come by my house and listen to some music; and to my surprise she actually accepted. Even more surprised was my mother when we entered the house and I introduced her to Anna. We listened to records and talked for what seemed hours, and before she left Anna told me her true passion was poetry. She took out her journal and showed me pages of poems illustrated by original artwork.

It was an early autumn day, and a deep red sunset filtered through the clusters of orange and yellow leaves of tall trees lining the streets. In the air there was a faint tinge of smoke, bringing with it that old familiar nostalgia such fall days brought. But now there was something else too. Something magic. And when I finally said goodnight to Anna and walked home alone, the magic transformed to a deep melancholy. I hadn't a clue about what to do next.

"Ask her out!" my friends all said. But I felt I had to have a good excuse to do so and couldn't just call her up out of the blue. I realized too that I still had a deep inner fear of being rejected. I wasn't sure why, but the thought of rejection seemed to paralyze me into inaction. (It would be years before I associated this fear with an acute sense of rejection due to an absent father.) Yet an opportunity to ask Anna out soon presented itself unlooked for.

I heard the announcement on "Magic 105" rock radio that the Canadian rock band "Loverboy" would perform a concert in Little Rock. They were an international super group with a recent top ten hit called "Turn Me Loose" that featured a solo bass pattern right at the start of the song. So I gathered my nerve and called Anna to invite her to the concert.

"Sure," she said. "Can I bring my sister?"

"Yeah, okay."

Not the perfect arrangement to be sure, but at least I had a date. I counted the days until the show, and that morning something extraordinary happened. When I got a phone call from the manager of Boyd Music store, I figured they were just calling to reschedule a bass lesson with Bob Lincoln, but it turned out to be something completely different.

"We got a call from one of the roadies for Loverboy. Turns out the band's bassist had a problem with his backup bass and told a roadie to find a Rickenbacker. The roadie called every music store in the phone book, and when he called us we told him about you and your bass. He wants you to call him ASAP. They want to use your bass."

I anxiously dialed the number he gave me, hardly believing for a moment this could be real. But when I spoke to the roadie and introduced myself, he sounded extraordinarily relieved when I said I had a Rickenbacker bass. He'd looked all over town, he said, and I seemed to have the only one in Little Rock. He'd hate to disappoint the bassist by coming back empty-handed. But what he said next nearly knocked me from my chair.

"Listen, would you like tickets to the show?"

"I already have the tickets."

"How many?"

"Three."

"Okay, if you'll let us use your bass, I can get you three backstage passes for after the show. How does that sound?"

When I hung up I felt those familiar butterflies return, this time along with a sense of disbelief. I'd seen a number of concerts, but the bands themselves seemed like gods, set apart on some high pedestal you could only glimpse from afar. I knew that a few lucky people occasionally got (or won) *backstage passes*, but such an opportunity always seemed like some mythical dream. It took a moment to take this all in—not only would I have backstage passes, but I'd actually get to see *my* bass up on stage being played by Loverboy's bassist. Unreal!

The first thing I did was call Anna with the news. She actually screamed over the phone with delight. Then I drove over to Barton Coliseum and parked in the back, where crews were unloading huge tractor-trailer rigs full of equipment. I gave the name of the roadie who'd called, and a young bearded man came up and greeted me enthusiastically. He gave me a VIP pass to wear and ushered me inside. The backstage area was a flurry of activity, and when we walked past a room with an open door, I saw a pretty blonde woman sitting with Loverboy musicians.

"Did you see the blonde?" asked the roadie.

"Yeah."

"That's Connie. You know, *sweet* Connie?"

I had certainly heard about Connie. Everybody knew about Connie. She was a famous local groupie who managed to party with every band who came through Little Rock. My band even played the Grand Funk Railroad song called "We're An American Band" that had immortalized Connie in rock legend:

Out on the road for forty days,
Last night in Little Rock put me in a haze,

Sweet, sweet Connie was doin' her act,
She had the whole show and that's a natural fact!

We then entered a room full of musical instruments, where a technician was tuning a bass made of beautifully polished light brown wood. I immediately recognized it as the same Spector bass guitar I'd seen in Loverboy music videos on MTV. Without thinking (or knowing, rather) the proper etiquette in such situations, I asked if I could see it for a moment. The roadie hesitantly handed me the bass, and I began playing note for note the opening octave bass pattern from "Turn Me Loose." It felt scintillating actually to be playing the same song on the same bass I'd seen the Loverboy bassist play countless times on TV. Clearly displeased, the roadie quickly took back the bass and set it on its stand. He then asked me to follow him to the stage with my bass, and as we walked down the hall I recognized the band's singer as he passed with a warm greeting. We went up the ramp that led onto the stage, where I finally met the bassist, a pleasant young guy named Scott Smith. I then experienced the thrill I'd been anticipating ever since the phone call that afternoon, when I watched Smith play my bass right there on the stage of Barton Coliseum. The roadie thanked me again graciously, and then handed me an envelope with the backstage passes.

"Just come to the back entrance after the concert," he said. "Enjoy the show!" This all seemed too good to be real. If I knew the word yet, I might have thought of it as *surreal*. But I doubt even surreal would suffice to describe what happened later that night.

After the concert, our ears still ringing from the satisfyingly loud performance of a full set of favorite of songs, I walked with Anna and her sister eagerly around the building to the back entrance. We were all full of anticipation for the experience of going backstage and meeting the band after the show. When we got there, a group of fans had gathered, some also with passes but many others just hoping for a glimpse of the band members. A large burly man came out and told everyone to leave, and when I confidently showed him our passes he waved them off.

"It's late and the band's not doing a meet and greet tonight. Go on home."

"But they said . . ."

"Did you hear me? I said they're not doing it. Goodnight!"

As he turned to go back inside I was seized with panic.

"Wait, Mister, they've got my bass!"

He paused momentarily and looked back, and I explained that they had my Rickenbacker I'd loaned the bassist for the show. He went inside and I looked at Anna; she seemed both disappointed and concerned. After a few minutes the man returned, carrying my bass case but looking even more annoyed than before as he brusquely thrust it into my hands and quickly turned and went back in and shut the door. I dejectedly led Anna and her sister back to the car in the middle of the parking lot, now packed with honking cars trying to exit. I felt extremely uptight as well as embarrassed for letting down the girls after getting their hopes up, which is probably why I wasn't thinking clearly about my driving.

When we got to the main entrance on busy Asher Avenue, I needed to take a left turn through heavy, unregulated traffic. Apart from a battalion of dizzying headlights, it was difficult to see clearly around the slow moving line of cars in the lane immediately in front of us. The cars behind me started honking their horns impatiently, and just as I began feeling conscious of looking even more helplessly indecisive in front of the girls, an opening appeared between two cars in front of me and I punched the gas pedal and swerved left. Just as I rounded one vehicle to enter the far lane, there was a hideous CRASH as I ran almost head-on into a car from the opposite direction. A terrible feeling of angst coursed through my stomach as I grasped what had happened. I looked quickly at Anna, who like me fortunately had her seatbelt on; then I looked back and saw that her sister was bent low with her hands on her head, crying. She was hurt.

The driver of the opposite car was a young girl who also appeared to be hurt; and whereas the car I was driving—Dad's large maroon Pontiac Bonneville—appeared damaged mainly in the front, it had plowed like a tank into the smaller vehicle and totaled it. The police arrived along with an ambulance, and after the injuries were assessed— Anna's sister being scratched but able to go home, and the opposite driver shaken up but otherwise not seriously injured—an officer took a report and handed me a ticket. I then drove the girls home in Dad's seriously compromised car.

Dad was naturally displeased at the damage I'd wrought to his Pontiac, and said that for insurance purposes, I'd have to go a full year without so much as a parking ticket. This meant I'd have to keep driving to a bare minimum, and also of course that my dream of getting a car of my own was now indefinitely on hold. (I was also required to attend driving classes featuring a weekly barrage of gruesome film footage.) Far worse to me, however, was the end of all communication from Anna. She did not return my calls, and she avoided me at school. Soon I saw her hanging out with other guys—older guys who were reputedly potheads and worse. But I couldn't get her out of my mind. Her smile, her long auburn hair and the deep brown eyes that hinted of her mother's Hispanic heritage, haunted me day and night. I'd never experienced anything like it. I wondered if there was something I could possibly do to regain her respect, or at least her attention. Then I recalled Anna's love of poetry, and the original poems of her own she'd shared with me from her journal.

In my mother's study there was a typewriter that she used for writing lesson plans. I sat down in front of it. There was a blank sheet of paper already wound into the scroll, and I began to type.

I'd never attempted such a thing before, but after several hours I had typed out an original poem. I wasn't sure if it was any good, but what amazed me was that in reading through it I found I'd expressed all my feelings about Anna in two pages of rhyming couplets, organized into a series of stanzas that arranged themselves as I typed, and incorporated imagery—and even metaphor—that had never even occurred to me before I composed the poem. It was my first true vista of the creative process outside of music. Just as with my first discovery of the magic of music performance, the thrill of creative writing left me mesmerized.

I then faced a tortuous inner debate whether or not actually to give the poem to Anna. She would, I supposed, probably just laugh at it; even worse, she might show it to her new friends, making both it and me a source of ridicule. Yet, on the other hand, the poem might just move her in some way; being a sensitive poet herself, maybe she'd appreciate the hours I'd spent laboring away alone to produce this composition inspired by and dedicated solely to her. Finally I folded the poem, placed it in an envelope, and slipped it into her school locker when nobody was looking.

Meanwhile, I had a welcome opportunity for a new experience which promised to help take my mind off Anna and recent events. I'd been invited by my uncle, David Cash, to join him and various other male relatives at their deer camp in the woods outside Crossett for the start of deer season. For years as a young boy I'd watched as all the men went off hunting, and I'd longed for the opportunity to join them. "One day, when you're old enough, you can come with us," they always said. Now that day had finally arrived, and I gleefully headed to Crossett for my first hunt.

Dad had taken me shopping for the necessary clothing, including a camouflaged hunting jacket and boots, though I still didn't have a gun. But Daddy Frank said I could use one of his. I was more than a little apprehensive about this, as I'd grown up gazing from a safe distance at the ominous rack of ancient looking shotguns on the wall of his bedroom, right next to the equally intimidating portrait of my great-grandfather Jesse Hancock, with his long bushy beard masking the many stories I'd heard of him as a Confederate soldier and subsequent outlaw. (Daddy Frank said that after the Civil War his father had once even ridden with the Jesse James gang.) Some of these guns came from his time. But Daddy Frank chose one of the smaller rifles, a Winchester Model 1912 16-guage that he said he'd acquired when he returned from the First World War. From the moment I held it, I felt a sense of majesty about it. Not only was it my grandfather's, but it came from a different era altogether. The date stamped upon the barrel was 1913, and I realized the Winchester shotgun I was holding was a palpable symbol of the fabled "Wild West" itself. There in that old bedroom, musty with the dust of countless decades, as I looked up into Daddy Frank's wizened face beneath the brim of his Stetson cowboy hat, I felt the sensation of belonging to a different age—an age in which that gun was a precious tool in the struggle for survival in a desperate land.

The gun was lighter than I'd feared, and I otherwise had confidence in my shooting ability after years of target practice with BB guns during which I frequently hit the bull's eye. So off I went to the deer camp, where at last I found myself in the company of a group of hunters. Along with Uncle David, Jim Bob was there as well as my Aunt Blanche's husband Slim. Uncle Slim hailed from Texas and lived up to his name as a "long tall Texan" (including a sense of folksy humor that made every story he told around the campfire in his thick Texan drawl an adventure in itself). One story he liked to tell was of an old uncle of mine who was all but blind, yet still drove around in a huge old car, gauging when to turn by having memorized how many "Mississippis" must be counted before making each necessary maneuver en route to the local Piggly Wiggly grocery store. Remarkably, he'd never had an accident; but everyone knew if they saw him coming to swing wide, just in case.

The camp itself had the makeshift feel of a temporary sylvan retreat. There was a large main cabin, along with several smaller ones for the various groups of hunters. A communal supper was served in the main cabin, where the cook made everything under the sun that could be prepared with venison. She served venison steak, venison burgers, venison sausage and (best of all) spicy venison chili. For breakfast we'd have venison and eggs, venison and pancakes, venison and grits, venison and spam and—well, you name it and there was probably venison served with it.

In the chill before dawn I trudged with Jim Bob into the deep woods, where he guided me to a small deer stand set up in a tall tree and told me to climb up. When I got there I was to sit motionless and in complete silence until I either saw an antlered deer or else heard a bell summoning the hunters back for lunch. As I scoured the edge of the small glade around me, dreaming of the huge multi-point buck that would soon be within shooting range, my anticipation quickly transformed to intense boredom after what seemed hours sitting motionless and silent in the dark cold. I shivered, fingering the rifle restlessly as a dim gray light began faintly to illuminate the clearing. I took off my glove and ran my fingers along the old polished wooden stem of the rifle. I itched to squeeze the trigger, to feel again the jolt of the gun's action that I had felt during some practice shots the day before—and to taste the acrid smell of gunpowder while listening to the powerful blast I'd made reverberate through the woods.

My thoughts drifted to the time, as a boy scout, another boy and I had fallen behind the group during an Ozark forest hike; before long we realized we'd taken a wrong path and split off from the group. We shouted in vain for hours, until darkness fell. Then we had to put our studied scouting skills into actual practice over the next couple of days until we found our way out of the woods. Despite the harrowing nature of that experience, I'd found it somehow liberating to be—for a brief space of time—completely severed from society, completely at one with (and at the mercy of) nature. On another camping trip, I had experienced nature a bit too up close courtesy of a prank by fellow scout Tyler (the boy who in third grade had incurred my wrath, finally averting a fight with a diplomatic bowl of ice cream). Having heard my confessed arachnophobia there in the midst of a forest seething with poisonous spiders, Tyler arranged things so that I felt one night the sensation of something crawling up my leg from deep inside the sleeping bag. I froze, seized in the grip of some primal fear, as I could feel the thing moving up my body—accompanied by the further movement of something else crawling around my feet. In a terrified panic I slid out of the bag and ran from the tent screaming. As other scouts gathered around, Tyler pulled out the sleeping bag and shone his flashlight upon it with a laugh. It was filled with baby frogs.

My thoughts raced suddenly back to the present at the sound of galloping hooves just to the left of me. Then silence. I ever so slowly turned my head towards the direction of the sound. A twig snapped, followed by a rustling movement in the brush, and a pair of antlers emerged from the thicket. I froze. It wasn't the grand buck I'd envisioned, but this deer was fair game nonetheless. And after so many hours of idle waiting, I knew if I had any chance of killing a deer and impressing the men, this was the one shot I'd get. But I didn't want to risk the embarrassment that would accompany firing and missing—or worse, wounding the animal without bringing it down. So I waited, watching peripherally as the creature took first one, then another cautious step forward until it was in the clearing, still some distance away but well within range. I closed one eye and squinted with the other while inching up the shotgun. Then, as if in slow motion, I twisted my torso until I could see the animal in full view ahead across the glade. I lowered the barrel until I was aiming directly at him. I felt the sensation of cold metal as my finger wrapped carefully around the old nickel steel trigger.

At that moment I recalled what Mama Doris had said the day before.

"You won't be able to do it," she had said. "The moment that deer looks up at you, and you're looking right into its eyes, you won't be able to shoot."

The deer abruptly looked up, its eyes staring straight at me. I knew that any moment now it would dart off swiftly into the safety of the dark woods.

And I fired.

That afternoon I watched with mixed emotions as my uncle flayed the hanging carcass of the deer I'd shot. One of the other men, a tall bearded fellow wearing a bright orange baseball cap, looked at me curiously.

"Was that your first deer, boy?"

"Yes, sir," I said proudly.

The man smiled with a nod and loaded a plug of chewing tobacco. As I watched my uncle nonchalantly toss the animal's extremities and entrails into a large tin bucket, I couldn't help but reflect upon the need I'd felt to stalk and kill this beautiful, helpless creature. If it had been a question of survival by putting much needed meat on the family table—as in the case of my ancestors—that was one thing; but what inner aggression led men to hunt and kill with neither need nor provocation? Was it, I mused, the same killer instinct that fueled the endless wars from antiquity down to our own time? After all, the war in which Daddy Frank had fought was dubbed at the time the "war to end all wars," and yet the rest of the century had been fraught with fighting ever since. Even then, we were in a bizarre "Cold War," with the perpetual dread that sirens might sound at any moment warning of imminent nuclear attack. That, surely, *would* be the war to end all wars. And given man's apparent predisposition to violence, could such a war be finally avoided given both sides' "mutual assured destruction"? Or then again, maybe hunting for sport merely enacted an inherent, primordial ritual fulfilling man's communion with the natural cycle of life and death.

My thoughts were quickly cut short by a sudden bloodbath right there at camp: As I stood lost in thought, someone grabbed my hands firmly from behind and pushed my head forcefully towards the ground. Then I felt something cold and wet pour over me from above. When I saw what was now all over me and dripping from my hair, I cringed with disgust. Someone had taken the bucket and dumped over my head the entire mass of blood, guts, organs and body parts of the deer I'd killed that morning. I looked up the see the man with the orange cap holding the empty bucket, while the other men around me—including my relatives—laughed and clapped. The man turned his head aside and spat a brown wad of tobacco, then turned back to me with a grin.

"Congratulations on killin' your first deer, boy!"

A few weeks later I received a package in the mail from Uncle David. He had framed the deer's antlers on a beautiful wooden plaque he'd made for me. Underneath the antlers was a metal plate on which he had engraved the details of my first hunt:

FRANK THURMOND
NOV. 12th 1983   1 SHOT
FIRST HUNT   FIRST DAY
DADDY FRANK'S 16 GA.

I proudly hung it on the wall of my room.

Not long afterwards, I met Estelle. I'd heard nothing further from Anna, yet despite my disappointment felt relieved my poem had provoked no negative fallout. (Years later, when we finally reconnected in college, she pulled my poem from her journal and revealed she'd always cherished it.) But soon my feelings for Anna would seem a distant memory.

Robert invited me to a party one Friday night over Thanksgiving break at our friend Lauren's house, the parent-free venue of the week where a small get-together inevitably turned into chaos as news spread of a "party." When we got there, Lauren (who, after once calling me

"Fred" by mistake, made it into an endearing nickname for me within her circle) asked if we'd like some "PGA Watermelon." This turned out to be a whole giant "Hope watermelon"—named for the small town in southwest Arkansas famous then only for its sweet melons of gargantuan proportions—that had been soaked for hours in a tin tub filled with pure grain alcohol.

"Sure," we said, and were soon on a porch full of schoolmates munching upon large, benumbing slices of juicy watermelon. It was there that I finally met Estelle. I'd seen her around campus, but our circles had not intersected. She was older at seventeen, but by virtue of a summer birthday was still a junior. She had struck me as being among the most beautiful girls at school; like Anna, she was a brown-eyed brunette with a dark complexion—due in her case, I would learn, to an Italian background. There was a coy sophistication in her manner, a hint of mystery in the demure smile with which she'd often glanced at me in passing. There was also something in her expression, a certain precocious wisdom that seemed to emanate from the depths of her eyes. A certain pain even.

Now we were finally talking, our discourse no doubt enlivened by the stimulation of spiked melon slices. After the party we agreed to collaborate on an upcoming research assignment for history. We started spending evenings studying together at the local public library. Estelle became increasingly coquettish, touching my arm as she spoke and sometimes even making innuendos—hints that her plans for me extended beyond helping my history grade. At the merest touch of her fingertips upon my hand, I felt sensations unlike I'd ever known. My whole body felt transformed into a grand network of goose bumps enshrouding a pounding heart. When New Year's Eve arrived, she said her parents would be out and, instead of having a party, she thought it might be fun if I came over to her condominium later to watch a movie, just the two of us to bring in the new year. I agreed, and then spent the rest of that afternoon in a daze of nervous sweat.

Estelle asked me to pick up a case of her favorite beer first; she said I should go to the liquor store on the corner near her condo, where the Asian clerk there would sell booze to anyone, no questions asked. So I went to the store and nervously put the beer on the counter despite being five years underage, and sure enough walked out with a full case of beer. This gave me a sense of confidence, despite being told anyone could have done it. I was also pleased to have accomplished the mission Estelle had given me and hoped she'd be impressed.

She was. We sat together on the floor sipping beer and watching a movie. Which movie it was I have no recollection, as I hardly saw any of it. We certainly hadn't watched it long before Estelle flashed me a mischievous smile.

"Do you like to wrestle?" she asked.

"Well, I guess . . ." I stammered shyly.

"Let's wrestle!"

Before I knew what was happening she threw herself upon me, grabbing my arms and pushing me backwards to the floor. I playfully fought back, thinking at first to fake a struggle before realizing her short frame was possessed of disconcerting strength. It wasn't long before she had me genuinely down, my back against the floor with my hands pinned behind my head as she sat on top of me, gloating triumphantly. Then suddenly she bent down and began kissing me. I'd never really kissed a girl, but when after a few moments I felt her tongue push through my lips, I knew this must be the "French kissing" Father Tribou had warned about. *A sin because it leads on to other things*, he'd said.

Estelle suddenly sat back and stared at me with her wide brown eyes, now transformed from demure to seductive.

"Let's go upstairs," she said.

She turned off the television, and we watched no more that day.

The year 1984 thus began with a rush of new sensations and, concurrently, of confusion. I'd never experienced such an intensity of feelings; nor was I prepared for the vivid palette of emotions now coloring my deepest sensibilities. Every aspect of life seemed suddenly enhanced with an acute awareness; everything, even inanimate objects, became suddenly endowed with symbolic meaning. The lyrics of every song that played on the radio seemed a missive in code sent through the airwaves directly to me.

A fresh snow had blanketed the city to begin the year, delaying the start of school and allowing afternoons of sledding down the steep hills west of town with Robert, Joe, and another boy named Ken who became a great friend. In the eerie quiet of the snowy winter landscape, the only sound was that of sled blades sliding through the slush upon empty streets. As my sled whizzed downhill and the cold wind bit my face with the tickle of snow flurries, I felt a sense of inner freedom like I'd never known. And all the while, the image of Estelle's smile, the sensation of her touch, warmed my heart.

But the snowmelt came quickly. Within a few weeks of our starting to date, Estelle's father got a job out of town and informed her they would be moving in February. She cried when she told me the news, and at that moment all the emotions to which I'd only just now begun to adjust were turned topsy-turvy with disbelief. What had seemed such an enchanting start to the new year quickly dissipated into angst. Nor did our parents help. We'd resolved to make the most of the few weeks we had left, but getting around parental restrictions proved difficult. We had to find a way to meet undetected in the evenings, but it proved especially difficult for me to sneak out, given the perilously creaking stairs at the top of which was my parent's bedroom door. But I found that by exiting through my bedroom window, I could jump from the roof at its lowest point over the backyard, and enter the garage from the back and so sneak unnoticed into the dark street. My 10-speed bicycle had recently been stolen, but Kate had got a new bike that Christmas decorated with the "Pink Panther" cartoon character, and so I rode it the three miles or so to Estelle's condo. (This must have been quite a sight to any late night observers.) Upon arrival, we'd sneak upstairs into Estelle's bedroom, wary of discovery by her ever-irate father. The glaring catch with my plan was that, upon my return, the only way back onto the roof and into my bedroom was by the use of a ladder—which having been left behind under the roof was of course a dead giveaway next morning. Sure enough, one night as I climbed into my room I was in for a terrifying shock. The moment I came in through the bedroom window, my mother sat up in the bed.

"Where have you been?" she demanded. That moment was so fraught with guilt and fear that I haven't the faintest recollection of how I replied.

As a parting gift just before she was to move, I surprised Estelle with two tickets to an upcoming concert in Memphis by one of our favorite bands, The Police. The performance was part of their Synchronicity Tour (after which the group would soon disband), and so on February 16 of '84 we drove to Memphis for a truly magical experience in each other's company.

On the dreaded night before Estelle's departure, she made a secretive late night visit to my house. I'd built a fire in the living room fireplace, where I often read late into the night long after my parents were in bed in the room immediately above. When Estelle arrived, I laid out blankets in front of the fire, and there, as the bright firelight flickered upon our bare skin, we made love until finally the flames died down to the last embers of glowing scarlet. We lay a while motionless in a resigned embrace, still clinging to some false hope that the moment would never end. But end it did, and more abruptly than we'd imagined: The doorbell suddenly rang, followed by a loud KNOCK-ING. Estelle's eyes widened in fearful apprehension.

"It's my dad!" she exclaimed, and then the stair light came on and we heard my parents' voices upstairs. If there was a world record for speed-dressing we must have broken it that night, somehow managing to get dressed before the three-way collision of ourselves and our respective parents. It was a climactic end to the most profound period, however brief, I'd yet experienced in my young life.

Although her new town was almost as far away as the Missouri border, Estelle was still in the state and so we were not without hope of meeting occasionally and even remaining together as a couple. We vowed to wait it out for the year and a half until we could enroll together at the University of Arkansas at Fayetteville, not far from where she now lived. One thing I needed in the meantime was a car so that I could visit her occasionally, and to that end I got a job bussing tables at the local Bennigan's restaurant, quickly realizing I'd probably be long-graduated before ever making enough cash for even a down payment on a decent car.

The rest of my junior year remains a haze of dark memory, my longing for Estelle and constant fixation on her image abruptly transforming to despair and intense jealousy—a new sensation provoked by word of her new boyfriend soon after she'd moved. The letter she wrote explaining this was long and painful to read, and included the vague promise that "there will always be a place for you in my heart," and the comment that "one day our paths may cross again." I was devastated, and—as usual when life seemed to have reached a hopeless impasse—I found consolation in literature and music.

This experience coincided with a slate of highly cheerful reading on our English syllabus which, after an enjoyable survey of American fiction and the poetry and drama of the "Harlem Renaissance" writers, now included *Crime and Punishment, No Exit, The Stranger, Macbeth, The Metamorphosis, Brave New World*, and—added to the syllabus in light of the current year, *1984*. Fortunately my outside reading interests were enhanced by the discovery of J.R.R. Tolkien's fantasy *The Silmarillion*, as well as the recent publication of *The Book of Lost Tales*, part of an extensive series of Tolkien's unpublished writings edited by his son Christopher Tolkien and called by him "The History of Middle-earth."

I otherwise found most of my joy playing with my band. We started practicing in the garage, and to his immense credit Dad put up with it, even though this meant my bass lines were now driven by Dan's drumming, with on top of it all Sammy's wild guitar solos. We even included little Will in a few jam sessions—he'd received a small keyboard for Christmas and had already figured out the opening notes of

Van Halen's song "Jump" from their new album *1984*. I'll never forget
Will's delight in playing with the "boys in the band." We also started
getting paid gigs at various clubs around town; and since Dan and Sam
already had their own DJ business, *Apollo III Productions*, along with an
impressive light show they'd put together from scratch, we had an array
of sound equipment and lights to compete with many of the best (and
older) bands in Little Rock.

Despite my personal difficulties that year, one influence I managed for the most part to avoid was that of drugs. Now that I was a
regular member of local music circles, I observed that many of my musician friends had an affinity for one of Arkansas' most notable crops:
Marijuana. It is a weed which grows so naturally in the state that it
can seemingly pop up anywhere unawares, and if it were legal it would
undoubtedly join cotton and soy beans as a staple Arkansas crop. My
mother even told me of the time when federal agents turned up at
the house in Crossett asking to investigate reports of marijuana plants
spotted growing wild in the pasture near the pond; denied permission
by my grandfather, when they trespassed on the land anyway in an attempt to extricate the plants, Daddy Frank emerged from the house
with a shotgun. The agents quickly departed, never to return.

Many of my friends grew their own at home. Local "skunkweed" it
was called, or simply "skunk." Even the local police were not immune,
having gained notoriety for confiscating the stuff from people (often
along with severe charges) only to smoke it themselves—leading to
a famous prank whereby a marijuana plant was planted on the front
lawn of the Little Rock police headquarters, its stalk reaching a significant height before finally being pointed out by the local media. (Later I
even met an Australian who said there was a popular song in Australia
called "Arkansas Grass.")

So I was constantly around the stuff. And I must confess that
when passed my way I sometimes smoked—and inhaled—from the
odd joint or pipe (sometimes even from a massive, gurgling bong).
But the effect did not suit me. I became immediately depressed, even
paranoid. And I was then also, I noticed, unable to play my music as
well. I resolved not to smoke the stuff further.

There were other drugs too. A number of friends began dropping
acid—"Vitamin A" they called it—and there were occasionally even
"acid parties" specifically for that purpose. I attended one once with
the idea that I might actually give it a try myself; but fortunately Dan
warned me against it:

"You shouldn't try it man," he said.

"Why not?"

"I'm afraid just one bad trip might be too much for you. You already get way too deep about shit as it is. It'd be dangerous for you man, don't even try it!" And thanks to that advice, I never did. The only thing I did really partake in was alcohol, although moderately enough at first. I should, however, have paid closer attention to my mother's warning when, one day out of the blue, she simply said: "Once you start drinking, you're flirting with disaster." She knew what she was talking about, too.

But some friends took things too far and too fast, and they paid the price early on. One of them was Donny. Since 8th grade, especially after all he'd been through with his parents, I had worried about Donny. His mother was in prison for attempted homicide, his dad was still the notorious abortion doctor, and he lived in miserable circumstances with his grandmother. I had noticed he was prone to such negative influences as drugs, and I'd managed thus far to exert a positive enough influence over him to dissuade him from turning to them. But as we advanced in high school, something seemed to snap in Donny. And it wasn't just drugs that he turned to, either.

A small crime ring had formed within the student body. In addition to the drug racket, the campus—particularly the lockers and parking lot—became a frequent target of break-ins and petty theft. Numerous students, including myself, lost property (usually in the form of sunglasses or jewelry). To add insult to injury, the ringleader of the group began setting up shop in the boy's bathroom. He'd put a table there, upon which he displayed his wares for sale—sunglasses and jewelry at discount prices. And on that table you might well have to buy back the very item that had gone missing from your locker or car. He was called "The Candy Man," and beneath his dark shades and wide, pearly smile was a dangerous young criminal who would one day die in the prison to which he was sent for murdering a prostitute he'd picked up, expecting a girl who turned out instead to be a transvestite. It was with The Candy Man and his cohorts that Donny fell in cahoots. My estrangement from Donny (notwithstanding his spoiling *The Lord of the Rings* for me in 8th grade, before later getting banned from my house for blowing up the family toilet with fireworks) was now all but complete; but the final nail was driven in by Donny's betrayal of one of our closest mutual friends. Donny had gotten into a bit of trouble with the law, and he made a deal with federal agents to help (temporarily at least) save his skin.

One day Donny invited Kyle to meet a drug dealer to buy some stuff. He took Kyle that night to meet the dealer in a dark parking lot, and the moment Kyle handed money over and accepted the small bag, the "dealer" flashed a badge. Kyle was promptly arrested and eventually prosecuted with felony drug charges.

Many years later Donny would get his comeuppance. I had just moved to Los Angeles when Joe emailed from home with a link to an online June 2006 *Arkansas Democrat-Gazette* newspaper article. The headline read: "Standoff Ends After Tear-gas Blast," followed with the statement that "A 39-year-old man engaged in a nearly five-hour standoff with Little Rock police Monday morning before surrendering after two volleys of tear gas were fired into his home." I was shocked to see that the man being described was Donny! The article continued as follows:

> After Donny [S] surrendered to police, Fire Department bomb squad officers disabled two pipe bombs found in his pickup parked outside the house . . . where he had recently moved in with his elderly grandmother.

> [S] ran into the house with a gun in his hand after police responded to a weapons disturbance call about 5:30 a.m. A special weapons and tactics team, squad cars and fire trucks soon filled the hilly, tree-lined neighborhood near John Barrow and Markham roads as hostage negotiators tried to persuade [S] to surrender.

> SWAT team officers entered the lower level of the split-level house and evacuated the grandmother, who . . . was said to be in her 80s or 90s and suffering from Alzheimer's disease. Neighbors peeked from behind curtains and doorways, cringing at the sound of tear gas canisters being fired.

> After three hours of fruitless attempts to end the impasse, police fired two volleys of tear gas through the windows of the house. [S] didn't immediately come outside. Bomb squad officers were readying a robot equipped with cameras to search the residence when [S] surrendered just before 10 a.m.

> Little Rock Fire Department Capt. Randy Hickman said the pipe bombs were made of plastic PVC piping, had fuses and were ready to be activated. [S] was arrested twice in December and January on numerous drug and theft charges while living a short distance away. [S] explained his actions to police by saying that someone had been sending him threatening e-mails.

After reading this, I realized Donny never really had much of a chance. Yet I couldn't help wondering if there might have been anything I could have done, as a childhood friend, which may have helped him avoid his tragic fate.

By the end of what seemed an interminable year, my fellow students and I already seemed afflicted with an early bout of "Senioritis" as we began to anticipate our final year of High School and the mysterious world beyond. Before school finally let out for summer vacation, we had to decide which elective courses we wished to take the following year. One day Mrs. Maddison stopped me in the hallway outside her classroom, pulling me in as if preparing to confide in me some great secret.

"Would you be interested in taking Creative Writing next year?" she asked. I'd heard much about her writing class from a senior named Isaac who'd become a great friend that year, and so I also knew that it was in that class in which students edited *The Inkwell*, the school literary journal published each spring. I'd never even considered taking part in such a class. But now Mrs. Maddison said she'd observed talent in my writing and thought I'd make a great addition to the class—open only, she explained, to students she personally invited to participate. Despite the great honor I felt at the invitation, I still had my doubts until Isaac explained what a great opportunity this was and convinced me to enroll in the course.

Then summer finally arrived, and along with it a chance for a much needed vacation. Joe had put together a trip to Florida, for which we had been saving up all spring by working at Bennigan's. And after a refreshing week on the Florida panhandle beaches, I turned my sights once more to getting enough money for a car, which I desperately desired for my senior year, even if it was a pile of junk. I sweated furiously all summer in the sticky Arkansas humidity mowing lawns. For some time I'd run a thriving lawn care service with Joey and Darryl, mowing springs and summers and raking leaves each autumn, and after Darryl's graduation we brought in Andy, one of Joey's Catholic High friends, as his replacement. Andy had a car with a hatchback which facilitated transporting our equipment. (This worked out well, apart from Andy's penchant for hell-raising, sometimes celebrating a completed job by abruptly burning rubber as we left in his car—once even exceeding 100 mph on an open city road.).

Joey and Andy had just graduated and wanted to put some money in their pockets before heading off to college—Joey to Texas Christian University in Fort Worth, and Andy to the University of Arkansas at Fayetteville. By the end of the summer, I was just about to buy a royal clunker when Dad surprised me with an offer to help me get something better. I'd now proven myself a responsible driver, he said, and by the time school started I had a sporty red Nissan 200SX to drive into the school parking lot. On Joe's advice I got a standard stick shift instead of the more common automatic, something he may have regretted as he helped me learn to operate the clutch while getting perilously stuck atop several of Little Rock's notoriously steep hills. And the car had a nifty hatchback for transporting my upright bass around town.

School finally arrived and it felt wonderful indeed as I drove onto campus—despite living just around the corner from school—in my shiny new car, unpacking my bass for band and gearing up for the new adventure of creative writing and magazine editing. This was a year full of promise, when I finally felt confident of my place within a community of friends and teachers and in which I felt genuinely happy. I also had, for the first time, friends in high places, thanks to my old third grade Cub Scout buddy Brian having been elected student body president. We were the Class of '85 and felt a sense of community and school spirit that would last a lifetime.

Not only did Creative Writing prove a delightful experience from the start, but Senior English was the ultimate capstone to the one thing that had been consistent since elementary school: excellent English teaching. My teacher in the Advanced Placement level English "Humanities" class, Gail Strange, brought her extensive knowledge to life through a wonderful sense of humor combined with a penchant for witty puns.

Perhaps it was this exposure to so many genres of creativity that inspired me to try out for the high school musical. The production that year was to be *Bye Bye Birdie*, and I actually managed to land a small part until the director announced the band was in need of a bass player. Someone told her I fit that description, and I found myself thrown into the orchestra pit with the stage band. I missed not getting the chance to dance and sing on stage, but made use of the extra time between songs to catch up on reading the novels *Of Human Bondage* and *Tess of the d'Urbervilles* for Mrs. Strange. During my short-lived career as a song and dance man, however, I made a striking new friend.

We had a foreign exchange student that year, a girl from Norway named Jeanette Fjeld. When I saw her on stage at the first rehearsal I was immediately taken with her—accompanying the beauty of her features, with her winsome smile beneath flowing blonde hair, was a certain gracefulness and *style* which set her apart from most of the other girls. I was at the same time intrigued by her "otherness," and by her knowledge of the wider world outside of Arkansas. After the rehearsal, I summoned up the nerve to speak to her and soon struck up a friendship. She seemed especially to appreciate my genuine interest in learning about her culture, rare among her classmates. But on one occasion she looked at me curiously.

"You don't sound like everyone else," she said.

"What do you mean?"

"I mean, you don't have the same accent the others here have. They all talk like *this*"—she gave a hilarious imitation of the Arkansas accent, dividing various monosyllabic words into two or even three syllables—"but you do not talk like that. Are you not really from here?"

It was true. Even when I was much younger, I'd once been startled by a sales clerk who had said, "You're not from around here, are you? You sound like you're from *New York*." (I didn't know at the time whether that was meant as a compliment or an insult.) But in high school I'd gotten this more often, even being asked by students from other schools if I was an exchange student myself. Occasionally going along with it, I'd ask them to guess where they thought I was from, and would usually be taken for Scandinavian, English or Dutch. But considering the healthy Southern accent of everyone around me as I grew up, I had no idea why I lacked it. (I read recently, however, that dyslexia can cause a type of speech defect, so I can only surmise this had something to do with it.) But later in life as I traveled widely, I'd often be asked the same thing, especially from fellow Americans—often quite annoyingly—with the comment: "But you don't *sound* like you're from the South." (Even worse, back home I still regularly get the following: "Where're you from, boy? You're not from around here, are you?")

Worst of all was an incident in California, where I was actually accused in Los Angeles of having completely fabricated my Arkansas background as a fake identity. Not only was this experience painfully insulting, but I was left baffled as well: Of all the places in the world a person new to L.A. might claim as home to impress people there, a city where glamour and sophistication—no matter how falsely contrived—seem prized above all, the backwater swamps of deep woods Arkansas might seem an unlikely first choice. Perhaps this is why I now feel most "at home" when visiting abroad, where being a genuine foreigner I can truly be myself while feeling understood and accepted as such.

Unfortunately, with Jeanette my innate shyness got the best of me my senior year, and I never allowed my relationship with her to blossom into what (in retrospect) might have been something truly special. I suppose I ultimately felt intimidated by that same beauty and style I so admired. And, as ever, I must have been too fearful of *rejection* even to try expressing my deeper feelings. So once again I turned to music, throwing myself wholeheartedly into practicing and performing.

The Jazz Band had gained a reputation around the city, and we increasingly performed gigs off campus, at other schools as well as for various special events. We were playing quite an eclectic mix of music too. In addition to jazz standards, we paid homage to the Michael Jackson craze by performing "Billie Jean" and "Beat It" from Jackson's recent album *Thriller*. (One kid at the school was so obsessed with Michael Jackson that he came to school every day dressed in Jacksonesque clothing—including a bright red jacket and single white glove as he "moon walked" his way around campus.)

I was also pleased that I'd been able to recruit my old friend Jason as Dan's replacement on drums after his graduation, along with a lovely girl named Judy on keyboards. On one memorable occasion, we performed for a state education event hosted by Governor Clinton, who came over to greet Mr. Smith along with a wave to all of us in the band. On another occasion we performed on local television, which I recall pleased my grandmother Francis Thurmond to no end.

Early that fall, Mr. Smith asked if I'd be interested in playing with the Marching Band. But how, I asked, could I possibly march with my electric bass and amp? The solution, he said, was simply to sit with the band in the stands and perform with them from there during the football games; and when the band marched during half-time, I could stay put and continue performing from the bleachers. (All were pleased apart from the tuba players, whose part I duplicated, and who glanced at me in annoyance as I rendered in vain all their huffing and puffing in the attempt to equal my amplified volume and be heard as well.) This led to the truly enriching experience of traveling with the band and football team every Friday night that fall to perform at games— where playing my Rickenbacker bass whilst donning the bright orange Hall High Warriors band uniform made me feel like Paul McCartney in full "Sgt. Pepper" regalia. I especially enjoyed the distinction this brought, as my band mates began taunting our opponents' bands across the stadium with a poster which read "WE GOT THE BASS!" On one occasion, though, the opposite band had brought a bassist and a similar sign, prompting my colleagues' exhortation to "Blow 'em away, Thurmond!" The ensuing "battle of the basses" was a night to remember.

Another key musical contribution made that fall by Mr. Smith was his suggestion that I try learning to play the double bass. He introduced me to a professional musician named Joe Vick, who performed in jazz ensembles as well as with the Arkansas Symphony Orchestra and who taught in the Fine Arts Department at the University of Arkansas at Little Rock. I became a regular at the various classical and jazz concerts in which he performed; before long, with Joe's help I actually had a double bass of my own and was taking weekly lessons on this grand instrument, whose neck stretched well beyond my own. And as I practiced the difficult art of "arco" (bowing) technique, I took pleasure in the warmth of sound that emanated from this giant, vibrat-

Performing at a Warriors football game, autumn 1984

ing "bass fiddle" (as my grandfather called it). I was soon playing the string bass parts with Mr. Smith's school concert band, and by year's end was awarded second place in the bass soloist category at a state competition for my performance of a Beethoven sonata movement. (The thrill of this award being only slightly qualified upon learning I was one of two contestants.) The contrast among styles I was playing all at once on two distinct instruments, from jazz to rock to classical, was truly exhilarating.

In the meantime, Excalibur continued to thrive with gigs around town and performances at local band competitions like "Magic 105's Battle of the Bands." In addition to playing the latest 80's hits the moment they appeared on MTV, we began writing original songs of our own. I found the process of creating my own bass rhythms and

melodies to complement Sam's lead guitar skills—and then the chance
to try out our new material on the public—the most satisfying aspect
of being in the band. Dan had a large red and white van in which we'd
load up his drums and our guitars and amps and head off to various
clubs to play. (And from which, admittedly, often plumed a trail of
smoke like something straight out of a Cheech & Chong movie.) But
our most memorable performance was one that became something of
a legend among my classmates.

Even though Dan and Sam had graduated, they were both still in
town—taking classes at the University of Arkansas at Little Rock—
and returned to perform occasionally at school. For one pep rally we
decided to play "Red Barchetta" by Rush, a particularly challenging
song to pull off. It featured the most difficult bass line I'd attempted
to learn to date. The distinctive vocal part was all but impossible to get
right, though admirably handled by our new singer, Dennis. But somehow we did pull it off, and this must have made quite an impression
on my fellow classmates assembled in the audience, as it immediately
earned me the flattering sobriquet of "Geddy" after the Rush bassist.
Still to this day I occasionally bump into an old schoolmate—one I

Performing with Dan and Sam (as Excalibur) on the high school stage.

might not even recognize—who'll say: "Hey, it's Geddy Lee!" before
launching into a vivid description of that day back in high school when
we played "Red Barchetta."

On another occasion, Tyndall and Rob came over to Hall from Central High for an impromptu jam session with Jason and me in the
school gym during lunch. Before long, we had an impressive group of
students gathered around us and dancing to our cover of the Stones'
"Sympathy for the Devil." This attracted the attention of the assistant

principal, Mr. Gadberry, who motioned for us to stop. This we ignored. When Mr. Gadberry began shouting, we responded by turning up the volume. Then, in a scene we fondly recall as being reminiscent of The Beatles' famous appearance on a London rooftop, other administrators swarmed the scene, dispersing students even as we continued playing until Mr. Gadberry finally thought to pull the plug on our amps—leaving Jason still momentarily drumming away to our now silenced guitars. But the legacy of that experience continues even today, as Jason soon joined Tyndall and Rob to form a band that—now known as "Mojo Depot" with legendary local musician Johnny "B" Wright on bass—still records and performs their eclectic, original music for local and national audiences.

In Creative Writing, meanwhile, my need for creative expression found an unexpected outlet through poetry. Mrs. Maddison began assigning various writing exercises, one of which was to compose a poem. This could take any form, with the condition that each stanza had to begin with the phrase "I wish." The result was a poem that seemed to impress Mrs. Maddison greatly. It also impressed Mom. She was now a part-time writing instructor at the University of Arkansas at Little Rock, and as an experiment she decided to give the poem to a bona fide poet in the English faculty for feedback, simply telling him the poem was by a "student" of hers. The poet, David Wojahn (then editor of the literary journal *Crazyhorse* based on the campus), wrote comments on the poem indicating he was impressed especially with the imagery of the language, along with the comment: "Encourage this student!" I was encouraged indeed, and continued writing the rest of that year with the satisfactory result of seeing both poetry and fiction published in *The Inkwell* student literary journal when it appeared that spring.

One day Mrs. Maddison announced that she was organizing a student trip to Europe that summer and held a meeting for students and parents to discuss it. The trip would constitute a kind of "grand tour" of major European capitals, with a particular focus on cultural and historical sites and institutions. It was the trip of my dreams. I hardly thought for a moment that my parents would consent to my going, much less help pay for it. But to my great surprise, not long afterwards they announced that I could go after all. It would be their graduation gift to me. I was ecstatic! Yet this made the rest of the year in between seem all the more like a lifetime away.

Later that fall, Joey called to say he'd be coming up from Texas for the Arkansas vs. TCU game in Fayetteville. Arkansas was, at that time, part of the old Southwest Conference of college athletics, and Texas Christian University was an old rival. Andy had pledged at a fraternity there and said we could stay at the frat house that weekend, so I eagerly agreed to meet them. Game day was on as beautiful an Ozark autumn day as you could want, resplendent with radiant autumn foliage. Getting to Fayetteville was half the fun too, as it involved driving northwest along a steep—and sometimes treacherous—climbing road through the Ozark Mountains known as "the Pig Trail" in homage of the Arkansas Razorbacks. The team was so named after the then-called Arkansas Cardinals shut out Louisiana State University 16-0 in a championship football game in Memphis in 1909, prompting Arkansas coach Hugo Bezdek to proclaim that his players had run around the field "like a band of wild Razorback hogs." The name stuck, as did the cardinal color of the team's uniform.

The stadium that day was packed. From the moment the "Hogs" ran out onto the field and into the crisp autumn air, I experienced that same magic I'd felt since a young boy when my parents took me to numerous Razorback games at War Memorial Stadium in Little Rock. The sense of anticipation of a good game—and hopeful victory—along with the brass and drums of the marching band performing the Razorback fight song during half-time and after every Arkansas score—titillated the senses and, for a few hours, brought thousands of people together as one in a profound sense of community. For this was never *just* a football game. The Razorbacks (in the absence of any major professional teams) are for Arkansans the ultimate symbol of our state: the source of our greatest pride when they win, and the crucible of bitter disappointment (even fury) when they lose. (Dad had once expressed his feelings about one such loss—due to a missed last minute Razorback field goal attempt in a big game—by putting his foot through the TV set.)

Now the game was underway, and the cheerleaders wheeled around the field a cage containing the team (and state) mascot—a particularly savage-looking wild Razorback hog (a species of Russian boar), its razor-sharp tusks protruding from the cage upon which the cheerleaders stood rallying the crowd. "Big Red" they called him. And at his appearance the crowd burst spontaneously into the ritual of "Calling the Hogs." This I won't even begin to try to describe; one has to experience it at a live Razorback game.

It can also be very daunting to the opposing team, making home games in Arkansas a dreaded away trip for most opponents. Needless to say, I was therefore somewhat vexed at Joey for calling *not* the Hogs, but rather the despised TCU Horned Frogs instead. Yes, he attended

TCU, but surely back home he knew where his true loyalties lay? Not so, he replied; he must now show team spirit for his new school. It was therefore with increased satisfaction that Andy and I enjoyed gloating as the Razorbacks trounced TCU in the first half of the game. And midway through the third quarter, with victory assured, we decided to leave early to get celebrations underway at the frat house. Joey however remained behind, insistent on seeing the game to the bitter end.

But I had a little adventure to attend to first. Before the trip, I'd decided to get in touch with Estelle—still living not far outside Fayetteville—to see if she could meet briefly while I was in the area just to catch up. She seemed happy to hear from me and said she'd love to see me, and so we made arrangements to meet for an early dinner that evening before I returned to join my friends at the frat. Her town was just outside of Rogers, home of Sam Walton and headquarters of Wal-Mart. (Originally a small family store, the low price wholesale chain was now moving swiftly through Arkansas towns while destroying countless small, family-run businesses in its wake, and it was already poised for its national—and ultimately *international*—rampage in the years just ahead.) As I drove down the long, dirt driveway leading to the small farm where Estelle lived, her father was outside chopping wood. The moment I got out of the car with a cheerful wave, his expression as he looked up nearly turned me right around and sent me packing without a backward glance. I still wish that it had.

He glared at me as I walked up. "She's not here," was all he said. I stood there in tense silence for a few long moments before the door opened and Estelle's mother appeared, her face betraying a look of concern. Her father continued staring at me, his face shifting to an expression of curiosity. He appeared to have suddenly had an idea.

"Why don't you come in for a minute," he said.

I was soon sitting with them in the living room, attempting a bit of awkward small talk when Estelle's father cut to the chase.

"Estelle's run away," he said. "She's apparently gone to stay with her aunt in Pine Bluff." I told him I'd just spoken with Estelle the day before, and she told me she'd be there expecting me. He glanced at his wife with a look that made me even more uneasy. Then he gave me a hard stare.

"How close were you and Estelle?" he asked.

"What do you mean?" I replied, hardly optimistic about how this would turn out.

"What I mean is, did you ever sleep with her?"

My face must have blanched white as a frightened vampire, because he immediately shifted to a gentler tone.

"I don't mean to make you uncomfortable," he continued, "but this is important, as I'll explain later. But let me rephrase this—was Estelle a virgin when you started dating her?"

Without thinking of the wider implications of my answer, I said that no, she wasn't. Then it hit me what I'd just inadvertently revealed.

"So," he said, "you must have been with her to know that, right?"

I supposed I could have gotten around this somehow if I'd been thinking more clearly, yet it appeared now that he had me. But I'd at the same time been brought up always to tell the truth, no matter how difficult or awkward, and had not yet learned how to plant a well-placed lie.

"Yes." I quickly dropped my chin, but then looking up again I was surprised that both of them seemed actually relieved.

"There's something I need to share with you," he went on. "Before she ran away, Estelle accused me of incest."

Time froze at that moment. None of us stirred for what seems an age in my memory; there was complete silence apart from a ticking clock. *Tick, tock* it went, ticking away into eternity. And my mind along with it, as if the whole world of my experience were suddenly one giant clock, its hour hand moving towards the dissonant chimes of the darkest midnight in memory. *Incest*, he'd said. I knew the word, more as a source of jokes describing the sordid lives of country rednecks. But it never seemed *real* as a concept, not something that really ever happened to people one knew.

They were both staring at me now. "Of course," he went on, "that's not at all true. She was just looking for an excuse to leave." He went on to explain that for some time, Estelle had been unhappy living up there in the country. She'd often blamed her father for her unhappiness, for forcing her to live there on a farm in the middle of nowhere, and they had been fighting about it for months. Then suddenly, just yesterday, she ran away to her aunt, who had called to say Estelle now planned to get an attorney and sue her father.

"Let me show you something," he finally said. The next thing I knew, I was walking with the two of them on a tour of their land. There were acres of pasture, a garden, a small barn house ready for livestock, a flower garden she'd cultivated along with careful landscaping. It seemed, on the surface, almost idyllic. Everything they'd been working for and dreaming about for years, he said. And now his daughter threatened to take it all away with a frivolous lawsuit.

"Unless," he said, "you might be willing to help." I remained silent, apprehensive.

Estelle, he said, had accused him of sexually abusing her since she was a young girl. She claimed that this had so ruined her emotionally that she would never be able to have sex with another man, and her life was ruined. However, or so at least ran his logic, since she *had* in fact slept with someone else, this proved she was lying and would protect him from the lawsuit.

"Think about it," he said. "This would help Estelle as much as me. She's confused, she needs help. You'll be doing *her* a favor."

He then invited me to join them for dinner. I should have left, then and there, but at the moment I was too overwhelmed to refuse.

"Okay," I said. "I'll think about it."

They took me out for a steak dinner at a local restaurant. And over dinner Estelle's father continued to press his case, to insist that this was all just a terrible misunderstanding, but that I was the key to setting everything right. Would I be willing, he asked, to talk to his lawyer in Little Rock? Just think about it, he insisted. Then he handed me his lawyer's business card.

The drive back to Fayetteville that night felt long and lonely. When I got back to the frat, I found the celebrations had taken a downturn. Joey jubilantly explained how, not long after we'd left the stadium, TCU made a startling comeback, blowing out Arkansas' top-ranked defense in a fourth quarter rally to beat the Razorbacks 32-31. But I was too dazed and confused to care. By the end of the night, the frat house was transformed into a scene of rocking hedonism. And I got, for the first time, truly drunk—finding it only too easy to drown my cares away. The last thing I remember doing was sitting in with the band on bass, playing the "Ghostbusters" movie theme song as throngs of wasted college students danced away the night.

Not long afterwards I got a call from the lawyer. He asked if I would come and "visit" with him at his office. Still completely confused about what was the right thing to do—and afraid to discuss what had transpired in northwest Arkansas with even my closest friends—I agreed to meet him one day after school. I vividly recall my intense emotional confusion and sickening sense of *dread* that whole day at school. I wished the final school bell would never ring. And that day in Creative Writing class, Mrs. Maddison looked at me gravely and asked if something was wrong.

"No," I said, "everything's fine."

"Okay," she answered, clearly unconvinced. "But do feel free to see me if you want to talk about anything."

"Thanks," I said. In my heart I wanted nothing more than to open up to her and tell her everything I was going through. But I didn't. I never expressed it to anyone for a long time afterwards. Mrs. Maddison probably also observed that my poetry had taken a much more introspective, darker turn.

The lawyer's office was in one of the few high rise office buildings in downtown Little Rock, and taking the elevator up to one of the highest floors made the visit that much more intimidating. The lawyer, dressed to the nines in a dark business suit and power tie, ushered me into his impressive office with a friendly, reassuring smile and offered me a Coke. After a bit of small talk, he asked if I wouldn't mind his recording our conversation. Just a matter of routine, he said. I didn't object. The conversation then turned to my discussion with Estelle's parents at the farm; he repeated what I had told Estelle's father in response to his questions about my relationship with Estelle, and asked me to confirm what I had answered. When I hesitated, he emphasized that I was doing the right thing, that it was in Estelle's interest that the truth be told. When I finally complied and corroborated my previous conversation with her father, the lawyer abruptly clicked off the tape recorder and stood up, thanking me for my time before sending me away with a firm handshake.

I felt terribly shaken and unsure what to make of the event, feeling even less certain than before whether or not I'd done the right thing. But I had the sinking feeling that I'd just been exploited, and that this would all do ultimately more harm than good to Estelle. What's more, there had been something unpleasant in the lawyer's gleaming eyes and behind his winning smile. What was that line from *Hamlet* I'd recently memorized for Mrs. Strange? *That one may smile and smile and be a villain.* I'd never before then so much as even met an actual lawyer in my life, but one thing I knew now for certain: I would strive to avoid them at all cost in the future!

Finally some good news arrived. In June I'd taken the ACT, at that time the main standardized college entrance test. After taking it, I was convinced I hadn't done well enough to get into any college, nor could ever do so even if I retook the test countless times. But when my scores arrived in the mail and I nervously pulled them from the envelope, I was amazed to find I had done quite well after all, even on the math and science sections as well as a strong score in Social Studies. But best of all was having got just one point shy of the perfect score on the Reading Comprehension and Writing section. I was further stunned to read the explanatory note provided with the scores: "Your

English score is 29 (out of possible 30), which has a percentile rank of 98. This means that you scored higher than 98% of the college-bound students taking the English test nationwide. Compared with all high school students (not just college-bound) your percentile ranks would be higher. The percentile rank of your composite score indicates that your overall educational development probably ranks in the top quarter of college-bound students. Your composite score indicates that you can probably do well in a wide variety of colleges and programs. You may want to consider several options before making a final choice." This made me eligible for college academic scholarships, a possibility that I'd never even previously bothered to consider. To celebrate, my parents took me, Kate, and Will to the restaurant of my choice: A new local pizza joint called U.S. Pizza.

Soon I began receiving offers from regional colleges and universities and began to realize I had a world of options. Especially now that my previous UA Fayetteville plans had clearly soured. One day my mother brought home a brochure describing the "Scholars Program" at the University of Arkansas at Little Rock (UALR). At first I merely scoffed at the idea. After all, why would I want to stay put in my hometown when college offered the chance finally to escape, to find adventure out in the world as I'd long dreamed? But when I read through what was on offer, including—in addition to full tuition and a generous stipend each semester for books and other academic needs—an expense-paid summer study abroad opportunity to study any language in the country of my choice, I got truly excited. This was clearly an innovative program, described in the brochure as emphasizing "critical thought, problem solving, and interdisciplinary studies." Then when I saw that most of the many applicants for the mere 20 places available had a perfect overall score on the ACT, and that the program had recently been identified as being "one of the top three honors programs in the nation" by the director of the Washington Center for Undergraduate Education, I hesitated. After all, what chance could *I* possibly have of being accepted? But the brochure also pointed out that "other students may be admitted on the basis of high school performance and activities, recommendations from counselors or teachers, and personal interviews with the UALR Scholars Advisory Committee." I decided I'd go ahead and give it my best shot, and put much effort into the application essay on the topic "What is a Scholar?" Rereading that essay now, I find it surprising how much thought I seemed already to have put into this as a 17 year old kid of limited reading and experience.

"The scholar," I wrote, "takes a great interest in learning, and he develops an appetite for information. His thirst for knowledge grows as he is introduced to the many branches of learning which begin to unfold before him while he progresses through school . . . Any person may be interested in learning, but without a strong dedication to knowledge he will ultimately achieve little or nothing. The average student is content to know only what he *needs* to know; rather than striving to achieve the most of his resources, he puts forth only a minimum of effort to achieve a minimum of results. The scholar is dedicated to his works and is therefore only content when he has achieved his *goal* . . . In my opinion, one of the most important goals of the scholar should be to strive, after much work and achievement, to make outstanding contributions to society. Whether it be through teaching, counseling, helping, entertaining, or any other field, the scholar's ultimate goal should be to make himself a good example for the rest of society in general." Having been asked to describe what I thought set me apart from other students, I pointed out that "I enjoy reading and studying great literary works for my own satisfaction, whether assigned or not," and that "in music I have developed a taste for any composition displaying talent and would attend a classical symphony or jazz concert with the same fervor that most students of my age group would only find in a rock concert . . . Finally, an important activity to me, and the main reason I was encouraged to apply for this UALR Scholars Program, is writing. I enjoy creative writing as well as research, and at school have succeeded very well in both of these fields. Whereas throughout high school I have had problems in the area of mathematics and in other areas I am weak in objective-type question and answer tests, I perform very well when assigned an essay and have made top grades on lengthy papers. These qualities of mine are what I feel make me a scholar and are what I think the UALR Scholars Program will greatly develop."

That last passage was clearly my best effort to explain my rather inconsistent grades, as I was well aware that I'd be competing with hundreds of other applicants who would have perfect grade points. My only hope was that the evaluating professors might be able to see something beyond the mere numbers of my academically mediocre transcript, and recognize that I might have something to offer beyond that of another student who might be perfect academically but in fact mediocre intellectually. But along with the essay, I had excellent references from Mrs. Maddison, Mrs. Strange, and Mr. Smith that attested to both my talent and my dedication in the areas in which I *did* excel. Mrs. Strange wrote in her reference that I was "completely attuned to the fine arts," and that "he has distinguished himself by the depth of his comprehension of pieces of literature and the insight he demonstrates in papers about literature." She also said of me that "a final proof of both his intelligence and intuitive grasp of literature is the fact that he can read a part in a play for the first time, aloud, and never misinterpret the meaning by even one false inflection. That I consider remarkable." She went on to praise my "intellectual curiosity" and "real insight" into literature as well as "a beautiful articulateness in writing." I had had no idea whatsoever that I might have made such an impression, and this brought to mind my bass teacher Bob Lincoln's words from over two years earlier. Perhaps I truly *was* better than I thought. So I finally sent off my application and knocked on wood. But to be safe, I continued applying to other regional schools as a backup plan.

I had also a burgeoning desire to study abroad, particularly in England. (Mrs. Maddison's stories of London and of studying English literature actually *in* England had excited my imagination and sparked a desire to do the same.) So during a study session at the UALR library one evening, I looked up British universities and photocopied the details and admissions requirements of every university in the book. But one place stood out, thanks to a combination of Mrs. Strange's description of the place and my awareness that many of my favorite writers— from Orwell and Auden to C.S. Lewis and J.R.R. Tolkien—had been there: Oxford. Something about it seemed truly enchanting, and the mere concept of spending time there took hold in my dreams and never let go. Oxford also happened to be on the itinerary of my summer European tour and promised to be a highlight of the trip. But when I read through the admissions process for Oxford as well as all the other British institutions, it became clear that applying for undergraduate courses as an "overseas" student from outside the British educational system seemed prohibitive. With this consideration (not to mention the question of my spotty academic record), it became clear that my chances might be better if I postponed the effort until completing my first degree. This would allow ample time to prove myself academically as well, and gave me great motivation to reach that goal even before ever having stepped foot out of high school.

One evening in the early spring of 1985, when my family sat down to dinner, my mother said she had a special announcement. She handed me a letter which she said had arrived that morning, and as I read it she said a proper celebration was in order and, for the first time ever at dinner, handed me a glass of wine. The letter informed me that I had been accepted into the University of Arkansas at Little Rock Scholars Program with a full four-year college scholarship, and I was overcome with joy as my family celebrated the news.

Not long afterward, another inspiring letter arrived. The envelope bore the "Great Seal of the State of Arkansas" beautifully embossed in shiny gold. Inside on fine stationary, with the gold seal again displayed at the top, was a letter signed by the Governor himself. "Dear Frank," it began, "I was very pleased to learn that you are among the students in the Little Rock School District who received a scholarship for outstanding academic achievement." The letter continued with words of commendation "on behalf of the State of Arkansas," before concluding: "I know you will continue to excel academically. Again, congratulations and best wishes for a bright and promising future. Sincerely, Bill Clinton."

I proudly showed the letter to my mother.

"You'd better hang on to that," she said. "He just might be President some day."

"Right," I said, with a sarcastic smirk. But I did hang on to the letter.

The final months of school flew by, and with the college question now resolved, I could throw myself into all my various projects and activities. Other opportunities came along too, which I eagerly seized upon. One was an invitation to hear President Ronald Reagan speak in downtown Little Rock. At the speech I could easily see why the so-called "Gipper" was known as the "Great Communicator." In person he had the ability to send his audience into a state of rapture. I got especially excited when he began praising the American space program and his vision for it. But then I realized that behind his words about space exploration was *not* in fact the idealistic, humanitarian dream I'd had about it since seeing the Apollo rockets blast off as a young boy; on the contrary, what he was really getting at was his desire to expend vast resources on developing a space based weapons program he liked to call "Star Wars." So what was on the surface a call to embark on a new, "grand American adventure" in space was in fact an absolute perversion of everything I believed with great conviction we *should* be doing. I was left with a feeling of disgust with the perception that the President was using his "communication" abilities, combined with his power, to manipulate the better nature of average people into believing in his narrow and unenlightened worldview.

Around that time, I was driving home one day listening to the radio when the broadcast was suddenly interrupted with an announcement by President Reagan speaking in a gravely serious tone: "My fellow Americans," he said, "I'm pleased to tell you today that I've signed legislation that will outlaw Russia forever. We begin bombing in five minutes." I was in such a state of shock that I almost crashed the car before Reagan suddenly burst into laughter. It turned out that the President had earlier been playing around in the studio before an address and hadn't realized that the mike was on. The recording got out and the radio station replayed it as a joke! But the incident obviously had immediate international repercussions and seemed to put a further chill on relations with the Soviets. Meanwhile the "Doomsday Clock" seemed to tick just a little closer to midnight and nuclear Armageddon. Great communication indeed.

By late spring the seniors were in full graduation mode. But before that, and not long after my 18th birthday, it was time for the Senior Prom. I had recently heard from Estelle, who was still living with her aunt and said she'd like to see me again. So I invited her to be my date at the prom. The event was set in the grand ballroom of the Excelsior Hotel, a modern high rise hotel in downtown Little Rock on the banks of the Arkansas River. I reserved a top floor room with a sweeping view overlooking the river valley. On the afternoon of Prom, I drove to Pine Bluff to pick up Estelle and despite the time apart—and everything that had happened in between—she seemed in good spirits and it was a pleasant reunion. Not a word was said, however, about what had happened with her dad and the lawyer, but I couldn't help sensing this lurking all evening as a distressingly awkward subtext beneath everything we said until later that evening when we were alone in the room after the dance.

"Why did you have to talk to that lawyer about me?"

I realized immediately that I should have thought my answer carefully through in advance of this moment. After all, it *had* to come up. But I hadn't. Instead I fumbled through, saying something about trying to help her out. Whatever I said, it was the wrong answer. And the more I tried to explain my actions, the more I confused myself as well as her.

"Look, I just didn't know what to do, what was the right thing. I mean, you weren't there and I didn't know who to believe."

"So you believed Daddy? Couldn't you tell he was lying?"

"But is it true?" I asked.

"Is what true?"

"What you said about your dad . . . Did he really do that to you?"

"Of course he did, how could I lie about *that*?" She started to cry. And then so did I. After months of repressed anguish, I finally broke down. It was Prom Night, and I wept.

Graduation day finally arrived. Commencement took place on the stage of Barton Coliseum, the same spot where I'd seen so many of my favorite rock bands perform. My family was there along with a number of friends, and I was especially pleased to see Joey and Andy high up in the stands. After the ceremony, I went out and celebrated with them before attending a graduation party at which Excalibur performed, now for the last time. I felt almost delirious standing on stage performing Alice Cooper's "School's Out" as my now former classmates danced ecstatically.

> *School's out for summer,*
> *School's out forever!*

Toward the end of the party, Jeanette came up and gave me a warm hug. She was preparing to return to Norway, she said.

"I want to tell you something," said Jeanette. She looked at me through teary eyes. "You are the nicest and most handsome boy I met during my whole time in America." She gave me a warm hug, and kissed me on the cheek before turning away with a wistful smile.

I would be forever haunted by the memory of her smile and her words, and the thought of what might have been.

PART II—SPIRES AND ASPIRATIONS

We cannot live better than in seeking to become
still better than we are.

—Socrates

5

"Trojazz"

The true goal of the traveler is not the exploration of the world,
but of the self.

—Thomas Traherne

In my 1985 high school yearbook, I found a message from my parents
along with a photo of me as a smiling toddler: "The road goes ever
on and on, down from the door where it began . . ." This was followed
by: "May yours, Frank, lead always to happiness and success. Love,
Mom & Dad." It was the perfect sendoff, and I wondered how in the
world they'd ever happened across that particular poem. *And I must
follow, if I can . . .*

This really was, I realized, the start of a new journey—one that
would take me from beyond the confines of security and predictability
into the uncertain realm of independent thought and complete self-
dependence. And with my "Grand Tour" of Europe around the corner
in July, the road was about to lead me suddenly quite far indeed from
the door where it began. But I was more than ready for it. In all my 18
years, hardly had I ever set foot outside the state of Arkansas, and certainly not from the South. Now, with Peter Gabriel's new song about
life being "one big adventure" filling the airwaves, I was determined my
road would be one full of adventure too. And I could barely stand the
anticipation of the trip to come.

Apart from one thing, that is. With all the emotion surrounding
my graduation, and all the reflection this spurred in me concerning my
life and future destiny, I couldn't help feeling the conspicuous absence

of the mysterious man who had sired me: the one whom I would have otherwise had so much to thank for a life already full of extraordinary experience and blessed with the chance to follow my heart and dreams. Why wasn't he here for all this? Until now, I hadn't thought much about him. And when I did, I found it difficult to speak to my mother about it. But now I did. I asked her where he was, and whether she thought I'd ever see him again. She looked both surprised and uncomfortable that I had brought it up.

"Someday, when you're ready," she said, "you may want to find him." And that was it. It was the last time I'd ever ask her about my birth father again. Not until much later, at least.

I was due to fly out in early July with a small group from Little Rock, who would be meeting a larger group of American students from different parts of the country upon arrival in Rome. Mrs. Maddison had originally planned to join us, but unfortunately a last minute glitch prevented her from coming. So we would have no chaperone until we arrived in Europe.

Finally, the big day came. I noted in my journal that I'd had a hard time getting to sleep the night before departure and had read until late that evening the details about the trip ahead. The next day, I felt a deep thrill of excitement during the drive to the airport to board an American Airlines flight from Little Rock for the beginning of a 21 day journey that would take us by land from Rome to London and every place that could be squeezed in between. But the trip did not go without a major hitch right off the bat. Fortunately I kept a detailed, daily journal of my first adventures abroad, and rereading it now twenty-five years later I realize I captured in large part the essence of that seminal experience of my formative years—and the first impressions of Europe from the eyes of an untraveled 18-year-old boy.

Later that summer I attended a special orientation session for the new UALR Scholars. There I met some of my new college classmates as well as professors, one of whom gave a talk in which she described one of the goals of the program being to cultivate the idea of "the Renaissance man" in students—inculcating through the deliberate structuring of an array of interdisciplinary courses a love of knowledge in general and the ability to use that knowledge for the common good in particular. Students would likewise, she said, be given encouragement and support to pursue their own outside interests concurrently with the core academic program. I left the orientation feeling truly inspired and full of anticipation for the year ahead.

We were also asked to consider where we wanted to spend our study abroad opportunity the following summer. For me the choice was clear. I wanted to get back to Europe above all, and the two countries not included on my recent trip that I'd especially wanted to visit were Greece and Spain. But given my new musical passions, there was only one possible destination: I would go to Spain to study Spanish and the Spanish guitar.

I prepared in the meantime to move into my new accommodation. My parents owned a rental house near the university campus. The opportunity to move out had always been a key priority of my college plans, and I'd at first felt concerned that remaining in Little Rock for college might mean I'd have to continue living at home. I was naturally ready for the opportunity to live on my own, as most of my other fellow graduates planned to do, while life at home had started to feel oppressive.

I moved out not long after returning from Europe and never looked back, hardly even visiting once I was settled into my new house. In later years this became one of the most painful regrets of my life, and remains so. By failing to "be there" as a big brother for Kate and Will, I allowed both time and distance to create an ever widening chasm between each of us (though much later circumstances would finally help narrow it). I now know that if I only *could* have the chance to go back in time and redo one thing, it would be this: I would relive those years intent to share more warmth and love as a brother and son.

But I eagerly packed my things and hired Joe's younger brother Charles to bring his truck over and help with the move. By late August, I was fully ensconced in my new place and ready to start my first college classes. These were structured into several "core courses" including "Rhetoric and Communication" (focusing on both written and oral communication); "History of Ideas" (history, philosophy, religion); "Science and Society" (a study of the history of science both as a mode of thought and a method of enquiry); and a "Scholars Colloquium," which included in-depth discussion of the themes arising in the various courses, along with guest lecturers on an eclectic range of topics. Students were also required to attend classes and labs in the foreign language of their choice—Spanish in my case—in advance of the summer abroad program (after which we were expected to pass an oral proficiency exam in the language).

The course which had the most profound impact on me was "Science and Society." I realized with some regret that my knowledge of science was quite limited, apart from basic high school courses which did little more than pique my interest. But this two semester course, co-taught by two distinguished professors—a physicist and a biologist—was intense, and by the end of the year I'd read so extensively within each branch of the sciences that both my understanding of the physical world and my worldview were irrevocably transformed. This journey began by reading the complete text by Thomas S. Kuhn titled *The Structure of Scientific Revolutions*, which served as the springboard for understanding the scientific method and the meaning and paradigmatic nature of the theory. From there we made an extensive study of many of the most significant figures and theories in the history of science, reading core texts as well as numerous analyses (and disputations) associated with various great minds of science. We further considered the impact on human culture of scientific thought and technological discoveries and progress—several years before anyone had even heard of email, the internet or even the cell phone.

Titles of some of the many papers I wrote for the class include: "New Views of Space and Time"; "The Influence of Einstein, Darwin, and Freud"; "The AIDS Dilemma"; "Loren Eiseley: Religious Scientist"; and "Darwin's Theory of Evolution." It was naturally Darwin who stirred up the most controversy within the class, with a number of students (and their parents) finding Darwin quite at odds with the fundamentalist Christian conception of man's place in the universe. Darwin had been neatly avoided at school, and I don't in fact recall his theory being in the least discussed in high school Biology.

The "History of Ideas" course taught by Dr. Tom Kaiser filled in serious gaps in my knowledge of world history and cultures (all but completely undeveloped since Mr. Marczuk's 9th grade history class), with readings that—in addition to a Western Civilization textbook—included a study of Hindu myths, Buddhism and Eastern cultures (both past and present). This opened up a whole new world—and lifelong interest—to me of which I'd previously been almost entirely in the dark.

In "Rhetoric and Communication" I had the best writing teacher I'd yet encountered in the person of Dr. Michael Kleine, whose sincere enthusiasm and friendly demeanor was as equally inspiring as his teaching. One thing he emphasized from the start was the dire need to safeguard one's writing, which in those days before the widespread use of storage retrieval systems led to his recommendation of saving all papers, as he did, in the freezer. Because, he explained, even if your house burned down, the one thing that would still be standing would be the fridge—with your papers intact inside.

Apart from the "Core" courses, I was free to take various other electives. These were for the most part all in the music department, where I could continue my bass lessons with Joe Vick for college credit. At the same time, I finally realized my dream of taking lessons on the classical guitar. I was taking lessons on four different musical instruments simultaneously: double bass, electric bass, classical guitar, and piano (on which I'd started lessons with Kate's teacher at the end of my senior year). There were numerous performance opportunities as well in the Fine Arts division, most prominently being with the jazz band, which I was invited to join. And to my delight, this brought a musical reunion with Dan, who was studying percussion at UALR with local drum legend Dave Rogers (with whom I recalled playing in the *Bye Bye Birdie* orchestra for our high school musical the year before).

The jazz band was directed by a professional trumpeter named Tom Richeson, who was famous for having played (and recorded) with numerous top artists, including Michael Jackson. Mr. Richeson challenged me to push the limits of my electric bass technique right off the bat, giving me a bass line which required me to "thump" (or "slap") the bass, funk style. This was intimidating at first—along with the overall standard of the older, often professional musicians in the band—as it was the one thing I'd seen done on the bass I in fact had no clue how to do. But one day at Boyd Music I saw a bassist thumping away on an instrument, and I asked how he did it. He showed me how to practice playing octaves by hitting the low note with my right hand thumb before rapidly plucking with the index finger. Before long and after extensive practice, I was able to impress Mr. Richeson and the band (as well as myself) with my newfound "funky bass" technique. Getting the right sound was facilitated by the acquisition of an old 70s Fender Jazz Bass I bought from local musician "Johnny B" Wright.

One day that fall Mr. Richeson told us the chancellor had requested we play at UALR basketball games, and we soon found ourselves loading up our equipment once or twice a week to set up in the gym and accompany the cheerleaders in providing "pep" for the school team, the UALR Trojans. Because we were suddenly the official team band, although still "jazz"-based (as opposed to performing the usual "marching band" style musical offerings), someone came up with an apt name for us: "Trojazz." (This led inevitably to occasional jokes of exceptional bad taste with reference to a particular brand of condom.)

To everyone's surprise, the basketball team rallied at around mid-season with a wild run of victories that eventually took them, for the first time in team history, to "the Dance": The NCAA (National Collegiate Athletic Association) basketball tournament itself, in which the 64 best teams in the United States compete for the national championship. They completely surpassed the Razorbacks that year, requiring sportscasters to hyphenate this underdog breakaway team as "Arkansas-Little Rock." After upsetting Notre Dame in the first round, UALR advanced to the second round and lost in double overtime on national television to the North Carolina State team of Coach Jim Valvano. We were one step short of advancing to the "Sweet 16" regional semifinals; but back home in Little Rock, we were all convinced that had Trojazz been present with the team on the road, the Trojans would have gone all the way.

With all the excitement of "Trojan Fever" that fall, our band began receiving invitations to play various gigs around town. The most exciting occasion had Dan and me pulling up in his old red and white van at the stately Governor's Mansion to perform for a grand reception the Governor was holding on the expansive grounds behind the mansion. Once again, I saw Governor Clinton come up and greet the band director, along with a warm smile and a wave of his hand towards the band before striding off back into the crowd.

6

HOMAGE TO ESPAÑA

The guitar begins
its weeping.
The cups of dawn are crushed.
The guitar begins
its weeping.
To silence it is useless.
To silence it is impossible.
Monotonously it weeps
as water weeps,
like wind weeps
over fields of snow.
To silence it is impossible.
It weeps for things
distant.
Hot sands of the south
longing for white camellias.
It weeps as an arrow without target,
an evening without morning,
and the first dead bird
upon the branch.
Oh, guitar!
A heart wounded mortally
by five swords.

—Federico García Lorca, "La Guitarra"
(Trans. F. H. Thurmond)

Even though I still lived in town, I saw less and less of my old high school friends as I threw myself headlong into my new college life. I did see Estelle a couple of times, but the connection was now clearly gone and we made no further attempt to rekindle a spent flame. Yet despite a full plate of academic and musical activity, I found time for a rich social life as well. This was in large part facilitated by having pledged at a "Greek" fraternity. I'd never originally intended to do so, especially after observing the antics on "fraternity row" in Fayetteville. I didn't see how anyone in a university social fraternity could ever get any work done at all. But when an old Catholic High friend named Ben—part of Joey and Andy's group of friends I'd gotten to know—called and invited me to pledge at *Sigma Phi Epsilon* (where he was now Chapter Secretary), I agreed to give it a go. After all, at UALR the fraternities and sororities were all non-residential—as opposed to larger campuses like Fayetteville—and Ben assured me this was purely a social network and would have no adverse effect on my studies. Also, having been founded at Richmond College in 1901, "Sig Ep" was among the older and more prestigious college fraternities. It boasted a number of distinguished members, the favorite then being President Reagan. I finally decided I would try it—just for the experience.

The first thing I found when I entered the Sig Ep house was the house "beer machine." On the surface it was your standard Coke machine; however, if you put your money in and pressed the button labeled "Coke" you got a Budweiser; selecting "Diet Coke" got you a Bud Light, "Dr. Pepper" a Coors, and so on. (I don't recall the machine ever actually stocking any Coke.) Any given hour of any given day found guys—and various local sorority girls—lounging around the house, drinking beer and getting high in front of the TV. The local frats also sponsored various extravagant parties during the year, Sig Ep being especially famous for its Halloween party. On one occasion a popular local band performed on a stage in the large backyard, and—as often—I managed to get up on stage and sit in on a song to the delight of my frat brothers and friends. All I otherwise recall of the party is that it made the film *Animal House* seem tame by comparison. One frat brother even bore a remarkable resemblance to John Belushi, in appearance as well as manner. This was all the more pronounced when, during one theme party, he burst onto the scene shouting "*Toga!*"

The "pledge" process itself also proved more like a traditional fraternity experience than I'd bargained for. This involved the infamous practice of occasional "hazing," as well as spending a semester being treated like servants—including having to clean up all the broken glass and puke after a wild party—and ultimately being forced to undergo a rather frightening ordeal as part of initiation into the fraternity: We were loaded, blindfolded, into the back of a pickup truck and driven to the midst of a dark forest outside town. En route we were instructed to come up with an original drinking song, a task my pledge brothers placed upon my shoulders. After all, *I* was the musician. When we arrived and were unloaded from the truck, still blindfolded, we could feel the heat of a large bonfire so close it was nearly painful. Then we were instructed to sing our song, which came off very impressively. Finally our blindfolds were removed and our individual "big brothers" stood in front of each of us with an outstretched beer and congratulations for being fully initiated into the fraternity.

As a full member, I was now free to come and go as I pleased, and the house became a welcoming home away from home, although its top amenity (apart from a popular ping pong table) was short-lived: Someone must have said something to the campus police, because one day they walked in and hauled the beer machine away. Perhaps this was prescient of the frat's ultimate future as well, because some years hence when I returned for a visit, not only was the fraternity gone from campus, but the house itself had been completely razed. There was just an empty lot where the house had once stood, leaving all my happy (if hedonistic) experiences there confined to memory.

At the end of the first semester, I was at the same time delighted and disappointed by my near-perfect academic record of 3.8. I had failed to get an A only in Dr. Robert Boury's Music Theory class, which, with its mathematical basis, required further study than I had been able to give, and I bitterly realized I could have had a 4.0 had it not been for pledging the fraternity. (I nevertheless became something of a legend within the frat itself, as no one else had come even close to an A average.) But socializing at the frat house can't bear all the blame for my extracurricular distractions, as there was another—and infinitely more important—aspect of my social life that first year of college. This was my membership in the International Student Club of UALR.

For a small provincial university, there was an impressive population of international students on campus. Most of them were there on athletic scholarships for sports including soccer, tennis, volleyball, and swimming. They came from all over the world, and especially from Europe, Latin and Central America, and the Middle East. Many of them were members of the International Student Club, which I now joined in my eagerness to meet people from around the world and learn about their cultures. The president of the club was from Oman, and at his request I hosted a club party at my house. There gathered under one roof were nationals of Oman, Iran, Iraq and Saudi Arabia as well as Guatemala, El Salvador, the Philippines and others I can't recall. I only realized later the true significance, especially at that time, of having students from these countries in one place. It turned out that a large proportion of the swimmers were from Spain, at UALR on swimming scholarships to play on the water polo team, and so it was that I was able to befriend a group of actual Spaniards even as my anticipation for visiting their country grew by the day. They all lived in a rented house just down the street from the fraternity, which meant that on a good night I could walk back and forth from one party to the other. I first got to know all of them after being invited to a Spanish party at their house that fall. The first thing I saw when I entered the house was a huge bucket in the kitchen in which two young men were pouring whole bottles of different wines over every type of fruit available at the local store. *Sangria*, they called it. "Because it's red, like blood," one of them explained.

Two of the Spaniards, Juan Antonio and Tomás, came from a city called Alicante. This, they explained, was on the East coast of Spain, south of Valencia along the *Costa Blanca*. The other two, Martin and Aldo, were from Tenerife in the Canary Islands. These two brothers were the most identical of twins I've ever met. And they knew how to use it too, telling me stories of how they would occasionally—if overbooked on romantic liaisons, which were many given the overwhelming power their suave good looks had on local women—fill in for each other, the unsuspecting girl never even noticing. (Or alternatively, an unrecognized woman might warmly approach one of them at a bar with flirtatious familiarity and—realizing it was his brother's work—he'd simply go with it, carefully gauging conversation with the young lady to avoid seeming clueless of previous encounters.)

Another young man from Tenerife, Fernando, needed temporary accommodation and I agreed to let him use the spare bedroom at my house the next semester. He insisted I visit that summer where his family lived on a different part of Tenerife than Martin and Aldo. There would in fact be a grand *fiesta* in Alicante that June, one of the thousands of annual festivals particular to each city in Spain, from Madrid to Barcelona and Pamplona and even the tiniest villages in between—and we all agreed to meet there for what they promised would be the week of a lifetime. And they meant it.

Later that fall was another event that had an impact I could never then have imagined. The head of guitar studies at the UALR music department, Michael Carenbauer, arranged for a young New York classical guitarist named Benjamin Verdery to perform a recital, along with a guitar master class in which I was invited to participate. It so happened that my mother had met Mr. Verdery the previous year when Verdery had performed at a special reception for a new bank opening in Little Rock. She later told me about the "haunting" music he'd played on classical guitar, and that she had in fact told him about me and my garage band.

"Is there any hope for my son?" she'd asked.

Verdery replied that he, too, had once been a rock musician before discovering the moving artistry of the classical guitar. So yes, he'd advised her, there was hope.

My mother got the idea to arrange a get-together with the guitarist during his visit, and Carenbauer—who was hosting Verdery—agreed to invite him. Finally, after Verdery's inspiring performance, we made an arrangement to meet at a local restaurant very early the next morning for breakfast with both Benjamin and Michael before Verdery's flight back to New York. The next morning, the two men clearly regretted having agreed to do so, as their eyes revealed a late night. But in the course of the conversation, I told Benjamin about my planned trip to Spain, where I hoped to find a way to study guitar performance. His expression lit up warmly and, his innate enthusiasm revived, he said he would in fact be teaching that summer at an annual guitar festival in Córdoba. He would be co-teaching a guitar master class with the virtuoso Australian guitarist John Williams, and if I called him after his return to New York he'd give me the details for enrolling in the course. This was a dream come true! And on top of this opportunity, he said he knew of a group of guitarists based in Dallas who took an annual tour of Spain that focused on guitar music and trips to famous *luthiers* around the country to shop for Spanish guitars—including the Ramirez shop in Madrid I'd been wishing to visit since first hearing about that famous name among guitar makers. Benjamin offered to put me in touch with the Dallas guitarists as well.

I called Benjamin soon afterwards, who gave me all the promised information and once again left me with inspiring words of encouragement for my guitar studies. "See you in Spain!" he said finally. I then immediately made a call to Dallas, finding myself on the phone with an equally enthusiastic gentleman named Carlo Pezzimenti, who said he was indeed putting together a tour of Spain that summer and that there was still a place for me if I wished to join. The trip would include a true cultural tour of Spain, including performances of classical as well as flamenco music by Spanish guitarists around the country. Also included would be private lessons along the way with Carlo and other professional guitarists leading the group. So before long I had the ultimate summer planned: I'd begin in Madrid with a month-long formal course of language study, followed first by the guitar tour with Carlo Pezzimenti and then visits to my new UALR friends in Alicante and

Tenerife before culminating in July at the International Guitar Festival in Córdoba. It was more than enough to look forward to, and it was all I could do to stay focused on my current studies while I waited for summer to arrive.

Before leaving, my mother told me stories she'd heard about two living Spanish music legends, the guitarist Andrés Segovia and composer Joaquín Rodrigo. Then she gave me her old dog-eared copy of Hemingway's *The Sun Also Rises* for the trip.

The first leg of the trip was the month-long Spanish course arranged by the Scholars Program. This was held at a language school in Madrid, and for room and board I was hosted by a local family in their home. I had no choice but to learn quickly how to communicate in their language. The head of the family, a retired history professor, was as eccentric as he was witty, friendly, and knowledgeable of all aspects of Spanish history. The first thing I recall him saying to me just after my arrival, speaking in English with a thick accent as we watched a heavy rainfall over the rooftops of Madrid, was: "And they say in Spain it only rains in the plains!"

I was also eager to get started with my guitar studies. I'd brought an old, cracked guitar I bought from Robert, and on which I had begun my lessons at UALR. (I planned to buy a proper Spanish guitar later on the "guitar tour.") So I went to the Madrid Conservatory of Music, where I was able to arrange lessons with one of their "Maestros," and was soon spending afternoons after class practicing my guitar lessons in Retiro Park, enchanted with the new melodies I was making alongside the sparkling waters that splashed from beautifully sculpted fountains.

The language course also included a cultural element, with trips to museums like the Prado and excursions to local historical sites in and around Madrid. It so happened there was also a major art exhibition in Madrid that month devoted to the Impressionists, and this combined with the Prado exposed me within a matter of days to more great art than I'd ever imagined seeing in my life. This experience, along with that of the previous summer, firmly secured a lifelong love for and appreciation of all aspects of art and artistic expression.

On one of the excursions, I experienced a most extraordinary coincidence. We were on the train to Toledo—which I'd been longing to visit since reading the novel *Of Human Bondage* in school with Maugham's vivid description of El Greco's artistic depiction of that city—when I met a Mexican couple in Spain on holiday. They were sitting across from me, and I enjoyed the opportunity to try out my newly acquired Spanish. As we compared our respective travel plans, when I told them of my upcoming trip to the island of Tenerife they said they too planned to visit there. Then I happened to mention my Spanish housemate, Fernando, who was from Tenerife and whom I'd be staying with there. They said they too knew a Fernando from Tenerife: They had met him in New York at the airport while changing planes when, not knowing a word of English and finding themselves in a bind, a young man who happened to be walking by saw their predicament and helped them out. They were so grateful they'd told him he was welcome to visit them in Mexico whenever he wished, and he likewise invited them to visit his family in Tenerife. Then they showed me the paper on which he had written his details: "Fernando Paniagua," my own friend and housemate! When I told Fernando about it later, he too was amazed not only at the coincidence of my being on the same train, car, and seat with this couple he'd met so randomly at the busiest airport in the world, but at the extreme odds of discovering the connection. (Especially given it was my first real-world conversation in Spanish.) Ever since, I've often wondered what personal connection I might possibly have—yet never even suspect—with any given stranger passing by in a crowd.

Before leaving Madrid, I heard that the flamenco guitarist *extraordinaire* Paco de Lucia would be performing at an outdoor concert. I wouldn't miss this for the world and was awed by the power this gentleman poured forth into his instrument, wounding gathered hearts mortally—to quote Lorca—with the cutting edge performance of his five right hand fingers (despite his hands being partially clothed in a thick glove for warmth on that chilly evening). After the concert, I went up to meet de Lucia and daringly asked if it might be possible to arrange a guitar lesson with him. In reply, he put his arm around my shoulder, and with a warm smile said, "One day, my friend, I will."

Following completion of the language course, I joined the "guitar group" as planned, and the ensuing tour was a great success for two reasons. I first of all did acquire a new guitar, although not a Ramirez— this being far beyond my present means (as I discovered at the Madrid shop) and, my teacher said, not at all justified until I reached a higher performance standard. A Ramirez guitar was something to strive for, to *earn*. For now, I bought a student guitar from the shop of respected luthier Manuel Contreras, whose store was near the grand *Plaza Mayor*. Still, the difference between my new instrument and Robert's old guitar was night and day, so I gave the latter to the professor, who quickly found an appropriate use for it: When I returned for a visit later that summer, he had nailed it up to the wall of his flat near the entrance as an appropriate furnishing to greet future students. I imagine it still hangs there to this day.

The tour also included, as promised, lessons with the faculty leaders, and this is where I first got to know Carlo Pezzimenti, with whom I'd spoken only briefly by phone when arranging the tour. Now I learned that he was a protégé of the legendary Maestro Andrés Segovia, with whom he had studied and cultivated a friendship during regular visits to Spain. And it was through Carlo that I learned Segovia's words of wisdom concerning music, art, and life in general that would inspire me for a lifetime.

The next part of my trip took me to Alicante, where I met up as planned with the Little Rock Spaniards in time for the *fiesta* known locally as *Fogueres de Sant Joan* ("Bonfires of St. John"). This traditionally starts on the first day of summer and continues for a full week. And what a week it is! The entire town essentially shuts down and transforms into the wildest party imaginable. And while it may not feature bulls running through the streets in hot pursuit of drunken tourists, it is equally both exciting and debauched. I threw myself into the festivities wholeheartedly, but even though I was a fit 19-year-old boy full of energy and enthusiasm, after only three days I began to ask if it would soon be over. "But no!" Juan Antonio would reply, waking me up for a game of tennis before lunch following a third all-nighter in a row full of drinking and dancing in the streets. "The *fiesta* is only just beginning! *Vamos!!*" Then I'd feel every single muscle sorely pleading with me to throw in the towel, only to find myself getting a second wind on the tennis court with a seemingly indefatigable Juan Antonio; this would be followed by a giant meal cooked by his mother featuring *paella del mar*, or perhaps *tortilla español* or even raw squid.

Then we'd go for a swim at the beach—or perhaps a bullfight with all its pomp and colorful splendor, followed by a dish of oxtail soup made fresh from the afternoon kill—then, finally, a long *siesta* lasting until early evening before the cycle began all over again. But to my alarm, and as Juan Antonio had indicated, each night brought an even greater level of intensity than before, so that I truly thought I'd completely and utterly collapse before the end of it. One night I even found myself in a tiny makeshift bullring with a small bull calf, very fortunately without horns, but sufficiently violent to ensure I'd never agree to such a thing again.

It all culminates in an explosive night—first the fireworks from over the ancient castle (*Castillo de Santa Bárbara*) that looms high above the city, and later the bonfires. Before the fiesta, each individual district of the city sponsors the building by local guilds of a large sculpture made of papier-mâché and wood; these often take the form of effigies devoted to particular saints, and they all together form part of a competition the winning of which brings great honor to the district it represents (reminiscent of the New Orleans *crews* during Mardi gras). Then, on the last night of the fiesta, every sculpture goes up in glorious flames. Crowds of people gather at each sculpture and dance in front of the huge bonfire it makes.

On this particular occasion the winning sculpture towered high above a small square, and we all converged upon it to take part in what promised to be a spectacular scene. As the sculpture caught fire, I looked up at it warily.

"Don't worry!" said Tomás, "it's designed to collapse straight down." When the bonfire reached its fullest potential, now a towering inferno of fire flickering high above the apartment buildings on either side of it, firemen moved in with high powered hoses to begin extinguishing the blaze. This was the cue for many, perhaps hundreds, in the crowd to run forward between the fire and water to enjoy the sensation of both the heat and the opposing coolness of drenching water. This was the fun part.

"Come on," said Tomás, "*Vamonos!*" He and the others ran forward into the chaos, but something held me back. I didn't like the way the sculpture appeared to be tilting dangerously near the top. Then, sure enough, it collapsed not downwards as designed but prematurely sideways. There was an explosion and loud flash as, to everyone's horror, it came down upon a power line next to which the sculpture had been built. So here was a burning mass of paper and wood resting upon a severed livewire, surrounded by crowds of people amid powerful streams of water. It could not and did not have a happy ending, and at least one person was electrocuted to death and others seriously injured before the catastrophe was over. (Fortunately none of my friends were hurt.) I felt grateful for the cautious intuition that had held me back. And I wasn't surprised to learn in later years that building codes for the annual sculptures had been significantly emended following this particular incident—namely, no more building them next to power lines.

The penultimate stage of my journey, to visit Martin, Aldo, and Fernando and their families in Tenerife, seemed relaxing and tame by comparison even though it, too, involved dancing till dawn at pulsating discotheques, followed by sunrise swims in the cold Atlantic surf. Getting there was half the adventure: The brothers came from a large fam-

ily, which still benefitted from a law instituted by the late Generalis-
simo Francisco Franco designed to encourage and reward particularly
large Catholic families. This included travel discounts, and as Martin
and Aldo came from a family of fourteen children they were obvious
beneficiaries. All I had to do, therefore, was to pose as a brother during
check-in (a sister worked for the airline and had arranged my ticket)
and I'd fly to the Canary Islands for next to nothing. "Just try not to say
anything," Martin advised. And sure enough, it worked.

By the time I finally got back to the mainland and arrived in Córdoba
that July, I'd almost forgotten this was the original point of my travel to
Spain. But soon I was immersed in the business of studying, practicing
and performing on the Spanish classical guitar. The International Guitar Festival was held at the *Centro Flamenco Paco Peña*, named after the
renowned flamenco guitarist who hosted the event. There were courses
in flamenco and flamenco dance as well as the classical guitar master class I took, in which students received hours of daily instruction,
inspiration and words of wisdom from John Williams and Benjamin
Verdery. I'd never imagined anything like it. The whole town seemed to
have become one giant guitar, with everyone living and breathing music and dance for almost two weeks. Every evening after classes there
was a concert in the city's formal concert hall, including back to back
performances by Verdery, Williams, Peña, the Familia Montoya, and
even a Latin American group called Inti-Illimani. After each concert
everyone, including the performers, instructors, students and a collection of locals would gather to eat, drink and mingle at the little bar
outside the old house in back of the ancient *Plaza del Potro* (described
by Cervantes in *Don Quixote*)—in which Paco Peña lived and hosted
the festival's guest musicians.

7

Big D

I know young people who play the piano as one can't play it better. But then, when I hear them play it that way, I have my little question for them. I ask them, when will you start to make music?

—Arthur Rubenstein

I saw the best minds of my generation destroyed by madness.

—Allen Ginsberg, "Howl"

When classes resumed at UALR for the fall semester '86, I took and passed my required proficiency exam in Spanish. Then I immediately had the opportunity to put my new language skills into practice, while at the same time gaining a memorable new cultural experience. I was in the International Studies Office filling in its director about my trip, when the phone rang and the secretary could be heard struggling to communicate with someone on the other end. Finally she held up the receiver with a look of desperation.

"Excuse me," she asked, "but can anyone here speak Spanish?" The director looked at me quizzically, and I said I might be able to help.

"Good," said the secretary. "The new student from Mexico is on the phone and can't speak a word of English!"

It turned out the student had just arrived by bus and was stranded at the station downtown. Due to a miscommunication, nobody from the university was there waiting to greet her upon arrival. She sounded quite stressed, and when I explained this to the secretary she asked if I would please drive downtown and assist the student.

When I got to the station, the student turned out to be a strikingly beautiful young lady and I was immediately smitten. Her name was Adriana, and she had just been on a grueling three day bus trip all the way from her home of Guadalajara. I could only imagine her feelings of dismay after coming all that way to find herself alone in a strange new land where no one spoke her language. I marveled at the chance that I happened to be there to take her call and be the one to greet her. She was so grateful that she offered to cook me an authentic Mexican dinner. I did not object.

The preparation for the dinner was an experience in itself. I went with Adriana to shop for her long list of ingredients, and became mildly concerned when she put everything *hot* available at the store into the grocery cart. But I was doubly concerned later when it all went in one go into the pot with the chicken. The ultimate concoction quickly taught me the delectable difference between the *tortilla Español* in Spain and its spicy Latin cousin, the *tortilla Mexicana*. But the meal's survival was facilitated with ample shots of the particular libation Adriana had selected: Tequila.

It so happened that I was currently studying a series of *Preludes* written for Andrés Segovia by the Mexican composer Manuel Ponce, and Adriana asked to hear my guitar music as an after dinner serenade. She seemed captivated as much by my ability to perform music by her country's national composer as with the sonorous beauty of the music itself, and to my surprise began kissing me passionately in mid-strum. The rest of that evening my quest for "cultural discovery" took on for me an entirely new—and sweetly romantic—meaning.

The UALR music department sponsored a number of impressive recitals by top musicians within a short space of time, including—as with Benjamin Verdery—master classes which allowed students to meet and study with the performers. In a short time, these guest artists included jazz percussionist Airto Moreira and drummer Jack Dejohnette, as well as a local concert by bassist Stanley Clarke. Clarke had become for me, along with Jaco Pastorius, a favorite jazz bassist, and I felt honored at the opportunity to meet and speak with him before the performance. During the concert I got directly in front of the stage in order to see Clarke's lightning fast fingers in action; at one point I held up my hand to wave, and to my great surprise he gave me a quick high five right in mid-performance of one of his furious bass riffs. He didn't miss a beat.

I also still occasionally attended rock concerts at Barton Coliseum, and took Adriana to see Van Halen, on tour that year with their new singer Sammy Hagar. Another entirely different musical experience was that of a recital at UALR by famed lutenist Paul O'Dette. This performance had, like Verdery's, been organized by guitarist Michael Carenbauer, and being familiar with the lute from Vivaldi's lute concertos—as well as the Bach lute suites—I eagerly attended. I was mesmerized by what I heard—as well as learned, as O'Dette gave the audience enlightening background knowledge concerning the Renaissance Italian and English music he performed. For the first time, I heard the sumptuously resonate music of such composers as Francesco da Milano and the celebrated Elizabethan lutenist John Dowland, performed authentically on O'Dette's elegant six and eight-course lutes. There was something about this music—and the lute itself as an instrument—which profoundly moved me, speaking to me on a deeper level than any other music (apart from that of Bach) had ever done. I felt an immediate longing to one day experience playing such music not just as transcribed for the classical guitar, but on an actual *lute* itself. (And thanks to Carenbauer, Adriana and I were able to meet O'Dette after the concert for an up close look at the lutes.)

In the meantime, I became further immersed in my guitar studies, and I arranged with Carlo Pezzimenti to have a lesson in Dallas. My old friend Joey had invited me to visit in nearby Fort Worth, where he lived with his girlfriend from Shreveport whom he'd met at TCU. We arranged for me to fly down for a visit, along with a meeting with Carlo in Dallas where he taught at Brookhaven College. Southwest Airlines had a special fare of only $15 each way to fly directly from Little Rock to Dallas, so I began traveling there biweekly for lessons—occasionally driving one way with Joey when he visited Little Rock and then flying back.

On one of these occasions, Joey said that since I was so serious about my guitar studies with Carlo, I might as well just transfer to school down in Dallas. It would also be good for me in general, he argued, to experience life out of state and in a bigger, more cosmopolitan city like Dallas. I needed little persuading, as I'd sensed the same myself for some time. To my surprise my parents were supportive of the idea, even though it meant giving up a great scholarship. Their only concern was that I should transfer into a full four-year university as opposed to the two-year junior college at which Carlo taught. On

Joey's advice, I therefore applied to Southern Methodist University (SMU), which had renowned faculty in the arts. By Christmas, I was fully enrolled at SMU as a double major in English and Music, and ready for a new adventure in Dallas—about 250 miles southwest, and popularly known to Little Rock residents as "Big D."

Before my move, tragic news came from Crossett: My grandparents' beloved old house caught fire in the middle of the night and burned to the ground. Very fortunately, however, Aunt Blanche saw the flames from where she lived in a house across Hancock Road, and Uncle Slim was able to rush over and help my grandparents out of the house just in the nick of time. Daddy Frank had had his leg amputated by this time—according to his doctor due to a clot that was possibly related to his having been a victim of a German mustard gas attack during a WWI battle in the trenches of France. (He'd just barely got his gas mask on in time to survive.) So he had been carried out of the burning house by my uncle. But even as they were exiting the burning house, Daddy Frank shouted to my grandmother: "Doris, get my guns!" She duly went back to the gun rack and was only able to save one gun from the flames: the antique Winchester .16 gauge shotgun I'd used for my first hunt. This was later willed to me as a gift from my grandfather, and remains one of my prized possessions.

Daddy Frank stubbornly refused to let a minor setback like the loss of his house, and almost a century of possessions, keep him down. (Nor did he curtail his smoking habit after learning the fire might be attributed to random sparks from his pipe igniting faulty old electrical wiring.) At 90 years old, he determined to rebuild; and by summer he'd had a new house built in the same spot.

I went down to see the site of the old house just after the fire. Everything was gone apart from the remnants of a chimney and—just as Dr. Kleine had predicted—the refrigerator, still standing completely intact right where the kitchen used to be. Also gone was the physical manifestation of my most poignant childhood memories. This was the only place I'd ever truly thought of as *home*, the place my mother had brought me after she split with my birth father. Now those old doubts returned, and I wondered if the time to search for my father had finally arrived. Yet still I took no action. I wouldn't do so for many years to come.

In that year also both my adoptive grandparents died, and Dad inherited their house on Sunset Drive with the impressive view of the Arkansas River valley. My parents planned to move with the family

*The old house in Crossett, painted from memory
by my aunt, Blanche Turlington.*

into it after a few months of remodeling, and as I departed for Dallas I knew I was leaving my childhood home for the last time.

When I arrived for classes that spring semester '87, there was an eerie pall over the SMU campus. This was because the school's football program, previously a national powerhouse based in the Southwestern Conference, was hit that February with the NCAA's Death Penalty. For the first time in the National Collegiate Athletic Association's history, it decided to punish a school for recruitment violations by forcing a complete shutdown of the football program for the next couple of seasons. It was widely perceived that SMU had simply been the chosen scapegoat to set an example for all the other schools nationwide using similar methods to attract star athletes—in SMU's case providing prospective recruits during visits to campus with cash, cars, and cheerleaders.

The loss of its football program had serious repercussions for the school in terms of both economics and reputation, given the unfortunate priority most American universities give to funding and promoting their athletic programs at the expense of actual learning. SMU football would not have a post-season bowl game appearance for 25 years. But in retrospect, the break from football seems to have done the institution a world of good in terms of some necessary soul-searching.

It was also at this time that the Dallas Cowboys professional football franchise was bought by Jerry Jones, who promptly fired Cowboys legend Tom Landry as coach and replaced him with Jones' fellow Arkansas Razorback teammate Jimmy Johnson. Jones would never be forgiven for this by local Dallasites—not taking kindly to an "outsider" replacing their beloved coach—despite, after years of lackluster seasons, soon taking the Cowboys to consecutive Superbowl victories in 1993-1994. Jones and Johnson then got into a public dispute over which one of them deserved more credit for the team's triumphs, leading Jones to fire Johnson as head coach and replace him with Mom's old Crossett schoolmate, Barry Switzer. After falling one step short of the Superbowl in Switzer's first year, Switzer coached the Cowboys to another Superbowl victory in 1996.

I had just begun questioning both my timing and my decision when the first classes I attended quickly dispelled my fears. There were professors in each of my chosen subjects who were nationally known as musicians and writers, and whose teaching was as stellar as their work. (There were also a few surprises: I found for instance that a "Core" course in Anthropology in which I'd enrolled for required credit was taught by an internationally renowned anthropologist, David Freidel, whose field research on the Mayan civilization was—and remains— cutting edge; this he was able to incorporate into his teaching of an otherwise general introductory course.)

I also began to revel in courses devoted to literature and creative writing. One of my favorite literature courses included a survey of American literature taught by Professor Pascal Covici, Jr. His father, Pascal Covici, was a famous editor who had helped discover John Steinbeck's work. During our study of Mark Twain, I told Professor Covici about my experience as a kid seeing the actor Hal Holbrook's "Mark Twain Tonight!" performance at UALR, when my mother took me as a kid to see Holbrook bring Twain to life. I'll never forget the way he appeared on stage in a white suit—looking and sounding every bit like the actual Sam Clemens during one of the author's famous lecture tours, even down to uttering witty aphorisms between puffs from a pungent cigar. Professor Covici said his father had actually seen Mark Twain himself give one of his lectures, and then lived long enough to see Holbrook's Twain impersonation and comment he'd gotten it just right.

It was in creative writing that I found, combined with my guitar studies, true fulfillment. My first course was a poetry writing workshop taught by Jack Myers, whose book *As Long As You're Happy* had recently won the National Book Award for poetry, for which it had been selected by future Nobel Prize laureate Seamus Heaney. (Myers himself would later be named Poet Laureate of Texas.) Jack, who often shared stories of the harsh circumstances of his youth, culturally informed by his Russian Jewish heritage, brought a warmth and spirit of openness to the classroom—a term used loosely since we'd often meet outside to discuss our poetry amid the voice of splashing water by the fountain. Or occasionally we'd even meet at a local bar such as Milo's, a popular pool hall off Greenville Avenue—sometimes with a visiting poet during the annual SMU Literary Festival.

This festival occurred each autumn and featured, over the course of several years, readings by some of the top poets and novelists in the country. These included Kurt Vonnegut, Donald Barthelme, Jay McInerny, John Barth, C.K. Williams, Gwendolyn Brooks, William Styron, Studs Turkel, Lawrence Ferlinghetti and Tim Seibels—who had previously studied with Jack Meyers and was a close friend of Carlo's. One of my favorite activities in those years was attending their collaborative performances, in which Carlo would perform classical guitar music to accompany Tim's poetry readings. These recitals inspired me to no end, and served as a prelude to my later interest in the classical—and Renaissance—theory of musical and poetic harmony.

As an English major, I was often invited to the receptions that followed these readings. They were usually held at a faculty member's house or at a local restaurant or bar. One poet—and future Pulitzer Prize winner—C.K. Williams, told of his life in Paris. (Several years later, I would cross paths with him at a reading there.) But perhaps the most exciting occasion was attending a party for Allen Ginsberg. After his exhilarating reading in his inimitable voice, the aging poet appeared old and frail beneath his mane of gray hair and stubbly beard. At one point in conversation with him, Ginsberg put his hand on my wrist and asked for help finding a seat.

"I'm a sick man," he said.

I showed the poet an old book my mother had given me called *The Beat Generation and The Angry Young Men*. It had been published in the 50s before the famous Supreme Court ruling (in the case of San Francisco's City Lights Bookstore) that loosened American anti-obscenity laws, and in the book Ginsberg's poem had been heavily censored. He seemed delighted to see it and signed the book for me and my mother.

Along with my courses in poetry writing with Jack, I took the fiction writing workshop conducted by novelist Marshall Terry. Marsh was already a legendary figure at SMU, having inspired (and exhorted) generations of students with his unique combination of classic wit and folksy humor—qualities which shine through in his novels and stories.

He'd recently published a collection called *Dallas Stories*, in which he captured the nuances of this oddly surreal city rising with gleaming skyscrapers from the arid Texas plains—a city sprung up around the oil industry and highly symbolic of both the best and the worst of American capitalism: On its surface Dallas is a shallow bastion of wealth, business, greed and corruption—reeling for two decades from the JFK assassination, until the popular TV show *Dallas* (featuring the iconic character "JR") gave the world a new, and ironically welcomed by Dallasites, image of the city. Yet conversely (or perhaps inversely) Dallas is at the same time a veritable Mecca for the arts and artistic expression.

Terry's stories and novels feature characters deluded with grand visions of their place within the cowboy mythology of the American West, including billionaire businessmen seemingly oblivious to the eccentric incongruity (especially in the boardrooms of Manhattan, Europe or Japan) of Stetson hats and sharp-toed cowboy boots combined with business suits and power ties. Marsh shared with students both his enormous enthusiasm and his talent for conveying written expression both as writer and teacher, and the experience of attending his workshop—in conjunction with that of Jack's on poetry—was nonpareil.

Counterpointing all of this was my work with Carlo. I had a weekly guitar lesson with him at Brookhaven College, where I also attended his weekly master class that provided students with a forum to try out newly learned pieces in actual performance. The first time I did so, it was as if all my rock and jazz band performance experience had come to naught, for—just as back in 10th grade when I'd first stood upon the stage in front of an audience—I completely froze when I found myself poised to perform in front of a group. But unlike managing in high school to navigate the four thick strings of an electric bass with the support of a band, I found to my horror that a shaking right hand proves deadly when attempting to play a complex solo on the delicate strings of a classical guitar. But that was the beauty of Carlo's class. Before long, I was able to perform in front of others—and, as Carlo taught, once a piece of music was memorized one could then focus on developing the many dynamic nuances and musical colors for which the classical guitar is uniquely suited in the hands of a competent musician. The guitar, as Segovia once observed, is an instrument that should be held and regarded as tenderly as a lover.

As a teacher—mentor even—one would be hard-pressed to find anyone more dedicated and genuinely inspiring (as a true artist in his own right) than Carlo. Part of this was certainly due to his personality, with his lively wit and zany sense of humor—complemented by a contagious smile beneath his dark Italian eyes and thick tufts of curly hair. He always addressed me as "Francesco" with an exaggerated Italian accent, ever since I reported being shouted at on the phone by the father of Antonella—a girl I'd met in Rome and been corresponding with ever since. (In a similar vein, Marsh Terry nicknamed me "Paco" after my penchant for writing about Spain.) Carlo also performed regularly around the Dallas area (solo as well as with poet Tim Siebles), while concurrently producing exquisite recordings of his wide-ranging repertoire. Above all was the importance of his philosophy of music performance, summed up in his admiration for the composer Gustav Mahler, of whom Carlo said: "He is a philosopher who uses notes instead of words." The ability to convey this philosophy through the medium of his guitar was an art Carlo learned from his studies with Andrés Segovia.

"An artist," Carlo once explained, "has to have a strong will not to allow himself the temptation of displaying only flashy technique." This, for Carlo, applied not only to the "flashy" dazzle of modern rock guitarists (the electric guitar having been only made possible, Carlo wryly observed, by Andrés Segovia's popularization of the instrument earlier in the century), but also the majority of classical guitarists themselves—many of even the best known ones putting technical prowess over the making of actual *music*. Carlo therefore taught the importance of concentrating on the musical subtext beneath each individual note, even at the possible risk of making the odd mistake during performance. The important thing was in preserving the musical integrity of a given composition. In this, he often made reference to the music and teachings of various "old school"—and romantic—artists including, in addition to Segovia, Jascha Heifetz (violin), Mstislav Rostropovich (cello), and Arthur Rubenstein (piano). I therefore began acquiring all the recordings I could find by these musicians—beginning with Rubenstein's exquisite Chopin performances—in hopes of learning from them a sensitivity of style I could bring to my own music.

Perhaps, in sum, the best way to describe Carlo's passion and philosophy is through reference to the Spanish concept of the *duende*. This, as Spanish poet and dramatist Federico García Lorca described in an essay dedicated to the subject titled "The Duende," is "not a question of aptitude, but of a true and viable style—of blood, in other words; of what is oldest in culture: of creation made act." By way of illustration, he quotes the great Andalusian flamenco artist Manuel Torres as remarking to a singer, "You have a voice, you know all the styles, but you'll never bring it off because you have no *duende*." Lorca likewise draws upon the wisdom of Goethe, who—in speaking of Paganini, effectively defined the *duende* as "a mysterious power that all may feel and no philosophy can explain." Duende, then, is for Lorca "the roots that probe through the mire that we all know of, and do not understand, but which furnishes us with whatever is sustaining in art." It is this life-sustaining quality of art which Carlo inculcates, with passion and devotion, through both his music and his teaching.

That first spring in Dallas, inspired by Carlo with an appreciation of Andrés Segovia's artistry, I flew to New York City for a concert by the Maestro at Carnegie Hall. At 94 years old, he was still touring and had just received great reviews following a recent concert in Chicago (which I had debated attending before deciding on New York). On the night of the concert, Carnegie officials announced that Andrés Segovia had just been hospitalized with heart complications and the performance was cancelled. He died soon afterwards—on June 2, 1987—in Madrid, and it turned out that the concert I'd missed was the only performance in Segovia's entire career (beginning with his professional debut in 1910) that he had ever cancelled.

Somewhat bathetically, I went instead to Broadway that evening for a performance of the current hit musical, *A Chorus Line.*

My time in Dallas was spent primarily devoted to my studies, a welcome change from the eventful years of high school and UALR. I tried initially to maintain my relationship with Adriana in Little Rock but eventually found out she had a new boyfriend. I generally found it difficult to meet people at SMU—both because I'd transferred in the middle of my Sophomore year and never experienced living on campus, but also because the majority of students there seemed to be grouped into cliques centered within the Greek system. One old Little Rock friend from elementary school days—Tyler—was at SMU but also caught up in a fraternity and I seldom saw him. All I had to do, of course, was affiliate with the SMU chapter of Sigma Phi Epsilon, which would have been as easy as turning up at their house and introducing myself with the secret fraternity handshake. Then I'd have had a guaranteed exciting social life. But that is exactly what I wanted to avoid. I had my eyes set on higher aspirations than the ephemeral pleasures of collegiate society.

I attended a number of music and theater events, plentiful in the SMU Meadows School of the Arts and elsewhere. All music students were expected to attend concerts and recitals almost weekly; these were meant to be strictly classical performances, and to this end the school provided free tickets to the Dallas Symphony Orchestra. One weekend

I attended both the Symphony and a concert by guitarist Carlos Santana back to back, and got called before the Dean after submitting the Santana ticket by mistake.

"So you want credit for attending a concert by Santana?" he asked incredulously. I reflected a moment, and then asked: "Why not?" He refused, however, to give me any credit for seeing Santana.

I eventually found a friend through the SMU music conservatory, where I spent much time both practicing piano and attending recitals. Michael was a viola player with a scholarship place in the SMU Orchestra, and we hit it off with a mutual love of music, literature, and girls. Michael was from Philadelphia and a self-described "Philly Jew," and so my unlikely best friend on this otherwise conservative Southern campus was a liberal Jewish kid from Pennsylvania. One day Michael pointed out an ongoing debate in the SMU student newspaper between Greeks and non-Greeks concerning the value (or lack thereof) of having social fraternities and sororities on a college campus. The argument had become progressively nastier, having finally reached a stalemate with the Greek side's argument that non-members (who insisted Greeks on campus did more harm than good through their staunchly non-academic, decadent and even debauched activities) had no right to pass judgment on something they had not experienced first-hand. Michael insisted that I weigh in with an article expressing my anti-Greek sentiments as an actual member of a national Greek fraternity. He finally convinced me that my unique take on the argument was something which needed to be heard, and I applied all my new-found knowledge of Swiftian satire in the composition of a piece which thoroughly eviscerated every pro-Greek argument that had been presented. I began by summarizing the arguments both pro and con, and expressing the desire that, "speaking as a member of a national Greek fraternity," I could prove that the Greek system did do more good than harm to university life as a whole. *But I can't*, I continued in a sudden reversal, and went on to provide a caustic satire of every pro-Greek point (all hinging on the "necessity of membership" argument).

After the article's publication, I nervously awaited an onslaught of angry responses. To my surprise, there were none—only praise from various professors who told me they couldn't agree more with what I'd written. I finally asked the newspaper editor what had happened to the debate, who replied that my article seemed to have ended it: There was nothing left for either side to say. I was something of a hero to non-Greeks, while clearly some kind of traitor to the Greeks—from whom the only comment I ever received was by Tyler, who simply said: "I read your article. Interesting . . ."

One day I saw a notice in the student union advertising international summer programs through the SMU International Studies office. And one of these immediately arrested my attention: It was called SMU-in-Oxford, and it offered a summer program of courses taught *in* Oxford by Oxford University faculty. Each course would earn required credit hours for my undergraduate degree, while providing a full month actually inside an Oxford college. My immediate thought was whether I could use this opportunity as a stepping stone to acceptance into Oxford University itself—a dream still very much alive since high school (and even more so as my studies in English literature progressed). But the first step was both to get accepted into *this* program, which had fewer places than applicants and required a detailed application along with references and interviews with the SMU faculty leading the trip.

My application was successful, and I would be spending the summer of '88 in Oxford, England. That spring, I spoke at length with one of my favorite professors, Dr. Kenneth Shields, who was also the International Studies advisor. Dr. Shields had studied at the University of London and was knowledgeable about British universities and the application and admissions procedures. I told him of my desire to pursue graduate studies at Oxford University. His advice was that I make the most of the Oxford summer program by, first of all, excelling in my chosen courses with actual Oxford academics, and then at the end of the course informing them of my interest in hopes of obtaining potential advice and even support. I resolved to do just that, and not to leave Oxford without having the groundwork in place for a return.

The summer went remarkably according to plan—far more so than I could ever even have imagined. It turned out that for conducting this summer program SMU had a special arrangement with the oldest college (and among the most distinguished) of the almost forty individual 'colleges' comprising the University of Oxford. This was University College (known to its members simply as "Univ"), and it was there that SMU students were able to live and study during Oxford's long summer vacation. We were even given temporary Reader's cards permitting access to the magnificent Bodleian Library.

As I settled into the pleasantly musty old college room at the corner of an elegant quadrangle, a tour bus passed by on the High Street below from which I heard the guide announce that C.S. Lewis had once studied—and taught—at University College. (It was a student of his, Tangye Lean, who started the literary group called "The Inklings"—whose senior members included Lewis and his friend J.R.R. Tolkien, then Professor of Anglo-Saxon at Oxford. They initially met in these very buildings, as well as at the nearby pub called "The Eagle & Child.") I felt a sudden deep thrill to realize I was now (unlike the young tourist passing by on that same street three years earlier), *inside* the place which, for me, represented the highest pinnacle of learning. From my window I could see the countless spires of Oxford colleges and churches reaching heavenwards in every direction. A chorus of bells seemed to chime ceaselessly, even furiously, adding a sense of rapid and blurred motion to the whole world around. *The city of dreaming spires*, they called it. And here I finally was: thrilled and enchanted at once.

On day one I was given an unexpected opportunity that was as daunting as it was exciting. This came courtesy of SMU faculty member Bonny Wheeler. Dr. Wheeler, a respected scholar of medieval literature, directed the program and led a number of excursions around Oxford and its environs. On these our guide was Bonny's husband, Dr. Jeremy Adams, a renowned historian who seemed literally to know the entire story behind every building, town, and monument we passed. In fact, he seemed to know everything about anything he was asked, on any given subject whatsoever. It wasn't surprising to learn that he was nicknamed the "know where man." But it was an exciting revelation to learn the true significance of this: When Adams had been at Princeton in the 60's, his reputation so preceded him that, through a colleague who knew George Martin, he became the real-life inspiration behind the Beatles' song "Nowhere Man" (an honor Adams himself found a mixed blessing due to the connotations of the song itself).

Upon seeing me arrive with my guitar, Bonny asked if I would give a formal recital for all the students and faculty at some point during the program. I cannot now recall if I initially agreed or (more likely) tried to defer, but I do recall seriously regretting finding myself officially on the program for a recital during the final week of classes. This meant I'd have to devote considerable free time in my room practicing. Yet this also brought a sense of exhilaration: My first full recital, something I'd been dreaming about for years now, would take place within the walls of an Oxford college. The question, however, was whether I could pull it all off.

Having a guitar had the effect of attracting the interest of fellow students in the program. One of these was a young man from Dallas named Mike, a business major with a passion for guitar. Thanks to Mike, I found a needed respite from my heavy-handed classical pieces as he taught me to play some popular acoustic guitar melodies by bands including Led Zeppelin and The Beatles. I was delighted to discover that I could apply my classical guitar technique to perform popular music as well.

Our academic program was in the meantime very demanding, with the need to complete within a month the material for two separate courses normally taught over a full semester. One course was taught by an SMU faculty member, and the other by an Oxford don. The SMU course I had chosen was entitled "World War I: The British Experience." I chose this because of my grandfather's own experience in that war, but now I learned that the British sacrifice during the so-called "Great War" was something that defied imagination—with a degree of horror and loss so great that it remains an intrinsic part of the British consciousness. The college itself bears witness to this with a War Memorial in the Chapel listing 173 names of college members who died in the war—far more than the number of young college men who perished in any other British conflict. Readings for the course, taught by legendary SMU professor Peggy "Twinkie" Lawhon, included A.J.P. Taylor's book on the war along with an anthology of British World War I poetry called *Men Who March Away*, my first exposure to the work of such poets as Wilfred Owen, Siegfried Sassoon and Rupert Brooke. The course also included a trip to France to tour the World War I cemeteries and battlefields (some with remnants of the old trenches still visible), which illustrated first-hand the vastness of death, destruction and sacrifice experienced by the British, French and Germans alike. We visited as well the monuments dedicated to all the many other foreign nationals who died on French soil, including Australians, Irish, and Canadians as well as Americans. (One of my grandfather's proudest moments was receiving—almost at the end of his life—a medal from the French Government commemorating his World War I service as a "foreign hero" who fought in France on behalf of liberty.)

Along with the intensity of this particular course, both in terms of work and intellectual demand, was my "Oxford" course. This was a survey of various plays by Shakespeare, taught by an eminent scholar of medieval and Renaissance literature named Helen Cooper. Dr. Cooper was a member of the Oxford University Faculty of English, and she was based at University College as a "Tutor of English" (where in addition to her academic work, she was important historically as being the first woman ever elected to a fellowship in the college's almost 750 year history).

So I applied myself to Shakespeare as fully as possible while balancing my studies of the Great War and rehearsing—with ever-increasing anxiety—for my approaching guitar recital. But the tutorials with Dr. Cooper went well, and she seemed to appreciate my first halting efforts to formulate original insights into the Bard's phenomenal artistry. Midway through the program, we took a trip to Stratford for a play, before which I had the opportunity of an enjoyable walk alone with Dr. Cooper to explore the town. She took me down to the pleasant green sward along the Avon, upon which floated the largest white swans I'd ever seen. We discussed current issues in the field of Shakespearean scholarship, and I finally took this opportunity to mention my interest in applying to Oxford for graduate studies. She said she would be happy to advise me concerning potential postgraduate courses and the application process. As we walked back towards the theater, I felt the same deep feeling of magic I'd sensed upon first entering Oxford and entering University College: the sense of experiencing something *real*—a sword of insight piercing more deeply than anything I'd experienced back home. This was an experience I wanted never to end.

On the way back to Oxford that evening I sat on the coach with the Chaplain of University College, Bill Sykes, who—despite the Dickensian connotations of his name—remains one of the friendliest gentlemen I've ever known. Bill had announced at the start of the program that he was interested in organizing something he called "Reflection Groups" and invited students to see him about this. Curious, I made an appointment to see him, and—being the only student who had done so—experienced something over the coming weeks that would make a profound contribution to my life. Bill explained that this was something he offered all University College students during term time. At the start of a "Reflection" session, he would offer a choice of tea, coffee, hot chocolate or Orange Crush. He would then distribute to each person in the group copies of one of his books containing hundreds of quotations—drawn from a surprisingly eclectic variety of sources, secular as well as religious—categorized under a series of topics representing almost every aspect of human experience imaginable. The students would be asked to pore over the topics until someone suggested one for that particular session. Then everyone would be given 25 minutes to read through the quotations in silence, while taking notes and munching biscuits from Bill's cookie jar. Afterwards Bill would call first upon the student who had chosen the topic and ask why he or she had chosen that particular subject. This would usually lead to a lively and wide-ranging discussion, using individual quotes as a focal point.

In my case that summer, since I was the only student participating, these weekly sessions took the form more of an Oxford "tutorial" session, being a one hour Socratic dialogue of give and take between

student and tutor. I would invariably leave each session feeling remarkably uplifted, often even enlightened, with my mind full of the many
quotes I'd just studied combined with the insights of wisdom and experience provided by Bill himself. I was truly lost in *reflection*, and that
was the point.

Another college figure I befriended over the course of the summer
was Richard, one of the assistant porters who worked at the Lodge in
the college entrance. Richard had a droll wit beneath the surface of his
ever-cheerful round face, and he took pride and pleasure in showing
off his model train sets. He was also a bassist in a local band, a topic
which led to an especial personal connection. I often found myself loll-
ing in the Lodge and chatting with him during free time. I confided in
Richard my hopes of returning to Oxford, and he gave me warm and
much-appreciated encouragement. I also made the odd acquaintance
of the proprietor of a fast-food van which arrived invariably early each
evening to park at the same spot. There "Ahmed's Kebobs" could be
found into the furthest reaches of the night—and into the early morning hours—serving up cheap and greasy kebabs and chips that tasted
like *ambrosia* following a few beers but would usually be regretted the
morning after. Whenever I walked up to the van, Ahmed would greet
me warmly: "Hello my friend! A mixed kebab for you, yeah?"

In the last week of the program, with my guitar recital almost upon
me, Bill had a suggestion for making the event something particularly
special. He would arrange for me to give the recital in the college Chapel, a marvelous Baroque structure especially famous for its stained
glass windows by Abraham van Linge, dating from 1641, with their
magnificent depictions of biblical scenes. When the day of my recital
finally arrived, Dr. Cooper allowed me the use of her room up above
the chapel so I could warm up before entering the chapel after everyone had been seated. From her window I could see all the students and
faculty entering the Chapel in the main quad below, where they could
enter from the adjoining Hall after dinner. Bonny Wheeler had made
attendance of my recital mandatory too, so they were *all* there, willing
or no. I had my work cut out for me indeed. But my greatest fear concerned my hands: Would they remain steady, or would the old nervous
shaking return the moment my first notes began to resound loudly
through the acoustically phenomenal Baroque chapel? It would mean
disaster if so. And what if I lost my place in the middle of a piece? I had
committed all the music to memory and would be performing without
a single page of sheet music—for a full half hour program including works by Heitor Villa-Lobos, Federico Moreno-Torroba, Manuel
Ponce and J.S. Bach. On top of everything, I learned that an Oxford

literary celebrity would be in the audience: novelist John Wain, who had been the guest speaker before dinner that evening and who had accepted Bonny's invitation to attend my recital. I was familiar with Wain as being one of the so-called "Angry Young Men"—the British counterpart of the American "Beat Generation"—some of whose work was included in my mother's book *The Beat Generation and The Angry Young Men* I'd recently had signed by Allen Ginsberg.

When I walked into the Chapel and down the aisle with my guitar, I was pleasantly surprised to find that Bill had lit all the candles lining the pews and illuminating the space before the altar, where a chair was set up for my performance. When I sat down to begin playing, my right hand did begin to shake—yet fortunately I'd begun the program with some fairly simple Renaissance pieces, and soon managed to tune out all the eyes upon me and focus on making music in the way Carlo had taught to do so well. As the flickering candlelight gleamed upon my guitar while I played, I knew the warmth of sound echoing through that noble chamber was truly something of my own creation.

Following the recital, Bonny held a party and I was overwhelmed with the genuinely sincere comments I received about my music and its effect. Most welcome of all though—in addition to praise from Bonny and Jeremy "Nowhere Man" Adams—was that of John Wain himself. Later, Mike—as a business major not usually one to wax poetic—especially moved me with his description of my recital (and that of Wain's response in particular). Mike described looking across the aisle from his pew and observing Wain's expression the moment the setting sun's rays filtered through the stained glass windows and illumined his face. I was in the middle of performing one of the mystical sounding pieces by Manuel Ponce, composed using the ancient Mayan scale, and Mike said Wain seemed at that moment profoundly moved, as if lost within another world. That image alone made all my hard work in preparation for my first formal recital more than worth the effort. I had now, I realized, fulfilled a long-standing dream in grand style. Now it was time to work on the next.

Just before the program's culmination, Dr. Cooper said that applicants to Oxford are expected to interview formally with a faculty member from their subject of interest. She kindly arranged for me to interview with Dr. Dennis Kay of Lincoln College, Oxford. Dr. Kay, an alumnus of University College himself, specialized in Renaissance studies. Just before my interview, Helen gave me a sealed envelope, explaining that it was customary for students interviewing for postgraduate courses to take along a letter of reference from their tutor. I felt nervous and overwhelmed as I walked over ancient cobblestones past the old Bodleian Library and its distinctive Radcliffe Camera for the interview. The moment I entered Lincoln College, the redolence of wisteria covering its walls took me back to the gardens of my youth. Dr. Kay proved, to my great relief, friendly and affable and the interview consisted of a lively discussion about the various postgraduate courses available through the Oxford English Faculty. He also wondered whether I was any good with computers—the "new thing" in academic research, he said. (I wasn't.) But after the interview was over, I left Dr. Kay feeling both encouraged and inspired.

After the Oxford program ended in early August, I visited St. Emillion in the south of France—the place where Daddy Frank had been based during the war in 1918 and about which he constantly reminisced. I was 21 years old, the exact age he'd been when he was there. When I called him from there and told him where I was, he was of course delighted. (All the more so when I reported the place hadn't appeared to change much since his time there, and the wine was as excellent as he'd remembered.)

When I got back to Dallas and looked carefully at the Oxford application materials, I balked. The amount of scholarly research and general academic achievement they required with the application seemed beyond anything I could ever hope to produce in time for the submission deadline. At first I despaired, but finally I decided the best thing might be to hold off applying for another year and spend the coming year preparing specifically for the Oxford application. I figured the interview would remain valid at least that long, and I also hoped that I'd made a good enough impression on Helen Cooper—having aced the final exam as well as the overall course on Shakespeare—to warrant an actual reference. But I'd still need several more references from the SMU end as well.

I still had one more year to complete, and I'd have to figure out what to do after graduation. I also couldn't be sure how my parents would react to the idea of graduate school (especially abroad). I spent the rest of that year focused on my studies, writing and music, socializing on weekends with friends. Mostly we'd gather on Saturdays to watch the latest episode of *Star Trek: The Next Generation*. Later, after its 1989 premiere, we watched the new animated series called *The Simpsons*. Along with its satirical depiction of the dysfunctional American family (something I knew about all too well), it was also refreshingly controversial.

Occasionally friends would come down from Little Rock to visit, including my UALR Spanish friends Juan Antonio and Martin, as well as old high school friends like Dan, Robert, and—on one occasion—Joe and Ken, who came to attend a concert by The Grateful Dead. This proved memorable as much for the carnival atmosphere surrounding the event as for the music of Jerry Garcia and the band itself. My friends were highly amused to find me during the concert out in the hall in the midst of a group of people, where—appropriately donned in my new tie-dye tee shirt—I ecstatically banged the bongos as tripping hippies swayed and danced. Later that year we also attended a memorable concert by the British band The Cure.

That year I met a lovely young lady named Michelle. She was a local girl from nearby Mesquite, Texas, and in what proved an unexpected 'cultural' discovery close to home, Michelle took me out to a Country & Western club called "Cowboys" and taught me to dance the Texas Two-Step to the tune of "The Yellow Rose of Texas." (I felt rather out of place as the only guy unadorned in cowboy hat and boots.) Later I would remember her rare combination of beauty, grace and intelligence with remorse, wishing I'd made more of an effort to know her.

Another interesting experience came in the form of a feature movie being shot on campus. The film director Oliver Stone had chosen the SMU campus as a location (as a stand-in for Syracuse) for his

Oliver Stone, Tom Cruise, and Kyra Sedgwick, on the set of
Born on the Fourth of July *(SMU May 1988)*

eventual Oscar-winning film *Born on the Fourth of July*, and students were invited to participate as extras. The film, a biopic set during the turbulent era of Vietnam, starred Tom Cruise and Kyra Sedgwick and naturally generated much excitement among students. I enjoyed the experience of being dressed in period costume and taking part in the action, although quickly also learned the monotonous boredom that can set in during multiple takes of the same shot. I did enjoy, however, seeing Oliver Stone in action and meeting the actors, including Tom Cruise: At the end of the shoot, I saw him standing alone near the set and so I walked up and introduced myself. I was surprised to find that the young man was significantly shorter.

"Nice working with you," I said. Cruise smiled warmly and shook hands.

"Nice working with you too, man," he answered.

When the film finally came out, I went to see it in Little Rock with Joe and felt the thrill of seeing myself on the big screen—even if it was just the back of my head as I climbed a flight of stairs with a crowd of other students.

With the arrival of spring '89, my attention became focused on graduation and future plans. My parents, Kate, and Will all came down for the occasion and to celebrate, and the commencement ceremony featured the iconic PBS newscaster Jim Lehrer as speaker.

With Mom and Dad after the SMU Commencement, May 1989

8

FROM RUSSIA WITH LOVE

I saw that, if you love, you must base your theory of love on something loftier and more significant than happiness or unhappiness, than sin or virtue as they are commonly understood. Better, otherwise, not to theorize at all.

—Anton Chekov, from "Concerning Love"

S MU had a continuing education graduate program leading to a Master of Liberal Arts degree, and as I looked through the program, I was excited to see that many of my favorite professors taught classes, developed from their own research interests, as part of the courses. Students were also able, with instructor approval, to choose from a variety of upper level university courses for credit towards the degree. I saw that one of the available courses was an extensive survey of Shakespeare's plays, and I began to conceive of a plan.

I managed to persuade my parents to support my idea of enrolling in the MLA program, with the assurance that I'd otherwise get to work on finding a proper job. But I of course had no intention of doing so. My goal was to stay focused on learning and creative expression as long as I could before having to join the rat race. That was always there, and many of my friends were now already distracted with the type of work that sucks you into time's vortex so completely and imperceptibly that you wake up one day twenty years later dizzy with regret at the time lost—the now impossible to realize dreams once so dearly treasured. I'd have none of it. I had even written a short story for Marsh Terry my senior year called "Sold Out," in which I imagined myself in middle age having given up all my dreams—only to realize I was living the mediocre, inauthentic life of every other disillusioned middle-class American lost within T.S. Eliot's spiritual wasteland. Simply the act of writing the story itself felt like a sacred contract I'd made with my soul never to betray it by getting pulled into an ordinary life—a life wasted within an ethos of mind-numbing consumerism and self-profit. But I'd quickly learn the need to tread carefully: The path of non-conformity can be fraught with lurking peril.

This became apparent especially with regard to my correspondence with a citizen of the then Soviet Union. I'd met Katya when I saw a notice in the student newspaper that a delegation of Soviet students from Moscow University would be visiting the campus to meet with students. Not one to miss such an opportunity, I turned up at the student union conference room curious to see what people from Reagan's "Evil Empire" were really like. And the first person I saw was a young woman who looked amazingly like the young Barbara Bach's Russian spy in *The Spy Who Loved Me*. This was certainly a girl who'd turn James Bond's head in a heartbeat, and I joined the group of students gathered around her to hear her descriptions of life in Moscow. During a quiet moment when she stood alone, I summoned up my nerve and introduced myself. "I'd like to speak with you," I said, and she said—almost as if I were a familiar acquaintance—she felt like sitting down after standing so long and led me to a quiet corner where we sat and talked for quite some time. I can't recall a word we said, being so taken with her beauty and, at the same time, almost otherworldly charm. But though she appeared around my own age, perhaps even younger, I perceived a level of depth and experience within her such as I'd seldom encountered in conversation with anyone before. I suggested we exchange addresses and correspond, to which she happily consented. I left the event with a thrilling sense of intrigue, almost guilt even—as if I were conspiring somehow with my sworn enemy.

Later that fall I visited Joey in Fort Worth to attend a TCU football game, along with drinks afterwards at the rather wild TCU Pub near the stadium. Joey asked about my Oxford plans, which took me by surprise as I hadn't recalled telling him of my desire to return there. He encouraged me to follow through with my plan to apply, and his words could not have been timelier, as I was just reconsidering once more whether to bother applying at all. But I did send off for the current application packet and Graduate Studies Prospectus 1990, and when the application finally arrived I realized this time I might actually have a shot.

I had an "A" essay on Chaucer I'd written for Dr. Shields' class, and he agreed to provide a reference letter. But I needed one more substantial piece of writing, and for that I was in the right place: Dr. Robert Hunter's Shakespeare course, in which I was doing well. So I waited for the next essay assignment, and then poured all my scholarly ability into writing the absolute best essay I could. Dr. Hunter had the reputation of being among the most challenging professors on the English faculty—and though I didn't know it at the time, his work and publications in the field of Shakespeare scholarship were known and highly respected internationally, including at Oxford. The essay that came back had received an A, along with extensive—and highly positive—comments. With this accomplishment, I successfully procured an agreement from Dr. Hunter to write a reference letter as well.

My last task was to write an essay detailing why I thought the Oxford teaching system was the right fit for me, and I was able to describe my first-hand experience with the intimate Oxford tutorial system as indicative of how the Socratic method suited my learning style perfectly. I also mentioned, as in the essay I'd written back in high school in application for the UALR scholarship, the ways I thought I could contribute to student life within an Oxford college through my music and other cultural interests.

Finally, in addition to indicating that I had already interviewed with Dr. Kay of Lincoln College, I was asked to list—in order of preference—my top four choices with regard to which of the many possible colleges I wished to attend. (Acceptance into Oxford involved getting admitted effectively twice: first by the relevant faculty, in my case English, and then by an individual college. It was possible to be accepted by the faculty and yet still not admitted into a college.) Dr. Shields advised that getting into one of the older colleges, particularly one such as University College, was almost impossible due to the disproportionately high number of applicants for very few places; he therefore suggested I might apply to one of the newer (and strictly postgraduate) colleges. Nevertheless, the place I knew and loved was University College, and so I placed it at the very top of the list despite the heavy odds.

Finally, the application was ready to go, and I kissed it goodbye at the post office as it headed off by airmail to England. I resolved not to jinx it by telling anybody about it and didn't tell a soul, including my family, that I'd even applied.

I spent most of the rest of that year immersed once again in my studies, reveling in the opportunity to take such a variety of courses at once.

The beauty of the Liberal Arts program was that I could combine science and humanities courses, and throughout the year I took courses in Astronomy and Biology concurrently with courses in Economics and Existentialism. Two of my favorites included a class taught by Marsh Terry entitled "The Myth of the West," in which he taught the themes he'd already explored so deeply in his fiction; and a course on the Spanish Civil War featuring a close study of Orwell's *Homage to Catalonia*. The latter was taught by history professor Dr. Luis Martin from Spain. He'd been recently knighted by King Juan Carlos—dubbing him *Don Luis Martin*. He also taught an invitation-only seminar on philosophy and ethics in which I was deeply honored to be invited to participate. It was in this course that I first came across the idea of the *two cultures* as analyzed by the Cambridge scientist and novelist C.P. Snow. Snow pointed out the danger inherent in isolating the arts and the sciences into disparate camps within universities and society in general. He argued that it is only by combining knowledge of both the humanities and the sciences, within the context of a broad interdisciplinary education, that people—including scientists, artists, and policy makers—can make truly informed decisions on all aspects of life. This, I realized, was why the interdisciplinary program in which I was participating was such a crucial opportunity.

Meanwhile, I needed a backup plan in the likely event my Oxford application fell through. I'd met the classical guitarist Benjamin Verdery, whom I knew ran the guitar program at the School of Music at Yale University, in Little Rock (and later at the guitar festival in Spain). I had already even broached the possibility of studying with him at Yale. So I called Benjamin and said I was thinking of applying to Yale specifically for graduate work in music and guitar performance, to which he replied, "Let's plan on it!" There it was then: If I got into Oxford, I would pursue my dream of studying English literature in England; if not, I'd go to Yale and focus on a career in music. Regardless, it seemed like a "win win" situation. It was now up to fate.

While I waited to let Oxford decide my future, I took my guitar studies with Carlo to a new level, both in terms of the music I was studying and the instrument upon which I played it. One day, Carlo called to say he had located the guitar of my dreams. When I arrived, he handed me one of the most beautiful instruments I'd ever seen: a José Ramirez guitar! The guitar had been handmade (and personally signed) at the Ramirez shop in Madrid. The body was constructed of Brazilian rosewood and Nicaraguan cedar, with a neck made of ebony and the fret nuts of ivory. The hand-crafted rosette was of an elegant

Arabesque pattern, and the mother of pearl tuning pegs sparkled iridescently in sunlight. Most importantly of all, of course, was the *sound*: The basses resonated through the wood, while the trebles sang with the sweetness of spring birdsong. With Dad's help I was able to buy the guitar, which in turn motivated me to study ever more challenging music—doing justice to the capabilities of the instrument itself. And I could wish for no greater challenge than the music of J.S. Bach.

I had first discovered Bach's music in my last year of high school, when my orchestral studies led me first to Vivaldi—whose *Le Quattro Stagioni* ("The Four Seasons") first ignited a passion for classical music, cemented with a recording I'd found of Vivaldi's concertos for lute and mandolin (which led to a lifelong love of early music—and instruments). This led me by chance to the purchase of a recording by John Williams on guitar of Bach's complete Lute Suites. But the power of Bach's music so transcended the performance medium itself that I was drawn to acquire more recordings of his music, most immediately a performance of various harpsichord concertos by Trevor Pinnock and The English Concert. At the same time, Kate was taking piano lessons and performing daily on the downstairs piano those charming pieces Bach wrote for his wife, Anna Magdalena. (I even wrote my senior research paper on Bach, entitled "Bach: The Man and His Music"— on which Mrs. Strange gave me an A+.) There was something about Bach's music that overwhelmed me, often even moving me to tears: the way layers of texture seemed to ebb and flow like waves crashing on some cosmic shoreline, melodies interwoven in modulations between major and minor—bright and dark—intonations of rhythmic harmony speaking a wisdom confined to the ineffable spirit of music.

Throughout my guitar studies thus far, I'd been working towards the day when I would be ready to undertake a substantial work by Bach. I had already learned the famous "Bourée" from the first (E minor) suite. Now Carlo gave me the music to Bach's first Cello Suite as transcribed for the guitar, to which I was soon giving my all—beginning with the mellifluous joy of its opening "Prelude."

By the spring of 1990, I had been corresponding for over a year with Katya in Moscow. And by an amazing coincidence, I found out the previous summer that the enchanting moment I'd first met her was forever captured in pictures: Mike called up just after the SMU yearbook, *Rotunda 1989*, came out and said—"Hey dude, so who's the Russian babe you're with on page 170 of the yearbook?" I eagerly flipped through the pages and found it, along with yet another photo on the facing page. Something seemed almost meant to be.

Katya wrote in perfect English, and her letters revealed her wide reading and love of literature, as well as a desire to read more of the American authors whose work was forbidden in Russia—although thanks to the policy of *glasnost* ("openness") under Mikhail Gorbachev, more Western goods (including books) were becoming available. But she sent an English translation of a book of stories by one of her favorite Russian writers, Ivan Bunin, with whose work I'd been previously unfamiliar. Another interesting aspect to receiving letters from the Soviet Union was the obvious fact that each had been carefully opened and resealed before reaching my mailbox. I wondered if this happened on her end or mine, or both. And I assumed that each letter I sent underwent the same fate, adding a sense of that same thrill I'd experienced when first meeting Katya, along with the temptation to play linguistic games in my writing for the benefit of these ghost readers.

Early that year, Katya wrote to say that she had won a prized posting to Paris, as an intern at UNESCO (the United Nations Educational, Scientific, and Cultural Organization). She would be there for a number of months, and she suggested I come to Paris to meet her. The thought was intriguing, but I'd almost forgotten about the idea until receiving a letter from Katya, this time from Paris, including her phone number there. When I called, she literally screamed with joy the moment she answered and heard my voice. We'd hardly begun a conversation when she cut right to the chase.

"So when are you coming to Paris?" she asked.

"Well, I don't know, I . . ."

"Oh, but you *must* come!" she insisted.

Katya had no time for vacillation, and before the conversation ended I'd found myself agreeing to come visit her during my upcoming spring break. But the moment I hung up the phone, I realized I could neither afford the ticket nor ask my parents for any more help. I was, after all, supposed to be getting serious about looking for a job. Then I saw my old string bass in the corner. I'd finally had to abandon my studies on that difficult instrument as I became more and more devoted to the classical guitar and realized it was one or the other—especially given the rather incompatible hand technique needed to perfect each instrument. I couldn't keep trying to practice mastery of both at once. So I managed to sell the bass for $800, and with this I bought a ticket to Paris.

Spring in Paris 1990 remains one of my most romantic memories. If I tried to describe that week in detail, I would inevitably have to summon up almost every cliché from each sentimental romance novel ever set in Paris—even down to our first kiss during a sunset walk along the Left Bank quay by the Seine. Then a candlelight dinner together at the famous café *La Closerie des Lilas,* mentioned by Hemingway in *A Moveable Feast* and where the fresh Atlantic oysters had the distinctive "metallic" taste just as he'd described. Katya lived in a fashionable area of Paris, near the Rue du Commerce and not far from the UNESCO headquarters. She took me with her there one day, where I attended a conference and experienced what it was actually like at an official United Nations event, including sitting at a place in one of those long rows of tiered desks I'd seen so often on television, while wearing headphones providing an English translation of the proceedings.

On another occasion, we visited Versailles and took a rowboat out upon the grand scenic lake behind the palace. Then Katya took me to a huge wine tasting expo to which she'd been invited, where neither of us knew the etiquette of spitting out the wine sampled at each table. (We saw others doing it and simply thought it a waste of good wine.) By the time we got back to her flat, we could both barely walk. The memory of that afternoon remains among the most erotic in all my experience.

As we sat in back of the taxi on the way to the airport on my last day, Katya took my hand and gave me a teary-eyed look that almost made me stop the taxi and throw out my return ticket. At the airport gate we kissed until the airline staff nearly had to haul me on board, and Katya continued to blow kisses towards me until I finally rounded the boarding platform and her image vanished. The whole flight back, listening repeatedly to the tape she'd given me of Rachmaninoff's 2nd and 3rd piano concertos, I was in a daze. Looking out the window at the sparkling blue ocean far below, all I could think of was the final expression in Katya's eyes.

Katya had to return to Moscow that summer, and we began making plans for my visit there at the earliest possible date. But as our correspondence became more heated, the "spooks" began to emerge from their lurking place in the shadows. My first direct experience with them happened when I tried to call Katya in Moscow. When I couldn't get the direct call to go through, I called the operator to ask for assistance.

"Where are you trying to call again?"

"Moscow."

"Oh," said the operator, "you'll need the special operator for that." She sounded nervous as she put me through to someone else. This new "operator" had a speaking style that reminded me of a character from *Rocky and Bullwinkle.* His voice was one of the most unpleasant

I've ever heard: sly, suspicious and patronizing all at once. When the phone on the other end finally rang and someone answered in Russian, I wasn't sure how to respond. Then came the voice again—"Aren't you going to say hello?" And I could hear laughter in the background.

On another occasion, I came home from classes to find two people inside my apartment. One was the landlady, who apologized profusely for coming in without notice to show my apartment—especially considering I wasn't even moving.

"I know it's our policy never to show an apartment without giving written notice first, but since you weren't here I thought it might be okay just this once." She seemed uncomfortable as she introduced me to a tall gentleman in a dark business suit. And instead of leaving, he proceeded to look around my apartment, even entering my bedroom, asking random personal questions all the while. When he finally left, I had an unsettled feeling, as if my private space had just been seriously violated.

I soon found that it wasn't only the FBI who took exception to my passionate preferences. During a trip to Crossett to visit my grandparents over Easter, I told my mother about Katya. She gave me the cold look (cultivated through years of teaching school children) that always froze my blood. I was taken aback by her response:

"If you marry a Russian girl, we'll disinherit you!"

"Who said anything about marriage?"

"Just keep it in mind," she said. "You can't trust the Russians!"

This wasn't the only time my mother had said such things, and it wasn't the last. But my Moscow plans were soon put on hold for another reason. I opened my mailbox one day to find an airmail letter with a stamp bearing the image of Queen Elizabeth II. I eagerly opened it, and found it was from the University of Oxford admissions office. Expecting the worst, I held my breath—then had to pinch myself to ensure I wasn't dreaming: It was an acceptance letter! My application had been officially approved by the Oxford English Faculty. I immediately rushed to campus to share the news with Dr. Shields, who after ebullient congratulations reminded me I was only halfway there. I still needed to be accepted by a college.

It wasn't long, however, before another airmail letter arrived, also brought courtesy of the Queen and this time with a large red stamp on the front which read: "University College, Oxford." I ripped it open and, sure enough, the news was beyond my wildest dreams. I had been admitted to University College to read for a Master of Philosophy degree in English at Oxford University.

9

CITY OF DREAMING SPIRES

And that sweet city with her dreaming spires.

—Matthew Arnold

Now it all came down to my parents. I could only hope that admittance into Oxford might be the one place that would inspire them to let me continue my studies. And I was right: They were delighted, and Dad said he'd be happy to help me with expenses. (It helped that the tuition was actually less than SMU's.) I now had to choose whether to abandon my current MLA degree, or alternatively stay the summer in Dallas taking a full load of summer courses worth enough credit to finish what I'd started. I opted for the latter. Time flew by until the end of August, when after one year of hard work, I managed to complete what was otherwise meant to be a two year course. I had a Master of Liberal Arts, and a month to prepare for the start of my Master's in English Literature course at Oxford. I also had to figure out how to make things work with Katya, my feelings for whom only seemed to deepen by the day.

When I at last walked into the University College entrance, now finally as an officially enrolled student, I stood a few moments in awe admiring the 17th century Gothic fan vaulting of the ceiling, at the heart of which gleamed the college's ancient coat of arms: a cross set between a group of martlets on an azure background (originally associated with the college's mythic founder, King Alfred the Great). Then I stepped up into the Porter's Lodge on the right and was pleasantly surprised to be greeted by a familiar face.

"So you made it back to Oxford, did you?"

Richard the porter flashed his winsome smile I'd so often fondly recalled. "Welcome back to Univ!" I suddenly felt as if I'd returned home after a long journey. This feeling was compounded upon seeing Dr. Helen Cooper, who immediately invited me for tea—which turned out to be a glass of sherry in celebration of my return—and a discussion of my upcoming course. Then I made a point to look up the Chaplain, Bill Sykes, and we agreed that with the start of term it would be good to resume the "reflection group," though perhaps this time with an actual group. He said once term got going, he encouraged the formation of separate groups consisting of students with compatible interests. Once I made some new friends, he advised, I could encourage them to participate in a group with me.

Later, as I stood at the Lodge admiring the main quadrangle, with its two swards of emerald grass divided by a walkway—and lined by two perfect rows of colorful flowers on its way to the Chapel and Hall—a gentleman in a tweed jacket and bowtie approached me. He seemed to know me, although I was certain we'd never met. He scrutinized my face a moment, and then:

"You must be Mr . . . . Thurmond. Frank, isn't it?"

This turned out to be the Dean of Graduates, Dr. Leslie Mitchell. Now I knew why I'd been asked to send a photograph in advance. Dr. Mitchell had actually memorized the names and faces of every new postgraduate student in advance of term so that he could personally welcome them by name.

Before that magical first day ended, I was in for a further surprise. Soon after I stepped out of college to walk up towards the City Centre at Cornmarket, from behind I heard a vaguely familiar voice shout: "Hello, my friend!" I looked back to see Ahmed waving from his kebab van. "It's very good to see you again!" he continued. I was amazed—over two years had passed (and countless new faces had no doubt visited his van in the meantime)—yet he instantly remembered me from summer '88 as if he'd known me for years. (He even remembered that I liked garlic chili sauce on my kebab.)

Shortly afterwards, new students gathered in the Master's Lodgings for the centuries old tradition of signing the college admissions register. Upon entering the imposing old house tucked away in the back of College, I was warmly greeted by the Master himself, Professor John Albery, who directed me to the line of students waiting to sign the book. I nodded nervously and started to move towards the queue. Then the Master added:

"But first do have a glass of the Master's punch, on the table there."

He pointed to a large pitcher and glasses on a table by a window looking out into the Master's Garden—a beautiful private lawn behind the Chapel, with scores of roses and tulips still in bloom in early October. Then he seemed to sway momentarily up and down on the balls of his feet, and I wasn't sure if he was speaking to me or to himself as he continued—"One mustn't miss the Master's special punch!" I noticed he himself had a glass of it in hand. So I stepped over to the table, poured a glass of punch, and with the first sip nearly fell backward from the strength of it. Special punch indeed!

When I finally reached the book of admissions, on display next to it was an ancient-looking leather bound volume open to the page where poet Percy Byshhe Shelley had signed his own name in 1810. Along with their autograph, students were expected to write out a detailed declaration involving their parentage and place of origin. But whereas Shelley and his contemporaries had been expected to do this in fluent Latin, we could fortunately write in modern English.

Once I'd completed this exercise, I turned to see the Master making his rounds among the guests with the pitcher, refilling glasses while chatting with individual students. From the moment I met him, I was immediately struck by the Master's natural exuberance. Tall and stout, albeit with a healthy paunch and a distinguished mop of white hair, he possessed the air of the senior professor he was—being an esteemed research chemist and Oxford teaching Fellow, as well as a Fellow of the Royal Society. But he wore other hats as well, including having once written for the 60s satirical television show called *That Was The Week That Was*. He had an acerbic wit coupled with a sly sense of ironic humor. And he was very shrewd, always looking for ways to bring recognition to the college over which he now presided. Finally he noticed my half-empty glass and came striding across the room to refill it.

"Frank, isn't it? From the States I presume. And from which State may I ask?"

"Arkansas," I answered. The Master looked momentarily perplexed, and then I added (almost as an afterthought): "I believe the Governor of my state once attended Oxford."

"He did indeed," replied the Master. "And he attended *this* college!"

I was taken by surprise. My mother had sent an *Arkansas Gazette* article to me before my trip which mentioned that Governor Clinton had once been a Rhodes Scholar at Oxford. But the chance of my attending as a fellow Arkansan the same college out of so many was remarkable. The Master seemed equally excited.

"Elizabeth!" he called, and when a charming lady appeared she was introduced as the Master's Secretary.

"Go find the Admission's Registry from 1969," the Master instructed her, and within minutes she appeared with the requested volume. The Master flipped through the pages and stopped excitedly.

"Look here," he pointed. And there was the declaration and signature of a young Bill Clinton from when he'd attended this same event in this same house. I then couldn't resist adding another thought about the matter.

"A lot of people back home think Governor Clinton might run for President of the United States—and that he'd have a good chance of winning."

I saw the Master's eyes light up.

"But first," I continued, "he has to get reelected this November as Governor of Arkansas."

The Master then conceived of a plan. He asked if I'd be going home over the Christmas vacation; when I said yes, he said to keep him posted about the election, and if Clinton were reelected he'd like to send a message from the college for me to deliver personally to the Governor when I went back to Little Rock. Intrigued, I happily agreed.

Following this success with the Master, I subsequently tried the same line about the Governor of Arkansas' presidential prospects in conversations with other new friends. I quickly found that no one else would take me seriously, and that my assertion even became something of a running joke. I would sometimes even be introduced with the following preamble: "This is Frank from Arkansas, home of the future United States President, the Governor of Arkansas!" I learned just to laugh along with everyone, although inside it was hurtful.

To my surprise, in fact, the fellow students I least connected with were my fellow Americans. In the graduate common room, a social gathering place for postgraduate students of the college, there were students from a variety of countries around the world. I'd simply assumed that my starting place socially would be with my compatriots; but these, most of whom were East Coast Ivy Leaguers clearly in Oxford just to bolster their resume, I found incredibly snooty and arrogant. They kept to themselves in their own cliques, and I was immediately made to feel quite unwelcome. The moment I said I was from Arkansas, they would make some patronizing or snide remark, often in the form of: "Oh, sorry for *you*." At first, I'd respond with, "So you've been to Arkansas?" The answer was invariably "no," and I'd suggest they might at least visit before insulting the place I called home—especially upon their very first meeting with me. But later I just realized that anybody who could behave in this way towards anyone, no matter who they were or where they were from, was not worth the time of day. So I focused on meeting the locals instead.

In retrospect, the Americans' treatment did me a favor. Since the majority of them made little attempt to cultivate relationships with the actual British students, my own efforts to do so seemed much appreciated. I found that while the British students did seem extra standoffish when it came to Americans—for reasons that had by now become very understandable to me, since I was now avoiding the "Yanks" as well—once they did accept someone as a friend it was truly genuine. Whereas many Americans had the tendency to seem unnaturally warm and friendly, as if a new acquaintance were suddenly the best of friends (only to give you a cold shoulder upon the very next encounter), with the Brits it was usually the opposite: They might seem to detest you the moment they first looked at you, but if you made a real effort to get to know them and came across as genuine, the friendship that might eventually develop would be of the highest caliber. However, one young British student felt I needed an apologist: Whenever he would introduce me to one of his friends, he'd say—"This is Frank. He's an American, but he's okay."

Most of the British students I met were undergraduates at the college; but although they were several years younger, their level of education and intellectual ability often made them seem much older. Sometimes the aristocratic backgrounds of certain students approached the Waughian stereotype of the conceited public schoolboy persona. This was especially apparent in the bar of the Oxford Union debating society, where 18 year old boys, wearing dinner jackets and smoking pipes while sipping vintage port, would address one another (and even me) as "my dear fellow" and "old boy"—as if we were all young Victorian squires.

Through the graduate common room, however, I became part of a highly diverse international group, including students from Germany, Japan, Greece, Ireland, Iceland, and Indonesia. This provided for a lively and invigorating social life outside the rigors of my new course, entitled: "Shakespeare and the Drama to 1640." I had chosen this specific course—out of a wide variety of options from Anglo-Saxon and Middle English through contemporary literary theory—due to my positive experience with Shakespeare studies, initially in Oxford itself and later with Dr. Hunter at SMU (whose reference, it now became clear, had been a seminal part of my being admitted at all thanks to his high standing in the international scholarly community). But perhaps also, despite the enormous challenges involved with getting a grip on Renaissance literary scholarship, reading drama was infinitely more accessible to me than the dense prose of novels given the slow pace at which I read. With a play, I could take time to consider and savor each individual line—which one should of course do with Shakespeare anyway. Then I would still have time to spare to research and read literary criticism.

The Master of Philosophy course (M.Phil.) was helpfully structured so that I had a combination of lectures, seminars, and individual tutorials with some of the top scholars in the field. As a postgraduate, I was free to attend any lecture given within the English faculty. Lectures were otherwise not required and all students—including undergraduates—were expected to take the lead with regard to their studies; there are in Oxford, after all, generally no "grades" in the American sense, and success or failure often depends on the final exam. In the case of my own course, this would be simply "Pass" or "Fail," and it was certainly disheartening to learn of previous students in my course who had studied diligently for two years or more only to fail the exam—and thus the entire course—at the end.

My tutors in that first year included the eminent scholar-duo of Professor Emrys Jones and his wife, Dr. Barbara Everett, both of whom were featured that year in Al Pacino's Shakespeare documentary *Looking For Richard*. I would meet with Professor Jones—whose own Oxford tutor had been C.S. Lewis himself—in his rooms in New College ("new" in 1349, at least), to read out my weekly assigned tutorial essay and discuss it (over a glass of sherry if the clock chimed noon). I also attended, along with a small group of other students in my course, a seminar with Dr. Everett at their house near Somerville College. (Somerville was then still an all-women's college, where Dr. Everett was a Fellow.) Occasionally the tutors would recommend various lectures currently on offer as a supplement to the texts we were considering. One very memorable series of lectures I attended was that delivered in his sonorous voice by Seamus Heaney, then Oxford Professor of Poetry and a future Nobel Prize laureate. Between lectures, I'd sit for hours in the medieval Duke Humfrey's Library within the Bodleian, a beautifully preserved reading room redolent of old books. There, I could call up from the old wooden book stacks centuries-old manuscripts, and often while reading could hear the faint strains of beautiful music being performed in the adjacent Sheldonian Theatre.

One young man in my course named Andy—a British student from London—and I began a tradition of attending lectures together. These included, thanks to Andy's particular interest in the subject, Terry Eagleton's course of lectures on Literary Theory. This tradition immediately expanded to include pints of beer at the nearby King's Arms pub (where hoards of students traditionally flock the moment a lecture, tutorial, or exam ends). We added a new activity too in the form of long sessions of snooker at the Oxford Union. It took me a while to get the grasp of playing upon what seemed at first a gargantuan pool table, but the game soon became addictive—as did British "bitter"—and by the end of term I actually beat Andy a time or two. During the hours spent shooting snooker we'd review our academic work, talking through research preparation for upcoming seminars and, ultimately, the final exam. After a few pints, Andy would often wax philosophical, with grand pronouncements upon such subjects as Heidegger, Marxist literary criticism, cultural phenomenology, and God. When I asked him once his thoughts on God, he replied in typical fashion: "I have no time for anyone with such an inflated ego as to demand to be worshipped."

After a day of lessons, pints, and snooker, it was inspiring to return to my room inside University College. To get to it, I had to walk through the passage that passed by the Shelley Memorial: This is in the form of a domed mausoleum with a skylight, centered within which is a ghostly sculpture of the poet, supported by a grieving Muse of Poetry, and depicted sprawled in nude death upon the Italian coastline where he'd washed ashore after drowning. In gold lettering around the dome above is an extract from Shelley's "Adonais"—an elegy to John Keats. Here Shelley is immortalized in effigy as a Univ student, despite having been expelled by the college in 1811 after only two terms for, among other things (including his reputation as a nonconformist rebel and prankster) co-authoring an initially anonymous tract entitled "The Necessity of Atheism."

I'd managed to interest my Univ friends in Shakespeare, and—in addition to helping organize trips to Stratford to see plays—I hosted parties in my room to watch various film adaptations available in the college library. One of our favorites was Franco Zeffrelli's film version of *Romeo and Juliet*, featuring in the role of Tybalt former Univ student Michael York (whom I later had the good fortune of befriending in Los Angeles). A particular highlight was making the journey to Stratford one weekend, with my good friend Joseph from Northern Ireland, to see Kenneth Branagh perform *Hamlet* on stage in an uncut, four hour *tour de force*.

Another film actor whose acquaintance I made through Oxford was Jon Voight. I happened to see a notice in a student publication that

Voight would be guest of honor at a dinner hosted by the Oxford Jewish Society. The reason this caught my eye was because Katya had told me that in Moscow, thanks to her perfect English, she was often asked to serve as an interpreter for visiting Westerners. She'd named a bevy of political dignitaries and celebrities encountered in this role, one of whom I recalled as being Jon Voight—with whom she had fond memories of attending a screening of the Voight film *Coming Home*, when she said they'd both even cried together at the end. So I called the Jewish Society and mentioned this connection, saying I thought Mr. Voight would appreciate the coincidence. To my surprise, they agreed, and I found myself the only non-Jew (apart from Mr. Voight himself) at the dinner. There, Voight did remember Katya and his experience in Moscow, and we had a lively chat about my own plans to travel there myself. Before I left, he wrote a warm message for Katya and me that I could take to show her in Moscow.

When I called Katya to tell her of this latest adventure, she was thrilled.

"So when are you coming?" she asked.

We finally agreed that I should visit Moscow before returning home for Christmas. I would need a formal visa to travel there, and this would require an official "invitation." Katya got around this by having a top academic at Moscow University officially invite me to give a lecture as a visiting "Oxford Shakespeare Scholar." This would require my actually giving a lecture at Moscow University, and I quickly agreed without realizing the implications. I then had to spend several different (and cold) mornings waiting outside the Soviet Embassy in London to deal with the incredibly dour-faced Soviet officials, so unfriendly and difficult I began to wonder why I would ever want to go to a country that willfully buried itself (and potential visitors) in such bureaucratic red tape. (My Oxford friends agreed, only half-joking as they teased that I would disappear in Moscow never to be seen again.)

In the Porter's Lodge, however, when I told him about my plans Richard took a more optimistic view: "Makin' memories," he said, with a reassuring smile. Then, just in time for my trip, the Soviet visa finally did arrive and I was soon headed East on a flight to Moscow.

Upon arrival in Moscow, I hummed to myself the lyrics of The Beatles' "Back in the USSR"—a song I'd never hear the same way again. Katya picked me up at the airport in a chauffeur-driven Russian limo ("Chaika"), and we were immediately whisked away for a performance of *Swan Lake* at the ornate Bolshoi Theatre. This first night in Moscow, like most everything about my brief visit to the Soviet Union in the waning days of the Cold War, was almost too surreal to describe. On the way to the Bolshoi, I got my first glimpse of the dull gray Stalinesque apartment blocks dominating the city skyline, permeated here and there with the glorious, multi-hued domes of old churches. Grandest of all was of course the magnificent St. Basil's Cathedral, which we would later visit along with Lenin's tomb and the "Eternal Flame" at the Tomb of the Unknown Soldier.

The interior of the Bolshoi was another world in itself contrasted with the city outside. But I could never have prepared for the splendor of the ballet performance itself, or the passion and even weeping of the spectators, as if the story were unfolding now for the first time on a grand living stage. During intermission, caviar and champagne were available in abundance—despite the general hardship outside for an average worker to procure so much as a loaf of bread (much less a ticket to the Bolshoi); while on television screens in the hallway, an earnest-looking Gorbachev spoke about solving the country's woes. I quickly perceived, as I surveyed the enormous sparkling chandelier dangling before the silk-curtained Czar's Box, that communal socialist equality was hardly evident.

While the authorities expected me to stay in a state hotel, where my actions could be monitored through one of those infamous bulky radios in every room, Katya's family got around this by bribing the hotel manager with a case of beer (for some reason a commodity hard to come by and a desired alternative to the omnipresent vodka). Her father simply drove Katya and me to the hotel, and handed the beer over to the pleased hotel manager, who stamped my visa with the dates of my putative stay at the hotel. And so, at a time when Westerners were strictly forbidden to stay in the homes of Soviet citizens, there I was doing exactly that: I experienced life in the home of a Russian family in the heart of Soviet Moscow.

This was, however, hardly a typical family. Part of the reason for their good fortune was that Katya's grandfather was a famous opera singer. And despite being Jewish, his artistry had once even impressed Stalin himself. He told me a riveting tale of his once being summoned last minute to replace a sick comrade for an operatic performance at the Bolshoi—and finding himself required to perform Stalin's favorite role in the presence of the tyrant (who on a whim might send a flawed performer to a Siberian gulag, or worse). But he had thrived, and successful artists were often rewarded with a large, comfortable flat and access to various goods and services—proving especially helpful at a time when one might spend fruitless hours queuing up in the bitter cold of the Russian winter for such basic items as bread, milk, or toilet paper. The house was full of music, including performances by Katya's grandfather with me accompanying on guitar. Another cultural highlight was seeing Rimsky-Korsakov's opera *Boris Godunov* performed by the Moscow Opera.

Despite the hardships, Katya's family clearly pulled out all the stops to make me welcome, including dinners featuring delicious *blinis* of caviar and sour cream, homemade Russian salad, and tasty black bread. This was all invariably washed down with Russian champagne and innumerable shots of *Stolichnaya* vodka—which came in flavors, such as lemon and peach, not yet available in the West. These shots came with passionate toasts, mostly expressing the wish for eventual friendship between Russia and America, symbolized by my presence in their home as a guest and friend.

One day something seemed wrong, and Katya and her mother ushered me frantically into the bedroom where I was asked to stay still and perfectly quiet. It turned out a senior KGB official from the foreign ministry was coming up for a visit. He was a "friend" of the family's, but they knew that if he caught me heads would roll. It was only then that I realized the degree of risk they were taking by having me as a guest. As Katya explained later, harboring a Westerner was considered a highly serious infraction. Many of their rights—including even their "domestic passports," needed for travel outside of Moscow itself—might be stripped away, along with the imposition of any number of other possible punishments. (I didn't think to ask what might have happened to me if caught.)

So I sat in fear, listening to a very official-sounding voice rise and fall in the otherwise musical inflections of well-spoken Russian. Finally, to my great relief, I heard the door close shut and heavy boots start to descend the stairs. Katya came in to give me a reassuring kiss, and then reminded me that I had a lecture to deliver at Moscow University the next day. This hit me with a bolt of trepidation, as I realized I had nothing prepared whatsoever to present.

I was also troubled about the family's evident connection with the KGB. Katya was reticent in her replies to my questions on the subject, but after pressing her she finally explained the "work" she sometimes did for the foreign ministry. It was they who in fact arranged her "interpreting" work for visiting celebrities and dignitaries, and she was expected to keep tabs on them and later submit a full report. (It was in exchange for this work that her family received further benefits, including the ability to travel abroad.) Just like I'd seen in the movies, here was a real-life instance of a KGB *femme fatale* employed to use her seductive charms for the good of the State. It was then I realized that not only did my girlfriend look and act like a Russian spy—she actually *was* one.

On the way to Moscow University we passed an impressive statue of cosmonaut Yuri Gagarin, and I suddenly felt far too down to earth than required for the adventure in which I'd found myself. Given my lack of a formally prepared lecture, we'd arranged that I would meet with students and faculty in a question and answer session about western Shakespeare scholarship. For the most part, this went well, and in the process I learned to my surprise that there was an entire school of Russian academic scholarship devoted to English Renaissance studies of which I—as well as my own academic comrades back in Oxford—was completely unaware. I also learned to appreciate that the heart of this work was Boris Pasternak's masterly Russian translation of Shakespeare's works; and I discovered that the best film version of *Hamlet* is in Russian, featuring a sublime score by Dmitri Shostakovich. (Later, back in Oxford, I attended a class entitled "Shakespeare in Film" which screened this version of *Hamlet*.)

Things fell apart at the end of the "lecture" when a faculty member suddenly began asking questions about esoteric aspects of Renaissance literary theory—questions which might only be answered by a professional expert on the subject. As I embarrassingly attempted to stumble through an answer, I felt like the character Holly Martins in Orson Wells' film *The Third Man*, a writer of cheap western novels inadvertently finding himself speaker of honor at an elite literary event. By the end of this ordeal, the faculty member glared at me with a look of such frightening penetration that I felt naked and exposed. As she stormed off, I realized she must have assumed me a CIA imposter posing as a scholar. I also resolved to brush up on literary theory before my next lecture.

Later Katya took me for a trip on the Moscow subway, where stations paved with marble and lit by sparkling chandeliers contrasted with the stark, gray miserable world just above the surface. Then we went for a walk through Gorky Park, where we had lunch at the new, unofficial "Hard Rock Café Moscow"—yet another tell-tale sign of the increased leniency under *glasnost*. The restaurant was run by a friend of hers named Stas Namin who was also, she said, a famous Russian rock musician—something indeed of the Russians' answer to Bob Geldof. In August 1989, he'd accomplished the feat of producing a rock concert (the "International Moscow Music Peace Festival") in Moscow featuring top Western and Russian bands performing together. This became known as the "Russian Woodstock," and Katya had been involved with coordinating this event with MTV. One of the headliners was the popular German band The Scorpions, and Namin proudly showed us a "flying V" style guitar signed for him by the band. Soon afterwards, The Scorpions released a beautifully melodic rock ballad called "Wind of Change," and I knew just whom they were referring to in the lyrics:

> I follow the Moskva
> Down to Gorky Park
> Listening to the wind of change
> An August summer night
> Soldiers passing by
> Listening to the wind of change
>
> The world is closing in
> Did you ever think
> That we could be so close, like brothers
> The future's in the air
> I can feel it everywhere
> Blowing with the wind of change
>
> Take me to the magic of the moment
> On a glory night
> Where the children of tomorrow dream away
> In the wind of change

After Namin showed us his impressive art studio, we walked back, and I was surprised to hear loud music—the newest by Madonna, as I recall—thumping through speakers set up around the park.

Katya's many connections led to further adventures. Knowing my interest in space exploration and my expressed admiration for the achievement of Gagarin—and my gratitude to the Soviets' efforts in space as the necessary catalyst to galvanize my own country into action after Sputnik—Katya took me to meet a senior Soviet space official at the space agency headquarters outside Moscow. The scene there reminded me of my childhood visit to Cape Canaveral, with its field of hulls from old spacecraft—though here surrounded by thick snow instead of sand. I took the opportunity to ask the official if the Soviets might be planning a manned mission to Mars, since the American program seemed to be going nowhere fast. But he confided that while the Soviet government spoke grandly about its plans for space exploration, it was incapable of getting beyond near-earth orbit anytime soon.

All I had to do, he said, was observe the country's chaotic state, with all its social disparity, food shortages, and long lines for even basic goods, to understand why. I began to see that the Soviet Union had as many hidden faces as a *matryoshka* doll. I was also struck by the Russian penchant for joking about their problems, distilling an inherent fatalism into biting satire.

I experienced first-hand a good example of this chaos. Katya took me to see the new McDonald's restaurant near where she lived on Avenue Tverskaya, and where an enormous line of people waited hours in the cold outside just to buy a Big Mac and fries. Katya of course knew someone at the door and got us right in—giving me a bizarre sense of guilty entitlement for dining at McDonald's as an invited guest. Soon afterwards, we heard a huge commotion outside and witnessed a large pro-Democracy rally marching through Moscow towards the Kremlin. Thousands of people carried posters with pictures of Boris Yeltsin as their preferred leader and imagined savior, chanting "Yeltsin, Yeltsin" as they went. We joined in and marched along with them just for the experience, while I wondered apprehensively if the group might be confronted by tanks as was the Soviets' wont. But nothing of the kind happened, and the protesters were allowed to march in peace all the way to the Kremlin. Along the way, I saw a sight that remains as a disturbing image and symbol of all that seemed wrong in Soviet society. We passed a figure lying on the street, and as I looked closely I saw that he was an old man—old, gray, and dead. He was frozen stiff on the snowy sidewalk, and people stepped nonchalantly over him, ignoring the desperate expression in his still-open, anguished eyes.

Before leaving Moscow to spend the holidays in Little Rock, Katya said she had one more person she wanted me to meet: A respected Moscow artist, she said, who'd agreed to paint my portrait. I'd never given any thought to having my portrait painted, but as with most things on this visit I decided just to go with it. He lived within walking distance, so we bundled up for the trip—she in the most extravagant mink fur coat I'd ever seen, I donning a furry Russian hat they'd given me to wear—and walked until we reached the artist's studio. There were numerous sculptures outside the house (he'd already sculpted Katya's face and displayed the sculpture in an exhibition), and the inside was full of canvasses. His wife greeted us and gave us hot tea, and after a few minutes the artist ordered the women to leave us alone. I then spent the next few hours sitting in a silent pose as the artist painted; I could feel his intense scrutiny as he labored at the composition, and I began to feel an anxious thrill about the process and longed to see the finished portrait. As he couldn't speak a word of English (nor I Russian, apart from the basic salutations), all was silent apart from the soft sweep of his brush over the canvas.

Finally, with a finishing flourish of his brush, he said he was done. I was at first taken aback, especially by the way he'd depicted my expression. When Katya returned, I asked her to inquire about this. The artist smiled and spoke in Russian to Katya.

"He says," explained Katya, "that he was trying to imagine whether or not you have slept with me."

"And what did you decide?" I asked the artist, who smiled mischievously as he answered. Katya laughed coquettishly and took my arm.

"He says the eyes in the painting say it all." I looked again at the portrait, and the interpretation was clear.

Portrait of the Author by H. Huker, 1990

The contrast with America startled me when I returned home. There, instead of scrounging for food on every corner, people were obsessed with the rapid pace of technological gadgets. The new thing was a communications device that my old friend Robert was now in the business of selling—he was one of the first salesmen in Little Rock to do so. Robert had a new Motorola 8000, one of the first portable phones, so bulky it was known as a "brick phone." He proudly carried it around as much as a novelty as something to sell at several hundred dollars a pop. For the first time since science fiction had imagined the possibility of "communicators" on the original *Star Trek* TV series of the 60s (not to mention Dick Tracey's watch phone), portable telephones were now a reality. The device was so bulky, however, that people told Robert it would never take off. I for one loathed the idea of individual privacy being eroded with the prospect of being always so easily accessible ("on call," as it were). But at least in the early days of what soon became known as "cell phones," there was an etiquette which everyone observed: Robert, like everyone at the beginning, would never even think about operating it in a public place such as a restaurant, and would politely excuse himself from company if he needed to make or receive a call. How rude it would seem otherwise!

I now often ache with nostalgia for those days, not so very long ago, when people managed quite well—as they'd done throughout the history of human civilization—without being so tied to instant communication: A time when you could actually have a full conversation with someone without being interrupted by a call—or a text or "Tweet" or new Facebook "friend" update. (Not to mention the forgotten benefits of undistracted driving.) Yet, for better or worse, society has irrevocably changed in just 20 years, and today's generation of children is all but born with a phone and laptop as requisite appendages for survival.

Soon after arriving, I needed to address the matter of the Master's letter. After Bill Clinton had been reelected as Governor of Arkansas, the Master gave me a letter he wished me to deliver personally to the Governor. The letter congratulated Governor Clinton on his success, and expressed the College's delight at having me as a fellow Arkansan at the college—causing me to blush in the Master's description of me as an "excellent Ambassador for both my state and country." It turned out my parents had connections with the administrator of the Governor's Mansion, and so it was a relatively easy matter to arrange an appointment for me to visit and deliver the letter in person to Bill Clinton.

When I arrived at the Governor's Mansion early one morning just before Christmas, I was met by a guard who confirmed my identity and then led me to the front entrance, where I was greeted warmly by the administrator, Ann McCoy. She said the Governor would be right down, and that she'd give me a tour in the meantime. Of most interest to me was the Governor's private library, where the shelves are stocked with books written by Arkansans.

"When you write a book one day," said McCoy, "it will be displayed here too."

The mansion was sumptuously decorated for Christmas, and McCoy explained that Arkansas First Lady Hillary Rodham Clinton always presided over the decorations—and the Governor, Mrs. Clinton, and their young daughter Chelsea had decorated the beautiful Christmas tree.

Soon we heard voices from the top of the elegant winding staircase, and I recognized Bill Clinton's voice I knew so well from his many years in Arkansas politics.

"The Governor may not want to be photographed," said McCoy, seeing me take out my camera. "It's still early and he's not formally dressed yet."

I watched nervously as Governor Clinton descended the stairs. He wore faded blue jeans and a plain shirt and, from the look of his face, didn't seem at all pleased to have such an early appointment. When he reached the bottom of the steps, he gave McCoy and irritated look and said: "So what's this about?"

Unperturbed, she introduced me and said I had a message for him from England. The look the Governor gave me was one of curious suspicion, so I just handed him the envelope from the Master and stood back with baited breath. Suddenly, Clinton's face burst into a delighted smile as he read through the letter.

"This is *great!*" he said. Then he looked over his shoulder back up the stairs and called. "Hey Hillary, come look at this!" Hillary Clinton appeared and looked at me curiously before reading through the letter. When the Governor introduced me to her, she asked—"How long will you be in Oxford?" I answered two years, and she turned to her husband and said: "We'll have to go back for a visit while he's there."

Bill Clinton smiled. "Yeah, we'll have to try and do that." Then he told me the story of his first trip back to University College after he'd first been elected Governor of Arkansas. When he arrived at the Lodge, the old Head Porter from his own time at Univ, Douglas Millin, took one look at Clinton and said he'd heard they'd made him "king" of some little region in America with two men and a dog.

"Sounds a lot like the current Head Porter there now," I replied. As we said farewell, I took a chance and asked if I could get a photograph with the Governor. He consented and McCoy took the picture with my camera. And as I departed the Mansion, I knew the Master would be immensely pleased.

Afterwards, during a visit to Crossett, my cousin Jon Cash said there was one thing he wished I'd said to the Governor at parting: "You should have said, *See you at the White House!*" I certainly wish that I had.

With Governor Bill Clinton at the Arkansas Governor's Mansion, 1990

10

AN UNEARTHLY ENCOUNTER

Heaven and earth are illimitable; to man a term is set. Furnished only with the scrap of time that is his span, he is committed to a place amid the illimitable. A flash, and all is over, like a racehorse seen through a crack. He who by the enjoyment of his senses can use this brief moment to the full alone can claim to have found the Way.

—Chuang-tzu

Upon my return to Oxford, I discovered with dismay that the airline had lost my suitcase—in which, along with all my clothes, I'd foolishly put all my academic notes from the first term. Worst of all, though, was the lack of my winter clothes in the midst of a particularly cold and damp English winter. There was a major snowfall that February, rare for Oxford, which—despite nearly freezing to death, remains as one of my most beautiful memories of the place: The inherent enchantment within and around the historical buildings and gardens of Oxford was enhanced manifold with the graceful tranquility and iridescent sparkle of a dreamy snowscape.

I had continued practicing my music too and could at last play the complete Bach cello suite I'd begun with Carlo in Dallas. I had also become a member of the University College Music Society, whose president had asked if I would be willing to give a formal recital that spring during Hilary Term (the second of three eight week terms at Oxford). I'd agreed, and got busy putting together a full repertoire for my most ambitious project yet. Once again, I intended to play everything from memory, and I still had a lot of work to do before I could play by heart the entire Bach suite. The recital was set two months hence, just before the Easter vacation—when I'd arranged both for Katya and my mother to be in Oxford for a visit.

I soon experienced another fascinating encounter. I walked into Blackwell's Music Shop one morning and stepped into a small room where they kept special collections of classical music recordings. There was one other person in the room, and I immediately stopped in my tracks the moment I realized who it was. He was in a wheelchair that looked like some strange spacecraft on wheels, complete with a small computer screen which rose in front of his face, although his head seemed permanently attached at a tilt on the headrest. His round glasses reflected the computer's glow, and his mouth gave the impression of a wry observation frozen just at the point of utterance between his lips. And I knew that behind the penetrating blue eyes now regarding me—the only thing about the gentleman which seemed animate—was a mind which comprehended like few others in all human history the infinite vastness of the universe and the bizarre properties of space and time that made it (and us) possible. I was looking into the eyes of Professor Stephen Hawking, and for me that precise moment in space and time will indeed exist forever.

I actually had a good reason to introduce myself. Two, in fact: I knew that Hawking had also studied at University College; and his daughter Lucy was an undergraduate there now—helping to organize my upcoming recital in her role as Treasurer of the Music Society. But it felt very odd at first trying to speak to the professor, as his face remained unmoving as I spoke so that I almost had the impression he wasn't conscious of me at all. Then I heard a light clicking sound, and recalled that his only means of communication was through his fingers, with which—after years of ALS-related muscular degeneration—he had just enough movement to operate a special type of keyboard designed specifically for him to communicate. I moved behind him and was able to read what he had typed on the keyboard about his daughter. I then mentioned that I had tried to attend his lecture the previous evening, but had been turned away in disappointment along with hundreds of other people due to lack of space. After more clicking, I read his comment that he hoped to return to Oxford soon, and that "hopefully they will give me a bigger venue next time!" Then I mentioned I'd read his recent book, *A Brief History of Time*. I started to make a comment about it, but then fortunately realized I was the last person on the planet to belong in a discussion of cosmological physics with Stephen Hawking.

A woman came in who appeared to be Hawking's nurse (and who I realized later must have been his wife) and I excused myself by telling the Professor what a pleasure it had been to meet him. As I walked out I heard, in that unmistakable computerized voice—"Nice to meet you too."

It wasn't long before Professor Hawking did in fact speak again in Oxford, this time as a guest speaker at the Oxford Union. I and my Univ friends made sure to get there early this time, and managed to get a good seat amid the huge crowd that filled the Union's famous debating chamber. It was an odd sort of lecture, with all eyes on the immovable Hawking as his monotone voice took us from the Big Bang to the Big Crunch. This was within around a year of the Cosmic Background Explorer (COBE) satellite's observations of the cosmic microwave background radiation indicating the universe will continue its expansion *ad infinitum*. But on that occasion Hawking described the current debate, including the possibility that our universe could be just one of an infinite number of such bubble universes within a much greater "Multiverse"—each expanding and collapsing repeatedly in an endless procession of big bangs and big crunches throughout eternity. He had a way of describing such mind-boggling concepts so that anyone with any degree of imagination could comprehend. Beyond elucidating the modern science of cosmology and its quest to discover a unified theory of physics as a "theory of everything" that predicts the very nature of the universe itself, he touched as well on the possibility of time travel: "The reason we know it is not possible to travel into the past," said Hawking, "is that we have not yet been invaded by a horde of tourists from the future."

He also waxed philosophical on the subject of technology and communication: "Our capacity for destroying ourselves is increasing, while our wisdom for using that knowledge is not." I later realized he was here paraphrasing the Oxford philosopher Bertrand Russell, who like Hawking spoke presciently of the impact—and potential dangers—of technology years before it came to dominate every aspect of our lives. In an essay titled "Is Everything Determined?" Hawking considered whether our intellectual evolution can ultimately keep pace with that of technology:

> One might hope that we could employ both the intelligence and the powers of logical thought that we have developed through natural selection. Unfortunately, natural selection has also developed other characteristics, such as aggression. Aggression would have given a

survival advantage in cave dweller days and earlier and so would have been favored by natural selection. The tremendous increase in our powers of destruction brought about by modern science and technology, however, has made aggression a very dangerous quality, one that threatens the survival of the whole human race. The trouble is, our aggressive instincts seem to be encoded in our DNA. DNA changes by biological evolution only on a time scale of millions of years, but our powers of destruction are increasing on a time scale for the evolution of information, which is now only twenty or thirty years. Unless we can use our intelligence to control our aggression, there is not much chance for the human race.

It is for this reason that Hawking seems at once both adamant and ambivalent about the possibility of human space travel. On the one hand, journeying to the stars is ultimately the only way the human race will continue in the long term. But our immediate concern must be with potentially fatal climate change, induced in part by the global warming exacerbated by human industrial activities. And there's at the same time the threat, in the near future, of a cataclysmic asteroid impact such as that which apparently wiped out the dinosaurs 65 million years ago. Then there's also the reality that our life-giving sun is an aging star. Or as Hawking's colleague at Cambridge University, Professor Sir Martin Rees, put it in a lecture entitled "Dark Materials" (quoted by Christopher Hitchens in a review in *The Atlantic*, January/February 2010):

> Most educated people are aware that we are the outcome of nearly 4 billion years of Darwinian natural selection, but many tend to think that humans are somehow the culmination. Our sun, however, is less than halfway through its lifespan. It will not be humans who watch the sun's demise, 6 billion years from now. Any creatures that then exist will be as different from us as we are from bacteria or amoebae.

The answer, then, is that we must see travel to the stars in the spirit of allowing our race the chance to continue its intellectual, spiritual, and even physical evolution beyond even the duration of our current solar system. (A more cynical alternative might be simply to consider—like the philosopher Schopenhauer—the world as inherently bankrupt and better not to have existed at all.)

I left the lecture with a profound sense of gratitude for the experience of being fully alive within—as I now comprehended for the first time—this overwhelming vastness of time and eternity in which each of us has the truly miraculous chance to taste of life but once. The sensation of this awareness was not entirely dissimilar from the cathartic realization I'd had after my near-fatal car accident in school. Only this time the inspiration was knowledge: There is an awesome power of imagination that can be wakened within the mind's eye like a sleeping giant. All it takes is the right spark, the presence and teaching of those who are both enlightened and passionate. Or, as Einstein once put it, "Imagination is more important than knowledge. For knowledge is limited to all we now know and understand, while imagination embraces the entire world, and all there ever will be to know and understand." This is what Professor Hawking clearly meant: With all our progress of scientific knowledge and the technology which is fast evolving from it, we must find a way to balance progress with the intellectual capacity to embrace it in ways which *benefit* our planet—without destroying it and us along the way. Such wisdom can provide both a practical and a moral basis for human progress, but only if it can transcend outmoded and destructive traits like aggression—and its expression through nationalistic flag-worship and racial and religious tribalism.

These no longer have any place within the wider universe we are just beginning to see, and we must strive to move beyond misinterpreting, as the mythologist Joseph Campbell demonstrated, archetypal symbols and metaphor as absolute fact (in contrast to their inherent value as guides toward a more enlightened human mythos). What we are most in need of, as Campbell points out in his book *The Inner Reaches of Outer Space*, is a "new mythology, which is to be of the whole human race"—one in which the universal image reflects the "immensity of galaxies . . . and superclusters of galaxies, speeding apart into expanding distance, with humanity as a kind of recently developed scurf on the epidermis of a minor star in the outer arm of an average galaxy, amidst one of the lesser clusters among the thousands, catapulting apart, which took form . . . as a consequence of an inconceivable preternatural event." For Campbell, this universal image might be most appropriately that of the earthrise photographed by Apollo 8 astronauts, in which "the rising earth shows none of those divisive territorial lines that on our maps are so conspicuous and important."

I felt a further sense of awe that, out of all eternity, I happened to inhabit *this* particular space, time, and self—despite all the infinite possible variations from the origins of the universe to this present moment that might have rendered Earth and life itself impossible, much less my individual existence and presence at that particular lecture. And, having come into the world in the first place despite the overwhelming odds, I thought of all the various directions my life could have taken—

Earthrise over lunar landscape. Apollo 8 Mission (1968)

from childhood through high school and college and the multifarious divergent paths I could otherwise have followed. Yet here I was, and oddly enough it was exactly where I'd somehow "willed" myself to be. The important thing was that I was now so vividly seeing the reality of it. The appreciation is all.

With this insight, I felt the extreme preciousness of each individual life—along with a new reverence for the human gift of consciousness. I envisioned in the flicker of a 14 billion year moment the primordial singularity bursting as cosmic light through the void; gas coalescing into galaxies, stars and finally planets pelted with bombardments bearing the carbon seeds of life—a life on Earth finally evolving until the first tetrapod hauled itself onto land to start the painfully slow (and yet geologically instant) development until, finally, reaching a life form with the singular capacity—in our solar system, at least—to contemplate our own existence. There is then ultimately only one key question to ask: What do we do with our capacity to think? Perhaps our truest hope lies in the possibility of transcending an attachment to material "progress" to allow our intellectual—and spiritual—capacities further to evolve and flourish. Or, as already expressed in the ancient Eastern philosophy of the *Tao*:

"To know eternity is enlightenment, and not to recognize eternity brings disorder and evil. Knowing eternity makes one comprehensive; comprehension makes one broadminded; breadth of vision brings nobility; nobility is like heaven." With this compare William Blake: "If the doors of perception were cleansed, every thing would appear to man as it is, infinite."

Hawking seems to hope that we will in fact eventually travel beyond this "pale blue dot"—as Carl Sagan once described our planet—floating like a precious jewel in the otherwise lonely, barren vastness of space. If we do, then perhaps we truly will fulfill the destiny of the primordial stardust of which each one of us is ultimately composed.

11

INTERLUDE

As he had been thinking for months about leaving his wife and had not done it because it would be too cruel to deprive her of himself, her departure was a very healthful shock.

—Ernest Hemingway, *The Sun Also Rises*

O, beware, my lord, of jealousy.
It is the green-ey'd monster which doth mock
The meat it feeds on.

—Shakespeare, *Othello*

During the months following my time with Katya in Moscow, I had become increasingly troubled by my conflicting feelings towards her. I felt powerful emotions that I considered true romantic love, and yet certain doubts had crept into my mind and begun to take hold, leaving me with a sense of profound anxiety. I had been increasingly concerned with the KGB side of her life in the Soviet Union, as well as with her easy ability to be quite dishonest when it suited her needs. (She explained this as a necessary corollary to life in Moscow, but I couldn't help wondering to what extent this trait was confined to "business.") This was compounded by a nagging jealousy that had taken hold after Katya's propensity to discuss her relationships with various other men—invariably much older men, who were both famous and powerful. I began to feel both deeply intimidated and, by comparison to those others upon whom she constantly harped, inadequate as her potential husband.

It was clear that the only way we could stay together in the long-term was through marriage. This was the reason I'd arranged for my mother's visit for my recital to coincide with that of Katya's: I knew that once she finally met Katya, my mother would love her too. My plan worked out, in fact, all too well. They immediately hit it off, and even my recital went better than I'd ever hoped, including performing from memory as planned the entire Bach Cello Suite #1 I'd been practicing since Dallas. A fellow student arranged to record the recital, and years later I'm still amazed with how well my ambitious repertoire went, especially considering the extreme pressures—both academic and personal—I'd experienced in the weeks leading up to the recital.

By the time she left Oxford, my mother was clearly taken with Katya and—despite her previous threats—I knew my "inheritance" remained secure even if I married Katya. The problem was now my own conviction about our relationship. Although she sensed my inner conflict and probed the reasons for my obvious doubts, I found it difficult to talk about my concerns and kept them inside. By the time Katya had returned to Moscow, a serious discord had taken hold between us, one which the long distance began to amplify until any hope of restoring harmony seemed moot.

That spring brought an exciting distraction with the annual "Eights Week" boat race. This is an Oxford tradition going back to the early 19th century in which each college competes for the honor of being able to call itself Head of the River for a year. Univ had not held this title since the race of 1914 until finally winning the Headship again in 1990. Retaining this title for a second consecutive year called for a major celebration indeed. That evening Master Albery hosted a grand supper in Hall, and afterwards opened up his lodgings in which the Master's punch poured forth abundantly. But the crowning moment of the festivities came when the Univ men's crew burned a boat in celebration right in the middle of the quad, and the Master himself joined students in leaping joyfully over the bonfire.

In early summer, Katya returned to Paris to take up a new post at UNESCO, and I flew there to meet her. My intent was to use the occasion to gently inform her of my wish to break up; and the same romantic city where our relationship had begun seemed the appropriate place to end it. Much to my surprise, however, Katya beat me to the punch. It was she who, over dinner at *La Closerie des Lilas* where our romance had first begun, informed me that it was over. And it was I who, after worrying so long how she would take my own departure, broke completely down at her rejection and begged her to reconsider. It was only by losing her that I understood at last the full depth of my feelings.

When I returned to Oxford, I was in an altered state of consciousness, my mind completely obsessed with Katya and unable to focus on any other thing—most especially my academic work. All seemed irrelevant apart from finding some way to win her back; and the only way to do this, I surmised, was to move to Paris and prove myself ultimately worthy of Katya's love. As emotionally perturbed as I was, I acted fully on impulse without making any arrangements with University College for time off. Rather, and much to my subsequent regret, I simply "disappeared" to Paris.

As rash as this decision was, I did have—thanks to a modest inheritance left to me upon his death by "Pop," my grandfather on the Thurmond side—sufficient funding for my new plans. And these included enrolling, first of all, in a French language course, followed by a course at the British Council in Paris leading to a certificate in TEFL ("Teaching English as a Foreign Language"). As for accommodation, the three month language course in which I'd enrolled provided room and board with a French family, after which I planned to find a small flat near the British Council while taking the TEFL course.

There was only one little hitch to this whole grand scheme of mine. Upon arrival in Paris in August, I found to my dismay that Katya was not, in fact, there. She was still in the Soviet Union, and the news that dominated the airwaves was that of the coup on August 19th (the "August Putsch") in which a group of Communist hardliners had placed Mikhail Gorbachev under house arrest and taken control of the Soviet government. These officials had felt threatened by Gorbachev's policy of *perestroika* and his attempt to restructure the USSR as a less centralized state, and they had now in one swoop banned newspapers, frozen political activity, and closed the borders. Katya, who had returned to Moscow in preparation for her move to Paris, was now trapped on the other side. Suddenly all the promise of both *perestroika* and *glasnost* seemed to have vanished in this new, unwholesome wind of change, along with the dream of freedom that had seemed at last within reach for the Russian people.

The coup was fortunately a short-lived affair. After Boris Yeltsin organized mass public opposition from his office in the Russian Parliament building (known as the Russian "White House"), the officials finally gave in after only three days and Gorbachev was restored to power. (He was, however, now significantly humiliated and weakened, even as Yeltsin emerged as a powerful new leader in Russian politics.)

In the meantime, while I waited for Katya finally to return to France, I settled into the French language course and my new life in Paris. There, I lived in the northern part of the city in a house owned by a lady who made a living by hosting students from the language school. My fellow housemates were German-speaking Swiss students, and it transpired that even though our landlady could speak fluent German, she had refused to utter a word of the language since World War II. Nor did she speak English, so we were all obliged to learn French fairly quickly in order to converse with her during meals.

One of the Swiss students, a stout businessman from St. Gallen named Caspar, became a good friend and we spent many evenings out enjoying the Parisian nightlife—mostly in the area of Les Halles and Chatelet near the banks of the Seine, but also occasionally in the rather seedy district known as Pigalle. There, not far from the *Moulin Rouge*, was a club called New Moon which featured live music by local and foreign punk and new wave bands. There was something fascinating for me about the young crowd there, most of them dressed all in black and bedecked with the most bizarre variety of tattoos and body piercings I'd ever seen.

A singular image from our neighborhood in north Paris is that of an elderly lady whom I one day saw fearfully trying to cross a busy street. After I helped her across, she pulled out a handful of coins and attempted to pay me for my help, and then seemed surprised when I refused to accept any money. I felt at once shocked and dismayed that the lady had felt the need even to suggest offering compensation for my doing what, surely, anyone would have felt obliged to do.

Then, that October, an announcement came for which I'd been anxiously watching the newspaper headlines for months. One day I finally saw it on the front page of the *International Herald Tribune*: Governor Bill Clinton of Arkansas had formally announced his candidacy for the office of the Presidency of the United States. This brought a profound sense both of home pride and anticipation for the year to come.

But in November there was an even bigger surprise. One evening I heard my landlady calling me from downstairs: "François!" It was a phone call from home, and I was completely thrown for a loop when I heard what my mother had to say.

"Katya's here!" she said.

"What?"

"Katya's here visiting, she called to say she was traveling in America and I invited her to Little Rock. She wants to speak to you."

The next thing I knew, I was hearing Katya's voice for the first time in months not from Moscow, but from my own home in Little Rock! And sure enough, before returning to France she'd had an opportunity to visit in America and—when she called Mom to say hello—had accepted an invitation to visit. She'd even agreed to visit classes at UALR and to speak to local media on a Little Rock radio program. Once again, the word that comes to mind in describing my feeling at that moment is *surreal*. When my old friend back home, Robert, learned about this turn of events, it gave him a running joke for years to come: "You moved all the way to Paris looking for a girl, who ends up calling you from your own home in Arkansas. That's fucked up, dude!"

That spring, the French classes complete, I enrolled in the course at the British Council—located near the impressive, gold-inlaid dome where Napoleon's remains are interred at Les Invalides. The course there led to the formal Cambridge University/Royal Society of Arts certificate in TEFL. This continued to be the cornerstone in my plan to win back Katya: I would get a job in Paris teaching English, while simultaneously mastering French and eventually landing a solid job in the international business sector.

Two eventualities soon derailed these ambitions, causing me completely to reverse course by early summer. First of all, there was Katya's substantial delay in returning. Having six months apart following the traumatic breakup proved the perfect panacea for a broken heart, especially for a young man left alone in Paris. By the time she finally did arrive in Paris to take up her new post, when we got together it was clear that the old spark had fizzled for both of us. The magic was gone. Nevertheless, we still enjoyed each other's company as friends, and found pleasure in going out to see movies and attend concerts together.

Then, just as I began to wonder what in the world to do next, I received an unexpected letter from Oxford. The letter was from Dr. Leslie Mitchell, the Dean of Graduates at University College. How he'd found me I have no idea, as I'd never given anyone my Paris address. But what Dr. Mitchell wanted to know was simply whether or not I ever planned to return to Oxford to complete my degree. The thought of being allowed to return at all after so abruptly disappearing had never even occurred to me. Yet this sudden opportunity to do so, combined with my changed circumstances in Paris with Katya, made returning to Univ the most logical course of action. So I replied to Dr.

Mitchell, apologizing for the inconvenience I'd caused and confirming my intention to return in October to complete my coursework and sit the exams the following summer. I'd already found a topic of interest for my studies: I'd research Shakespeare's use of music in his drama. Fortunately, it turned out the British Council in Paris had a good library, including material related to my chosen topic, and so I was able to get a head start on my research in advance of returning to Oxford.

I still had several months to enjoy living in Paris. As my mother expressed in a letter: "You're in Paris in the springtime and fancy free. Enjoy it!" And this I certainly did, enjoying all the art and architecture on offer in the "City of Light," along with a carefree lifestyle at times approaching the Henry Milleresque. I'd found a tiny room in the 6th *arrondissement* near the Tour Montparnasse—a room so small, in fact, that I could hardly practice my guitar without bumping one end of it against the farther wall. But the moment I walked outside, I was in one of the best locations in Paris. My room was at #16 Rue de Fleurus, and just after moving there I realized it had featured in Hemingway's memoir of life in Paris in the 1920s, *A Moveable Feast*. Just as he'd recounted, when I walked down the street to #27 Rue de Fleurus, a plaque indicated that this was where Gertrude Stein had lived for many years, along with her brother Leo and her friend Alice B. Toklas—and where she was visited by "a number of artists and writers from 1903–38."

At the corner of the street was a *Tabac* called Le Fleurus, where I would read the *International Herald Tribune* over an espresso and hot buttered croissant each morning, and often have a baguette with Camembert cheese for lunch. (I learned quickly that if you stood at the bar instead of taking a seat at a table, everything cost several francs less.) I also learned that actually *living* in Paris came with distinct advantages. During my previous visits, I'd decided that Parisians matched pretty well the general stereotype of the French as being, as Jon Stewart once aptly put it, experts in the art of "condescending scorn." Yet I also found that, once they perceived I was actually a "local" as opposed to a mere tourist passing through, I began to be treated as such—especially once I could address them in French. At Le Fleurus, for example, whereas during my first couple of visits the barman welcomed me with a haughty smirk, by the fourth or fifth time I entered he'd begun shaking my hand with a sincere smile and a hearty "bonjour, monsieur"—before promptly serving my usual coffee without a further word. (During a recent visit to Paris almost 20 years later, I dropped by Le Fleurus and was greeted with warm familiarity by the same old barman.)

Often after the morning coffee I'd drop by the nearby *Boulangerie-Patisserie-Sandwicherie*, called Boulangerie D'Assas, where the scent of freshly baked pastries proved irresistible. I'd pick up a warm *pain au chocolat*, or perhaps a quiche just out of the oven. Then I'd walk back down my street and, passing through a large gate tipped with golden spikes, enter the *Jardin du Luxembourg*. There, the beauty and *joie de vivre* of spring in Paris is at once fully manifest, with its colorful flowers, statues, splashing fountains, and old men playing *boules* from dusk to dawn. I'd sit on a bench and enjoy my pastry while reading a book of stories or poetry—or perhaps even practice my guitar in the bloom-scented breeze.

I'd found a job playing guitar at a local Left Bank Irish pub on Rue de Mirbel. This was called Connolly's Corner, a place I'd discovered after hearing of a poetry reading there one night. Its proprietor, Liam Connolly, invited me to perform one evening to "test the waters." My performance was well-received, and I was subsequently invited to perform at various other Irish pubs around the left bank. This work resulted in a much-needed subsidy of both cash and Guinness.

After my weekly performance at Connolly's, I'd walk around the corner to the Rue Mouffetard, an old street paved with bricks in an elegant circular pattern. Down this street were a number of bars popular with university students, one of which was the aptly named Le Bateau Ivre ("The Drunken Boat"), complete with an iconic picture of the composer of that poem, Arthur Rimbaud. Another bar across the street, The Mayflower, featured foreign car license plates hanging from the walls and ceiling. (I later sent them one of Kate's old Arkansas plates, customized with her name "KATE T", which still hangs there prominently to this day.)

Late that spring I organized—along with a British poet named Simon whom I met in the TEFL course—an ambitious evening of poetry and music held at an Irish pub called Sweeney's. Recalling the wonderful performances in Dallas when Carlo and poet Tim Siebles combined poetry readings with guitar music, our program likewise featured this same combination of artistic expression with pleasing results.

Before leaving Paris, I discovered something that seemed a perfectly symbolic transition from France back to Oxford to resume my study of Shakespeare. One day while browsing at the venerable Shakespeare and Company bookstore near Notre Dame Cathedral, I read that there would be a performance of *The Merry Wives of Windsor* at a place called La Jardin Shakespeare. Intrigued, I attended and found that this was in fact quite an impressive garden, located in the Bois de

Boulogne forest outside Paris. And in this garden was planted every type of flora mentioned by Shakespeare in all his plays. I could imagine few things better than seeing a good performance of a play in the "Shakespeare Garden" in the spring.

I finally left Paris with a deep conviction that the city is, truly, a moveable feast.

12

An Inaugural and a Commencement

I was a modest, good-humoured boy. It is Oxford that has made me insufferable.

—Max Beerbohm

When I returned home that summer, my city was full of excitement. Governor Clinton, now the official Democratic nominee for President, had located his official presidential campaign headquarters right in the heart of downtown Little Rock, and my mother encouraged me to "drop by." This I did, and I was enlisted as a full-time volunteer, which gave me the opportunity to reconnect with the Arkansas Governor and First Lady in person. I also had the opportunity to host a European visitor: One of my good German friends from Oxford, Juergen, came to Little Rock for a visit. (I had already visited him in his beautiful city of Regensburg in Bavaria.) Juergen particularly enjoyed the unique experience of seeing the inside of an American presidential campaign in action.

I later wrote, at the Master's request, a brief description of this experience for the *University College Record*. On a whim, I also sent it to the *International Herald Tribune* global newspaper, and was surprised when it appeared there in the editorial section on December 16, 1992:

"A Grass-Roots Insider"

Late one hot, muggy evening in July, there was a flurry of excitement on an otherwise empty airfield in Little Rock, Arkansas: The newly nominated Democratic candidate for president of the United States, Governor Bill Clinton, was returning home.

It was almost two hours past midnight, and the governor was hours behind schedule. The time of his return had not been made public, so the small airport stood empty and silent save for the "advance team" and a handful of local volunteers. I was a member of the latter group. Mr. Clinton returned often to his home base in Little Rock, so this would not be the first time I would receive a last-minute summons to the airport in the middle of the night, where our duties ranged from holding back reporters to unloading the plane. My solace was that, as an acquaintance of Mr. Clinton, I had only to call through the din of reporters a simple "Hi, Bill," and he would come over with a handshake and warm greetings.

None of us minded the midnight toil. It was rewarding enough just to be there, playing a part in the American political process in our own small way. But there was another advantage. I was free to roam around the campaign's national headquarters, in a modest building in downtown Little Rock. A short tour gave one a sense of awe at the intricate organization involved in one of the most underestimated presidential campaigns in U.S. history.

For one who has seen the inner workings of this campaign, it is possible to feel sympathetic to Dan Quayle's election-night remark as he conceded defeat: "If Bill Clinton runs this country as well as he ran his campaign, we'll be all right."

When I finally got back to Oxford and to Univ, I immediately took the opportunity to explain to my friends there what had happened. When I told Dr. Mitchell about my extreme emotional distress the previous spring that had led to my drastic actions, he pointed out that I should have come to him and the Chaplain, Bill Sykes, to express my difficulties and benefit from their support. "That's what we're here for," he said.

At this time University College suddenly found itself in the media spotlight, as reporters as well as political operatives began to investigate the young Bill Clinton's activities while a student at the college in 1968. A particular point of interest was Clinton's known trip to Moscow during that time, even as he'd taken part in public protests against the Vietnam War. As the Republicans became increasingly desperate to find dirt on Clinton in advance of the election, portraying him as some sort of Communist traitor became a key part of their strategy. And one day just before the first presidential debate, two women found their way into the graduate common room in college, where I happened to be sitting alone reading the newspaper. A student had brought them, and when he introduced me to them he pointed out that I'd been working with the Clinton campaign. When after a bit of small talk they asked if there happened to be an archive with old newsletters describing Bill Clinton's protest activities and Moscow trip in '68, their manner seemed suspicious.

"Why do you want to know?" I asked.

"Well," one of them replied, "as you know, the presidential debate is tomorrow, and we want to make sure Governor Clinton is prepared for any dirt the Republicans might throw at him." Then the other woman joined in:

"We want to *help* Clinton," she said; then they looked at each other and nodded.

I told them there were no such documents that I knew of, and then as they began looking around the room I called the porter and arranged for these ladies to be escorted from the premises. (Dr. Mitchell later informed me the college was fielding numerous such inquiries from "these nasty Republicans.") The Master was on top of things, however, and had quickly established an efficient public relations network. He, like most of the college (and Oxford University itself), eagerly anticipated the potential advantages of having—for the first time in history—a former Oxford student as United States President.

When Election Day 1992 arrived that November, I helped organize an Election Night party in the graduate common room, which proved a night to remember. Especially memorable was when early on, after the BBC commentators had bragged in detail about the efficient color-coded system they'd set up to indicate election results for each candidate, their initial results from American exit polls indicated half the country had in fact just gone to Ross Perot. This led to momentary chaos at both my party and with the BBC announcers, until it transpired that a "glitch" had mistakenly confused Perot with Clinton. Finally it was over, and it was one of the most exciting moments of my life to see on British television Bill, Hillary, and Chelsea emerge from the beautiful Old State House building in Little Rock to celebrate his victory—in front of thousands of locals, including my mother and friends, gathered there to hear Clinton's acceptance speech. The next day, the Master had the American flag flown from the college over High Street—albeit placed under that of the college flag, as if indicating a captured ship. At the same time, the phone on my desk started ringing. All of my old friends—including the Clinton naysayers from two years earlier—called to congratulate me with the same refrain: "You were *right!*"

The media, British as well as American, kept visiting the college, intent to hear its members' thoughts on the success of its illustrious alumnus. When word got around that there was a bona fide Arkansan in residence, I found myself being sought out for interviews. The first such interview was with a reporter from the regional news, who had also interviewed the college Master, John Albery. The evening of the broadcast, I was invited to the Master's Lodgings for a watch party. As my own interview ended, I was relieved it elicited a "Well done, Frank!" from the Master.

Another interview was an extensive one with the American C-Span network, in Oxford putting together a special about Clinton's time there. They interviewed me in the college beer cellar, and said the interview would air in its entirety as part of their coverage of the Presidential Inaugural.

When I returned home in December, upon landing in Little Rock—the location of President-elect Clinton's transition headquarters—I was bemused to overhear a fellow traveler comment: "Welcome to Little Rock, center of the Free World." Then I received as a Christmas present tickets to both the Inauguration and the Inaugural Ball in Washington, D.C. This had been arranged courtesy of a family friend from church, Mack McLarty, who had just been named by President-elect Clinton as White House Chief of Staff. So I remained home through January in order to attend every possible event associated with the Inaugural while in Washington, including the Inauguration itself featuring an inspiring address by the new President, and—for the first time since Robert Frost read a poem at the Kennedy Inaugural—a poetry recitation, this time by Arkansas poet Maya Angelou. This was followed by the afternoon parade, and then the "Arkansas Inaugural Ball"—a late night, black-tie affair with famous bands and celebrities in every corner of a grand ballroom.

The next morning, the Clintons had a special "open house" at the White House, starting with a reception specifically for Arkansans. The moment I stepped inside the White House, I was greeted by the President's mother, Virginia Kelley, who said, "I saw you on C-Span!" and gave me a warm hug. She was particularly pleased to hear about my own experience at University College. Then I had the opportunity to greet the new President and First Lady on their first official day in the White House—an occasion which, coincidentally, was captured on camera, as I discovered upon arrival home in Little Rock when I learned that the clip of the event broadcast on local news had shown the exact moment of my shaking the newly-inaugurated President Clinton's hand.

After this experience, returning to Oxford seemed almost anticlimactic, until I realized I had only a few months to write up my dissertation and prepare for final exams. These came all too quickly, but by mid-June the work was done, and when the examination results were finally posted, I was on the list of successful candidates. I'd passed! And suddenly another childhood dream was fulfilled: I had earned a degree in English literature from Oxford University. That meant quite a long night with friends at the King's Arms pub.

My mother came over for the formal commencement ceremony at the grand Sheldonian Theatre, where I and my fellow Univ graduates were ushered before the Vice-Chancellor by the college Dean of Degrees, George Cawkwell. The pomp and splendor of the ceremony was almost overwhelming, and my mother said it was one of the proudest moments of her life.

Before leaving Oxford, the Master announced that I had been awarded one of his "Master's Travel Scholarships"—a fully-funded trip to travel around Britain and visit host families consisting of University College alumni. This was a deep honor as well as a fitting way to end my Oxford experience. As term finally ended, I met with Bill Sykes for one final "Reflection Group."

"It's the end of an era," he said, as I prepared to say good-bye. So it seemed at the time, but I could never have imagined that this was in many ways only the beginning of a much larger journey ahead.

PART III—FULL CIRCLE

If your daily life seems poor, do not blame it;
blame yourself, tell yourself that you are not
poet enough to call forth its riches.

—Rainer Maria Rilke,
Letters to a Young Poet

That it will never come again is what makes
life so sweet.

—Emily Dickinson

13

HOMEWARD BOUND

When I was at home I was in a better place; but travellers must be content.

—Shakespeare, *As You Like It*

Following graduation from Oxford in July '93, and before embarking on my Master's Travel Scholarship, I traveled with my mother to Ireland to visit relatives in Dublin. (My cousin, Donald Noble, had married an Irish girl with whom my mother became close, and her parents warmly welcomed us at their home.) On the way, we visited Wales to attend the Welsh National Festival—the "Eisteddfod"—and then travelled on to Ireland by ferry. It was my first attempt at driving in Britain, and my experience navigating my first "roundabout" was evocative of the film *European Vacation*, when American tourist Chevy Chase becomes trapped interminably in one with his family.

After Dublin, Mom returned home and I visited Galway to experience its famous music scene before heading to Edinburgh for the grand International Arts Festival there. I then traveled around various other places in England, where I'd made arrangements to visit "Old Members" of Univ as part of the Master's Scholarship. Unfortunately, I failed to keep a detailed journal for the Master (the only requirement associated with the travel scholarship), but I did keep all of my receipts as requested and resolved to write the journal afterwards. I would later regret this.

When I finally arrived back home in Little Rock, my parents said I could live at home in the spare bedroom downstairs until a job came through. I was convinced that the White House speechwriting job I'd applied for—or another suitable position in the Clinton administration—would come through soon, and from my encouraging conversations with officials in the office of Presidential Personnel, I had every reason to believe this to be the case. Along with writing samples, I had provided strong, relevant references, and these combined with my campaign experience and new Oxford degree were all in my favor. Meanwhile I enjoyed life at my grandparent's old house on Sunset Drive, with its inspiring view of the river valley just beyond the tops of tall pines along the bluff below our backyard.

I even enjoyed an occasional personal correspondence with the President. I found I could get letters directly to him through the administrator of his "White House Arkansas Office," where President

THE WHITE HOUSE
WASHINGTON

January 26, 1995

Frank H. Thurmond
13 Sunset Drive
Little Rock, Arkansas 72207

Dear Frank:

Thanks for your letter and for letting me know about the first meeting of the Arkansas Branch of the Oxford Society. I passed your letter along to my scheduler, Billy Webster, and asked him to look into your suggestion.

Hillary sends her best regards.

Sincerely,

Bill Clinton

Glad you're doing this.

Letter from President Bill Clinton, January 1995

Clinton had a small version of the Oval Office from which he could work during one of his regular visits to Little Rock. On one occasion, I wrote inviting the President to officially join the local branch of the Oxford Society alumni group, of which I was now in charge. He wrote back to accept my invitation, along with a handwritten note expressing his appreciation of my organizing an Arkansas branch for the society. The President's letters always arrived in a large brown envelope addressed from "The White House, Washington"; and the elegant stationary, headed with "The White House" in bold blue lettering beneath an embossed presidential seal, was centered—and unfolded—on a layer of thick cardboard to facilitate framing. But despite the unique opportunity of this connection, I never mentioned directly to President Clinton my interest in a position with his administration. This, I knew, would have been highly inappropriate, and it was at any rate something I wanted to achieve on my own through the regular channels.

But time continued to pass, and by New Year 1994 I still had no job. Yet whenever I called the White House personnel office, I got the same reply—I needed to be patient; when something became available, they would call me. All I really needed was a simple "yes" or "no": Would I eventually get a job or not? (If not, I could get busy looking elsewhere.) What I got instead was always a frustrating deferment.

In early spring I got a surprise call from Oxford. It was from two of my best friends from the previous year, Dan and Mitsuhiro, but their news from University College was grim. They were calling to inform me that my friend Richard the porter had died of a sudden heart attack. The attack happened as Richard ran up the stairs beyond the Shelley Memorial in response to what turned out to be a false alarm. His funeral had already taken place, and Bill the Chaplain had spoken eloquently of Richard's kindness and popularity within the College. I learned later of his warm send-off by the entire college community.

However, Mitsuhiro had more joyful news: He planned to marry his Tokyo girlfriend in April, and for the sake of his many friends and colleagues in Britain would have the ceremony at University College, with Bill Sykes presiding in the Chapel. Both he and Dan then insisted I had to be there, to which I readily agreed—even though it would all but break me financially to do so. But my unexpected return to Oxford within a year of my departure would prove a bigger adventure than I'd ever bargained for.

I had a month to kill before my trip, and help came unlooked for thanks to the Arkansas Razorbacks' basketball team. They had managed to burst onto the national scene with a near perfect record, dominating their division and then winning out the entire Southeastern

Conference to become the top-ranked team in America. The so-called "March Madness" of the NCAA basketball tournament's "Dance" took the Razorbacks all the way through the "Sweet 16," "Elite 8," "Final Four," and finally down to the National Championship game itself. For each of these games I gathered with friends at a local bar called Pizza D'Action, where the cheering and excitement of "calling the Hogs" nearly blew the roof off the place by the end of the final game. And in that championship game the underdog Razorbacks had to play, of all teams, Coach Mike Krzyzewski's seasoned squad from Duke.

Our coach, Nolan Richardson, had managed to recruit a dream team of the best athletes from mostly local high schools, and now suddenly there they were—alone with #1 ranked Duke on the national stage to vie for the championship. Even President Clinton was in the crowd, the first sitting American President to attend a college basketball championship game. And this game was a whopper, with the two teams so evenly matched that it all came down to the last minute—and whoever had the right combination of strategy and talent (and luck) to prevail in the end. Finally, in the last few seconds of the game, star Razorback Scotty Thurman made a three-pointer that secured the Razorback's victory over Duke in a climactic finish that had President Clinton himself rushing the court to congratulate the team. The whole state of Arkansas was now officially in *Hog Heaven*.

Just before my trip to England, I visited Crossett and told Daddy Frank of my plans as he thoughtfully smoked his pipe. When we said goodbye, as he turned away in his wheelchair, he said—"Kiss lots of pretty girls for me!"

"You can count on me for that, Daddy Frank," I answered. He chuckled warmly as I watched him wheel down the hall and disappear around a corner. It would be the last time I ever saw him.

At Mitsuhiro's request, I brought along my guitar to Oxford and performed at a party the night before the wedding. The next day, following the service in the Chapel, there was a grand feast in an elegant college dining room. There I found myself placed next to the Japanese Ambassador, with whom I had a surprisingly easy time speaking. (Mitsuhiro afterwards admitted he'd seated us together deliberately, confident of my ability to keep the Ambassador entertained.) Once we'd established a mutual literary interest, he spent the dinner quoting haiku by Basho, to which I responded with corresponding quotes by Shakespeare.

The only hitch of the whole occasion came during the formal toast being given by, at Mitsuhiro's request, Dr. Leslie Mitchell. During the course of his—as usual—impeccable toast (Mitchell being rather renowned for his *bons mots*), it became alarmingly obvious to all present that no one had a drink with which to toast. The servers whose job it was to fill the glasses had been taken off guard by the toast, and were now standing aloof at the dining room entrance with full bottles of wine. Observing this, Dr. Mitchell—who had just made a grand pronouncement about the long-standing and respected tradition of hosting Japanese scholars at the college, added: "It is not, however, an Oxford tradition to propose a toast with empty glasses." The servers immediately took their cue, and to his enormous credit Dr. Mitchell managed to extend his toast until the exact moment the very last glass—which happened to be mine—was filled.

The next day was April 23rd. It was an annual treat for me to speak with my grandparents on my birthday, and I made a point to call them. Mama Doris said Daddy Frank was keen to speak with me, and it made my day just to hear their voices.

After that, I went on a "punting expedition" with Dan and other old friends. It was a gloriously green, sunny Oxford spring day, and as we drifted along the placid (apart from a disturbed swan or two) waters of the Cherwell, Dan said he had an idea for me: Come back to Oxford and work on a doctorate. The thought of doing so had never even occurred to me, even though my particular Master of Philosophy (M.Phil.) degree was mainly designed as a stepping stone to an Oxford doctoral degree (D.Phil.). Dan's idea was that, since for my Master's I had researched and written about the use of music in Renaissance drama, why not develop a proposal for a doctoral dissertation in that very subject? Dan was working on a doctoral project in American history, and he went on to share his own interest in the subject of Renaissance musicians and music due to a fascinating discovery he'd made in his work as a professional genealogist: His own family was descended genetically from two interconnected families of famous Renaissance musicians, the Bassanos and the Laniers.

The Bassanos, a family of Italian musicians of apparent Jewish heritage, had been invited to England from Italy by King Henry VIII in his quest to rival other European courts of his day as a bastion of art and music. The Laniers, originally Huguenots who had fled to England, likewise became prominent court musicians. One of them had even married Aemilia Bassano, who as Aemilia Lanier (also Lanyer) is celebrated as one of the first English women poets. The Bassanos are recorded to have performed at the coronation of Elizabeth I, while Aemilia's nephew, Nicholas Lanier, became in turn "Master of the King's Music" for King Charles I—and later, as an old man, in recognition of his loyalty reinstated in that role by Charles II following the Restoration. In the meantime, however, a number of Laniers had fled to Virginia during the English Civil War as Cavaliers escaping the retribution of Cromwell, where they lived throughout the South while continuing their work in music and poetry. Two of them have achieved lasting fame in American letters: The Georgia poet/musician Sidney Lanier, and the dramatist Thomas Lanier Williams (aka Tennessee Williams).

That punting trip down the river would prove fateful in more ways than one.

As I started—regretfully—to prepare for my return home, news came which suddenly shook the college with excitement. During an upcoming trip to France for celebrations commemorating the 50th anniversary of D-Day, President Clinton decided to use the occasion to stop by Oxford to receive the honorary doctorate he'd been offered. It is generally a tradition of Oxford to award such recognition for former students elected as heads of state, and the Master had managed to help convince the University Congregation to do so with Clinton— despite controversy around the fact that the Master himself had helped block approval of an honorary degree for former Prime Minister (and Oxford graduate) Margaret Thatcher. (As the Master put it: "I could not in good conscience so recognize a woman who'd ruined science for Britain"; but in the case of President Clinton: "The problem with Thatcher was that we waited too long to get round to it; let's give it to Clinton before he has a chance to screw up!") Arrangements were made for the President, First Lady, and a delegation of other senior members of the Clinton administration to converge upon Oxford— and University College in particular—for a day. I duly made arrangements to stay in Oxford through this exciting and historical event. After all, I'd nothing better to do back home—and besides I wouldn't have missed it for the world.

When I first saw the Master again during Mitsuhiro's wedding, he expressed his displeasure at my not having yet submitted the journal. "Where's the Master's journal?" he had asked, rather gruffly. I assured him I'd get it done as soon as I got back, but he was implacable. "Humph!" was his only response. Now, as it was the Master himself I'd have to see to request an invitation for the presidential reception he was organizing in the Master's garden, I was loath to approach him. But on the day before the President was due to arrive, I entered the office in the Master's Lodgings, where Elizabeth informed the Master I was there to see him. He did not seem pleased to see me.

"Frank," said the Master, "today I have a list of priorities, on which you're at the bottom!"

I cautiously made my request for the invitation, and he suddenly smiled. "You've done good things for the College," he said, and recalled my delivery of his letter to Governor Clinton that had helped reconnect the Clintons and Oxford. "That worked out remarkably well, I must say," he said, and he promised to include my name on the list.

The next day dawned with brilliant June sunshine, and the crowd of guests—all specially selected by the Master for the event—gathered in the Master's Garden to await the arrival of the President and First Lady. Everyone with an Oxford degree was expected to be dressed in appropriate academic regalia, so I borrowed the colorful accoutrements I'd never expected to wear again after the previous summer's Commencement. When the Secret Service announced they would disguise themselves in Oxford academic dress, the Master put his foot firmly down: "No one may wear Oxford academic attire without possessing an Oxford degree." To everyone's surprise, the Secret Service actually backed down, resorting instead to standing on street corners and at bus stops "disguised" as British gentlemen. (However, given their enormous build and height, nobody would have been fooled even if they weren't wearing ridiculous Victorian bowler hats over their dark shades.) We could, however, spot snipers on the roof, where once again the Master flew the American flag for the occasion. But the Master had to confront the Secret Service yet again when they attempted to frisk, as he hobbled up the steps with his cane, the eminent historian Isaiah Berlin. "Sir Isaiah Berlin is *not* carrying a weapon!" insisted the Master.

The wait in the garden was long indeed, as the President and his entourage were quite late, but no one seemed to mind given the weather, ample refreshments, and the thrill of anticipation. There was a roar overhead as the President's helicopter swooped over with a whir of blades and descended in the direction of Christ Church Meadow. After a few minutes, people began to appear through the back entrance, and there finally were the President and First Lady Clinton themselves. The Master introduced them to a few people there to greet them, including Univ Classics Fellow George Cawkwell and his wife, Pat. Cawkwell, the Dean of Degrees during my own time at Univ, had been Dean of Graduates during Clinton's time there and was, as Clinton says in his autobiography *My Life*, an important advisor.

I managed to catch the Master's eye, and he gestured for me to come forward.

"I believe you know Frank Thurmond from Arkansas?" said the Master. "He worked in your campaign."

"Yes, and he did a super job!" said the President, along with a firm slap on my shoulder.

Hillary Clinton greeted me with a smile, and then threw me for a loop with a question: "So what are you doing now?" asked the First Lady. I stumbled through some reply about traveling before returning home to look for work. I felt a strong temptation to mention my efforts to get a job in the Clinton administration, but very fortunately thought the better of it. Soon afterwards, I got into a conversation with the President's personal aide, to whom I did mention it.

"Oh, then you should speak to George Stephanopoulos, over there," she said, pointing across the garden. So I walked across the garden where Stephanopoulos stood with several people including Robert Reich, who had attended Univ with Clinton as a fellow Rhodes Scholar and was now his Secretary of Labor. (Clinton gives a humorous anecdote in his autobiography concerning his and Reich's reception upon arrival at the college by the celebrated head porter, Douglas Millin.) Also there was a British gentleman I'd met previously named Jonathan Powell, then First Secretary at the British Embassy in Washington. I knew that Stephanopoulos, a senior official in the Clinton administration, had himself attended Balliol College, Oxford, and armed with all this information I was able to join their conversation. I finally mentioned to Stephanopoulos my interest in working in the Administration, and he asked me to write and send my resume directly to him.

The honorary degree ceremony in the Sheldonian was full of Oxford pomp and splendor, and as per tradition the "Public Orator" delivered a speech completely in Latin. When it was President Clinton's turn to speak, he managed to joke about this, saying—"I thought after my recent travels in Europe I was finally in a place where I spoke the language. Yet here I am, just another Yank in Oxford, one step behind."

I managed to join the "Convocation" of Oxford academics as they processed from the Sheldonian into the "Old Convocation House" of the Bodleian Library, where the Chancellor presided over a further reception for the Clintons. Here I had the opportunity to introduce Helen Cooper personally to Hillary Clinton.

Then I saw the President heading across the room in my direction, and when he saw me he held back his hand in what was clearly the beginning of a major high five. I reciprocated, but—just at the moment when our hands were about to collide in mid-air—a hand grabbed the President's arm from behind and jerked it back. We turned to see standing there an otherwise distinguished professor who, clearly unaware of the sacred ritual of the American "high five," now perceived from the angry glare of the President's eyes upon him that he'd just committed an egregious *faux pas*.

"So sorry, terribly sorry!" the don mumbled.

President Clinton turned back to me and gave a regular handshake. (I'd never forgive that old don for screwing up my high five with the Prez.) But there I was standing one on one, for the first time, with the President of the United States, and I could say anything in the world I wanted. But what? Then, in a flash of inspiration, it hit me.

"We're good Razorback fans," I said.

The President grinned. "Sometimes I wish I could just go back to Arkansas and stay there," he said.

I knew then I had gotten it just right.

With President & First Lady Clinton, along with Master Albery and George Cawkwell, at University College, Oxford, June 1994.

14

TEA WITH THE TOLKIENS

When I got home, I was confronted with loss. The moment she greeted me at the airport, I knew my mother had bad news. As we drove home, she told me: A few weeks earlier, Daddy Frank had died. I was immediately grief-stricken.

"Why didn't you tell me?"

"I didn't want to spoil your trip," she said. "And there's nothing you could have done anyway."

"I could have come back for the funeral." We sat in silence the rest of the way home; I was too shocked to ask how he'd died or for details of the funeral. Later I learned that he'd died peacefully, just a few months after celebrating with my grandmother Mama Doris their 70th wedding anniversary, and the funeral had actually been more of a joyous celebration of his long life than a time of mourning. I knew I could at least always treasure my final image of him—sharing an intimate moment of laughter together as I embarked upon my recent journey. I'd forever recall the sound of his voice in our last conversation, as I celebrated my birthday on a fateful day in Oxford.

Mama Doris would follow just a few months later, as if they were truly inseparable. They had been so for over seventy years.

Now, out of money and desperate for a job, I started considering my options. I did write to George Stephanopoulos with my resume, but I'd learned not to get my hopes up in my dealings with Washington and began looking for potential teaching positions. And it wasn't long until I found one: There was a vacancy for a part-time Freshman Composition instructor at a small liberal arts college in northeast Arkansas called Lyon College, and there I would have a full load of classes starting later that summer. By then it would be clear if I'd ever hear anything definite back from Washington (I didn't), and my backup plan was to teach for a year while applying to undertake doctoral studies back at Oxford.

I had a delightful year working among the faculty and students on a beautiful campus in the foothills of the Ozarks. But oddly enough, even though Paragould—the town of my birth and source of my earliest memories—was just a short distance north of me, I never bothered to visit it. For all I knew, my biological father still lived there. (The thought also crossed my mind—disturbingly so—that I may even have further siblings, as closely related as Kate and Will, of whom I knew nothing.) But I recalled my mother's words after my high school graduation that, when the time was right to meet my father, I'd know it. And I knew I was not yet ready to look for him.

I busied myself instead with another Oxford application, this time requiring a detailed exegesis of my proposed research—the dramatic use of music in Shakespeare's plays. Before leaving Oxford during my recent trip, I spoke with several members of the English and Music faculties about my ideas, which had resulted in favorable encouragement. I also had strong references, this time from Dr. Kay himself, who remembered a presentation I'd given during one of his seminars—illustrated with an actual performance of Elizabethan music on my guitar. When I called him to discuss a reference, he said—"Certainly, and I'll tell them you're the man for the job!"

This time I carefully reconsidered my choice of college. Several friends had suggested that, as a doctoral research student, I might find one of the newer and purely postgraduate colleges more suitable both academically and socially. While I feared doing so would seem a kind of betrayal to my friends—especially the Master—at University College, I finally requested a postgraduate college instead and sent my application on its way. As a colleague at Lyon College pointed out, I was precariously "putting all my eggs in one basket." But I had faith that this was somehow meant to be. (Financially it was the only way doctoral work would be possible anyway, given the fact that my two year Master's course counted toward the Oxford doctoral degree, and I'd thus be responsible for only one further year of tuition.)

I managed to make life interesting despite my current small town restrictions. I had by this time racked up enough air miles on the American Airlines frequent flyer program to earn a free trip, which I planned to use for a holiday over Christmas vacation. I could go anywhere within the United States, including Hawaii—or even to various locations in the northern part of Latin America. So I decided to visit the most exotic place possible: Venezuela. This resulted in an adventure worth another book—including a tour of Caracas and a trip to the jungles along the Orinoco River, where from a camp called Canaima I visited the other-worldly landscape and waterfalls around the magnificent Angel Falls.

Sure enough, that spring I did receive another round of acceptance letters from Oxford—first, as before, from the English faculty, and then from a college: this time a small, postgraduate college called St. Cross College that had been recommended by Dan (whose work had involved him with faculty there). I managed in the meantime to secure additional funding in the form of student loans, and I could now look forward to a return to Oxford.

On my first day at St. Cross College, there was an orientation session for new students. Being a purely postgraduate college, most of the students appeared to be from international destinations—and quite a variety at that. Two young men who sat in front of me, one with a baseball cap, seemed to be Americans, and based on my previous experience with Oxford Americans in general—apart from Dan—I had made a note to avoid them. The college had quite a lively bar, however—a bit *too* lively, it would prove—where when I met these two it turned out only one of them (he of the baseball cap) was American and the other a burly Norwegian named Thomas. But upon learning that the American, named Brad, was from Georgia, my innate defenses abruptly fell and I sensed immediately that he would prove as genuinely real as he seemed on first impression. It also ensued that Thomas and Brad both played guitar, and before long I even had us a gig at a local pub on Walton Street in the section of Oxford known as "Jericho"—once the hub of a Victorian factory and accompanying red light district, but now a trendy student residential area of pubs and restaurants and the headquarters of the Oxford University Press.

The pub was just around the corner from my college accommodation in Wellington Square (in a house where—I'd been told—the poet Philip Larkin once lived). I had gotten to know the proprietor of the pub, an Irishman named Noel Reilly (himself worthy of a character in a novel in his own right) just as he managed to rile up locals by changing the name of the pub from its original "Prince of Wales" to "Jude the Obscure"—playing on references to Oxford's Jericho in Hardy's novel. Noel made me his new pub's official "music manager" and asked me to organize events. So the first performance I organized was that of myself, Brad, and Thomas performing a variety of rock covers with our acoustic guitars. In compensation, Noel said that each Sunday afternoon we performed we would receive 40 pounds and 20 pints of beer. This ensured at least a small crowd of "fans" from the college, and a group of British friends named Mike, Alex, Chris, and Manoj—along with a Brazilian called Adolfo—happily imbibed free beer all afternoon while cheering us on.

The first year of my doctoral work included a number of required seminars and classes, in which students were expected to share their initial research with one another in the form of presentations. I found once again the virtues of being able to illustrate my discussion of the relationship between Renaissance poetry and music through an actual performance to accompany my essay. But this time, instead of merely playing transcriptions of Renaissance lute music on the guitar, I took it a step further: I learned to play the lute itself.

There was a Fellow at St. Cross College named Hélène La Rue, a charming woman who was at that time curator of the Bate Collection of Historical Instruments at the Music Faculty. When Dr. La Rue heard about my field of study, she said they had a Renaissance lute on display in their stringed instrument section and invited me to see it. (While there are no fully intact surviving lutes from the period, this was an exact replica.) Then, after I told her of my desire actually to play the lute as part of my overall project, she went so far as to loan me the instrument indefinitely. As she put it, "We much prefer our instruments actually to make music rather than gather dust behind the display cases." I was then referred by the eminent Oxford musicologist John Caldwell to a local lutenist and teacher named Christopher Morrongiello, who helped me make the surprisingly challenging transition from guitar technique to that required for the lute.

My debut as a lutenist came when it was my turn to present my research to the class, and it was so well received that I felt afterwards I could have gotten by without an essay at all. What mattered most was the bringing to life of the Renaissance world that my lute so strikingly symbolized.

At the end of my first year, I had a run-in with the Domestic Bursar of St. Cross College—a rather notorious figure among students when it came to various issues of student welfare—and remembered wistfully my days at University College. I had visited once or twice for dinner, and as feared was all but accused of treachery by certain Fellows for having chosen a different college upon my return to Oxford. On one occasion, when Dr. Helen Cooper invited me to dine as her guest at the High Table in the college's 17th century Hall (and to perform my lute afterwards for Fellows and guests in the Senior Common Room), there was an ugly scene the moment I was spotted by the Master.

"Frank!" he said, with raised voice from across the room, "where's the Master's Journal?" Before I could reply, he proceeded to lambast me in front of all present until suddenly Alexander Murray, the college Medieval History scholar, came to my rescue.

"Master, Frank's got a good spirit. I've heard him play his guitar."

"He's got a good spirit," concurred the Master, still glaring at me. "But he's weak in the flesh!"

Fortunately, just then the Steward announced that dinner was served, and we filed behind the Master into the Hall. I was not invited to sit in the place of honor.

So when I pondered attempting to transfer, I knew I couldn't approach Univ without the Master's Journal in hand. Fortunately, I had brought all my notes and receipts from the trip (now almost two years hence), and sat one day in the St. Cross Library and wrote it all out from memory. I then made an appointment through Elizabeth to see the Master, and when I arrived at the Master's Lodgings in Univ was glad to find him in good spirits. It was also clear he'd already enjoyed a breakfast cocktail or two.

He was certainly pleased to be at last presented the Master's Journal, which he said he looked forward to reading before depositing it permanently in the college library. And when I broached the possibility of returning to Univ, he waxed ecstatic.

"Elizabeth, call the University Admissions office forthwith to enquire of the necessary arrangements. Tell them the Master wants Frank back!"

I was soon back in the St. Cross Bursar's office informing the Bursar of my desire to transfer to Univ. He stared at me incredulously for a few moments. "They'll never let you," he said. "It's simply not done."

I pulled out an official letter from a distinguished University College professor then serving as Tutor for Admissions, and handed it to the Bursar. He sat back in disbelief as he read the letter accepting me back into Univ.

Now back in the Univ graduate common room, that fall I was asked to help organize another election night party, this time in hopes (for the Master and most of the college at any rate) of celebrating President Clinton's reelection. Our guest of honor was former Senator and presidential candidate Gary Hart, who was in Oxford undertaking doctoral research. Dan was there, as well as Brad and Thomas whom I'd invited from St. Cross. I'd arranged for the Master to greet Senator Hart when he arrived, and when Hart entered the room I introduced him to the Master. Hart soon had more than he'd apparently bargained for when he made what might have seemed elsewhere an innocent (and *apropos*) comment.

"I understand," said Hart, "that University College is one of the oldest colleges in Oxford."

"Humph!" came the reply, and Dan and I could sense what was coming as the Master stood up tall and began to rock back and forth on his feet.

"It's not just *one* of the oldest colleges in Oxford," the Master exclaimed. "'Tis *the* oldest college!" The Master's exuberance took Hart by surprise, and he took a quick step back with a look of dismayed bewilderment. Fortunately the election results started coming in, and everyone gathered around the television.

Brad was a Republican, and we'd had some heated political debates over rounds of snooker and beer at the Oxford Union. I'd found it refreshing and helpful to debate American politics with a friend of opposing views, sharpening my own in the process—whether it be such issues as the environment, health care, or gun control. Despite my pride in my old Winchester shotgun, in recent years the trigger-happy nature of American society—including a recent spate of horrendous school shootings (one even close to home in Jonesboro, Arkansas)—convinced me that something must be done to stop the barbaric slaughter wreaked on innocent civilians by uncontrolled gun ownership. I also knew that, despite National Rifle Association propaganda, the type of "gun control" being advocated (an effort to curtail assault weapons in the hands of criminals) posed no threat whatsoever to Americans' constitutional right to bear arms—including hunting rifles such as mine.

Yet over time Brad did succeed in making me more conservative in certain respects (primarily economics) even as I helped liberalize his own views in others. But to Brad's dismay this night was to be, again, Bill Clinton's, and it was not without a clear sense of irony that we celebrated Bill Clinton's victory with Gary Hart.

That year I moved into privately rented accommodation elsewhere in Oxford. It was a part of the city where I'd heard numerous "celebrity" academic and literary figures lived, including the reclusive film director Stanley Kubrick and *Inspector Morse* mystery author Colin Dexter, who frequented the nearby Dewdrop Inn and joined me for a memorable High Table dinner at Univ one evening. But I also heard that another neighbor was in fact the daughter of one of my favorite authors, J.R.R.

Tolkien. As a kid I'd read *The Letters of J.R.R. Tolkien*, and so I was familiar with the names of Tolkien's immediate family in addition to his son Christopher (who had edited *The Silmarillion* and other literary as well as academic work by his father). I wrote a letter to Priscilla Tolkien introducing myself as a neighbor and a fan of her father's work, and to my great surprise she invited me to come for tea one afternoon.

Her house was just around the corner from where I lived, and when I arrived she greeted me warmly and took me out to her back garden. There she gave me a tour of her impressive variety of flowers then in full early spring blossom. She had set out a table with a teapot and cups, and showed me to a comfortable lawn chair; as I settled into it, I nearly fell right back out when she explained the chair in which I was sitting had been her father's favorite chair when he visited her there in the garden. I felt the same sense of awe when she said the teaspoon I was using, its stem shaped in the form of a dragon, was likewise J.R.R. Tolkien's favorite and that he'd even made up a legend about it. She then served a tray of homemade scones she'd made for the occasion, and I realized that this was in fact my first ever proper English tea. And how appropriate, I thought, that I was enjoying it along with some of the most stimulating conversation I'd yet experienced in Oxford courtesy of Ms. Tolkien. Especially gratifying was when she said: "My father would have liked you." Then she added, "He too was a Romantic."

A few months later, I received an invitation from Priscilla to attend an event she was hosting for the Tolkien Society to commemorate the 23rd anniversary of the author's death, at which she hoped I might also be willing to perform on my lute. But on top of this she said she wanted to include me as her guest in a small Tolkien family dinner after the party. She also said I was welcome to bring a guest along, so I invited Brad—himself a doctoral student of Anglo-Saxon literature—knowing of his own love of Tolkien's work.

When we arrived, we saw through the window of Priscilla's house a group of people sitting around an elderly gentleman puffing a pipe and telling stories.

"It looks like the Professor himself decided to turn up for his party," said Brad. It turned out that that the gentleman was in fact the author's eldest son, Father John Tolkien, and he was recounting his memories of his father reading to his children as a bedtime story what would ultimately become *The Hobbit*. Outside in the garden, Priscilla showed me to a bench set up under a "favorite tree" of her father's, where I could perform my lute music as guests enjoyed refreshments. For a fleeting moment as I struck the delicate strings of the lute, whose sounds resonated from the pear-shaped wooden body of the instrument to bring forth melodies from four centuries past, I felt I'd entered a portal into Middle-earth itself—for if it existed anywhere beyond the fantastic realm of its author's imagination, it was here in his daughter's secluded Oxford garden that he himself loved so well.

Afterwards, Priscilla took Brad and me to a local Italian restaurant, where we joined Father John and a small group of other family members and friends for a lively meal which included, at its heart, a toast in memory of the Professor.

"To J.R.R.," said Priscilla, holding up her glass.

"To J.R.R.!" we all answered, and for Brad and me it seemed a moment from a dream.

15

ATONEMENT

The woods are lovely, dark and deep,
But I have promises to keep,
And miles to go before I sleep,
And miles to go before I sleep.

—Robert Frost, "Stopping by Woods on a Snowy Evening"

In the summer of '97, I returned to Little Rock for a particularly special occasion. My sister Kate married her fiancé Jason (a wonderful gentleman whom she'd met at college) in a beautiful ceremony in grand Southern style—including an elegant reception attended by all of my beloved surviving Crossett relatives. But back in Oxford, as my 30th birthday came and went, the beginnings of a deep depression began to take hold. At the heart of this, I finally realized, was the fact that I was entering an important new phase of life and yet had still not resolved the question of my birth father. I began to feel tormented, for the first time in my life, by the hole left in my sense of self by growing up without an inkling of who (or where) the man who sired me was. I didn't so much as know if he was even still alive, and I wondered again whether he may have had further children whom I might also call siblings.

In brooding upon these thoughts, I turned increasingly to alcohol—an easy thing to do in Oxford, where the culture of drink among both students and faculty can seem at times as intrinsic as books and learning. And along with this I sought consolation through a series of superficial relationships, another easy thing to do given the frequency of social events—from college bar "bops" to extravagant, all night black-tie balls.

I realized with disgust that this wasn't a reflection at all of who I wanted to be—of who indeed I *had* once been—but that it was nevertheless the face I was presenting to my new friends and everyone around me. Occasionally, however, someone who had known me years earlier would comment that I seemed to have changed—and negatively, too. I became increasingly aware of the fact that I seemed to have lost my way. And I was desperate to get back on the path upon which I had set out—including my ideals and my love of pursuing knowledge and creative expression for its own sake. But for now, at least, the flame seemed to have burnt completely out. Despite the genuine friends around me, I still couldn't bring myself to discuss with anyone the deep despair swirling within my heart.

It was just at this time that the phone rang out of the blue one bright spring afternoon. The call was from my mother, and she had a message for me from my birth father.

As I sat in the rose-filled garden of Wellington Square reflecting upon my life, seeing the course of it play out in a tapestry of images recounting a narrative I'd almost forgotten, I nearly lost track of the time. 2:55! The call from my father was set for 3:00, so I ran around the corner and upstairs to my room and sat staring, breathless, at the phone on my desk. A thousand thoughts ran through my mind at once. What would he say? What would *I* say? At any other point in my life, I'd have had a thousand questions ready at hand. Now, moments before the call I'd both longed for and dreaded over the course of my entire life, I suddenly felt at a loss for words. But then, at exactly 3:00, the phone rang. When I picked up the receiver, the voice on the other end was that of Robert Mitchell, my birth father.

I tried to act and sound as if this were just any casual phone conversation with an old acquaintance. I could never have prepared myself for the emotional maelstrom upon hearing, as a grown man, the voice of the father I'd never known. But it was a voice in pain, this I could tell. He was in the advanced stage of lung cancer, and—whether because of this or the context or perhaps a bit of both—his words did not come easily. I found myself doing most of the talking, and what he wanted to know was how I'd spent the last 30 years of my life. This I tried to answer in a nutshell, and he seemed impressed that I was currently living in England and studying at Oxford. He had been to England himself, he said, to indulge an amateur interest in archaeology.

Finally he asked what seemed like an odd question, but it seemed important to him: "Girls or boys?" It took me a moment to gather he was interested in my sexual orientation.

"Strictly girls," I answered. "And I've been pretty successful too."

"You ever been married?"

"I nearly married a Russian girl once, but the relationship proved a disaster."

"Never marry a girl east of Vienna," he replied. I laughed, but realized I had no idea what he meant.

He then abruptly changed the subject. "Do you smoke?" he asked.

"Only sometimes, when I've had a few drinks."

"Don't," he said, and as if by illustration fell into a fit of coughing. "It's not worth it, let me tell you. I quit smoking ten years ago, but it still caught up with me now."

I could tell it was getting difficult for him to continue the conversation, and I recalled Brad's advice that I must try to meet my father at all cost. Despite my fear of rejection even at the last, I told him I wanted to fly home to Arkansas and meet him. He answered that this wouldn't be necessary. Yet there was something in his voice that seemed uncertain. So I said again that I really meant it—I wanted us to meet while we still could.

"If you want to come," he answered, "we'll be glad to have you."

Since I knew that in a matter of days it would be too late, I went immediately to a travel agency and booked the trip. During the flight home, I thought mostly about what I would say to Dad. I had asked my mother to ensure that he, Kate and Will were all present for dinner on the night before my journey to Hot Springs, and I knew I had this one chance to express things just right. The weight of this challenge felt almost overwhelming; in our whole life together as a family, the subject of my biological father had not come up even once in conversation—not even after Dad formally adopted me, and never with Kate and Will. But I'd always felt it as a topic hovering just beneath the surface, waiting for the moment when it (or my birth father himself) would suddenly and unexpectedly appear. And that moment was now.

As we sat around the formal dining table enjoying casual conversation about my latest adventures abroad, the sense of expectancy was palpable. Everyone knew why I suddenly returned home, but the onus was on me to bring it up. Finally, I did. I explained that I'd learned my birth father was on his death bed with a matter of days to live, and that I'd decided I must meet him before he died to close this empty gap in my life. Then I turned and looked at Dad.

"I want you to know that I'm only meeting him because he's my biological father, and that I have to do this before he dies. But it's you I consider my real father. You're the only one who was there for me. You've always been, and always will be, my only true father."

Dad nodded with understanding. "You're doing the right thing, son," he said. "You need this sense of closure."

My old friend Robert offered to travel with me to Hot Springs so I wouldn't have to journey there alone. We drove up the day before my appointment with my father and stayed the night in a hotel on beautiful Lake Hamilton. The next morning we drove to the house where my father had lived with his girlfriend and her family for many years. I was greeted in the front yard by a man of about my own age named Randall.

"I know exactly what you're experiencing," he said. "I met my own birth father later in life too." By the time we entered the house, Randall explained how he had instead been brought up as a son by my biological father. (My father had otherwise had no further children.) I was still processing this when I was greeted at the door by Randall's mother, Monica. She welcomed me graciously and led me into the living room, where several other women—including Randall's wife and sister—waited.

"He's in the back room," said Monica. "He's expecting you." Robert waited with Randall as I followed Monica into the back of the house. We entered the back room, and there he was, sitting in a chair waiting for me. Randall had quickly explained that the only reason my father wasn't in a hospital bed hooked up to a ventilator was that he'd wanted to meet me with dignity. So they'd had the machine set up here, next to his chair.

Monica showed me to a seat and then discreetly left the room. I didn't know what to say, but I knew an attempt at small talk would seem, under the circumstances, bathetic. But he spoke first.

"You're studying English literature?"

I could tell from his voice that his health had already declined rapidly in the three days since we had last spoken.

"Yes, I'm studying medieval and Renaissance drama."

Then to my surprise he began to recite Chaucer in Middle English:

Whan that April with his showres soote
The droughte of March hath perced to the roote . . .

I suddenly realized the room we were in was a private study full of books. There were books everywhere, with every imaginable title from Dostoevsky to Chomsky to a treatise on the art of growing marijuana.

He told me of his archaeological research in England and showed me photographs from his travels. He then commended me for my academic success, and said he'd been pleased to hear it.

"I guess you gave me some good genes," I said.

"You got your genes from your mother."

Then he finally asked me about her. I told him what a wonderful mother she had been to me, and how she'd encouraged and supported me in my every endeavor throughout my life. And now he revealed that he had in fact once made an effort to contact me, many years earlier, when I was still a young boy. Monica had even turned up at our house on Cleveland Street to discuss this with my mother, and said she'd greeted me as I was playing outside. My mother, however, had refused his overture, and asked that he not try to contact me again. Suddenly he began coughing violently, and Monica rushed into the room to adjust the ventilator. It was clear that conversation was becoming extremely difficult for him.

I looked into his eyes and was struck by a strange sense of familiarity, and then realized they seemed the mirror image of my own. But his eyes betrayed something else too—something he would finally express before we said goodbye. I told him I'd brought my guitar in case he'd like to hear some of my music, and he said that he would. "Play for everybody," he said. So Robert brought in my guitar, and everyone present gathered around as I described my studies on the classical guitar and gave a short recital.

"Can you play any Deep Purple?" my father asked. I complied with some of the first chords any rock guitar player learns: The opening of "Smoke on the Water." When I looked up, my father was applauding with a smile.

It seemed an appropriate moment for bringing the visit to a close. I told my father how glad I was finally to have met him. I told him that I would one day write about our meeting, so that this occasion (and he) would not be forgotten. It was now my turn to quote poetry, and I recalled two lines which seemed to fit the sentiment perfectly:

> So long as men can breathe, or eyes can see,
> So long lives this, and this gives life to thee.

My father nodded. Then I said: "I want you to know that as you are my father, I love you."

I started to leave, but he seemed to be struggling to summon up one last word so I waited.

"Don't die bitter," he said. Then he looked deeply into my eyes before saying the last words I would ever hear from him:

"I regret."

With this he abruptly dropped his chin to his chest with a look of final resignation. As I turned away my eyes filled with tears, and when they saw my face the women in the room began to weep. Randall accompanied me outside where Robert was waiting at the car, and I thanked him for helping make my visit such a warm one. Then Monica came out and embraced me, and said she had something for me from my father.

"He insisted on this." She handed me a check to cover the cost of my trip from London. On the check he had written: "For love and travel."

The next day Randall called to say that my father had died that night. It was if he had held on just long enough for my visit. The funeral was, as he'd wished, meant to be a highly informal affair and an old friend from Paragould would preside over a ceremony on the banks of the White River in north Arkansas—where my father had always enjoyed fly fishing for trout. There his ashes would be scattered over the water. But he'd warned in advance—alluding to a scene from the movie *The Big Lebowski*: "Just be careful about the wind so I don't come right back at you."

After the ceremony, I met a previously unknown Aunt named Kaye—my father's sister—who lived with her husband Herky in Jackson, Mississippi. (I later got to know them better while living for a time in Jackson, along with the additional pleasure of making the acquaintance of my first cousin Mitchell, the son of Kaye and Herky and a gentleman of around my own age.) Randall offered to take me to Paragould to visit for the first time since I'd left the house of my infancy. There I understood why the old house made such an impression that I'd seen it in dreams for many years afterward. The 1930s era house was of such striking architecture, it had even just recently been nominated to the National Register of Historic Places. According to the National Registry, the house "set the standard for a surprising number of Spanish Colonial Revival-style residences. With its stuccoed exterior, low-pitched clay tile roof, arched window grills, second-story overhand and hieroglyphic [Mayan] fireplace tile, the Beisel-Mitchell House is a textbook example of a Spanish Colonial Revival-style residence." Perhaps this explained, I thought, my affinity for Spanish architecture (especially given my vivid memory of the red clay tile roof—something I'd innately appreciated while in Spain).

Finally, Randall said my father had left something for me. He'd been worried about what to do with all his books, and at the end said he was pleased to find he had a son who read.

"He spent the last few days of his life trying to tie up all the loose ends before you arrived," Randall explained. "We told him he should just rest and save energy, and that we'd take care of everything. Yet he insisted, and just kept saying—*but I have promises to keep.*"

I smiled, and said I'd be happy to have my father's books. Then I recited softly to myself: *And miles to go before I sleep.*

That night, when I told my mother about the experience of meeting my father, she agreed that going to meet him had been the right thing to do after all. And after a lifetime of repressed questions, I was at last able to speak openly with her about my father and the reasons for their separation right at the start of my life—thanks in large part, as it turned out, to his alcoholic and often abusive behavior.

By the time I left Little Rock on a flight back to England, I felt an overwhelming sense of life having come full circle. Yet I couldn't help but wonder how my life would have turned out if—just if—I'd gotten to know Robert Mitchell in my youth.

16

A Royal Celebration

When I got back to England, everything appeared in a new light. Summer had come, and the sun glowed warmly yellow upon the ancient sandstone of Oxford's majestic buildings. Inside I felt like a heavy weight had at last been lifted, as if I were truly free to live my life fully for the first time. And what a year I had in store.

The year 1999 was the 750th anniversary of the foundation of University College—having been established in the year 1249 with a benefaction from a northern cleric, William of Durham, who bequeathed money for maintaining "ten or eleven or twelve needy Masters of Arts" in their study of divinity. Now, a year of rather extravagant celebrations was being presided over by the college's new Master, Sir Robin Butler (now Lord Butler), who was elected after John Albery's retirement.

During the course of the year, I'd realized that my funding (primarily in the form of student loans) would barely last the year, and it was clear I'd not be able to afford the further years necessary to complete my research and write up my doctoral dissertation. On a friend's advice, I therefore began applying for teaching positions at schools through an international teacher recruitment agency. Meanwhile, I had a part-time job teaching creative writing at the Oxford Centre for Medieval and Renaissance Studies, an organization associated with Keble College.

The rest of my time was devoted primarily to music, including performing at pubs and at college balls and parties with Brad and a Univ friend named Tom. During a previous visit over the Christmas holidays with Brad and his family in New Orleans, he and I had enjoyed a night out on Bourbon Street. We now began calling our little band "Bourbon Street" and began getting regular gigs around Oxford.

One of these performances was at the University College 750th Anniversary Commemoration Ball—at which the Domestic Bursar of the college, Elizabeth Crawford, asked me to perform on my lute. I also assisted a couple of British friends, playwright Nick Thomas (aka Thomo) and composer Nick Kenworthy-Browne, with the production of a musical called *Jericho Place*. This led to the memorable opportunity of dining with lyricist Tim Rice when he visited the Oxford Union that spring.

By this time, I'd also made a remarkable discovery, thanks to my friend Dan and his work as a professional genealogist. Through his research (combined with that of my Aunt Blanche on my own family) we discovered that an ancestor of mine, Nicholas Lanier, had been "Master of the King's Musick" for King Charles I. My connection with the Laniers—who had come to America during the English Civil War and lived throughout the South—was through my maternal grandmother's side: Mama Doris' own grandmother, Sarah Brewer Noble, was a descendant of Sarah Lanier Brewer. It was through her line that

Sarah Brewer Noble, wife of Mark Noble, as a young woman.

I found myself genetically descended from the famous Lanier family of musicians about whom Dan had already done so much research (see p. 197). He now established that not only were he and I in fact cousins, but I was also in the rather bizarre situation of learning that my skill on the lute performing 17th century music was in direct parallel with that of the livelihood of my own ancestors—including the Laniers and the Italian Bassanos (who'd performed in the court of Elizabeth I).

On top of this was the fact that, during the English Civil War, Nicholas Lanier was based in Oxford when the king had set up his court there, in nearby Christ Church College. So here I was, 350 years later, playing the same music on the same type of instrument in the same exact place! And it was naturally an awesome experience to discover I was somehow interconnected with the very people and music I'd been passionately drawn to as a schoolboy before ever leaving the narrow confines of Arkansas. There seemed something almost atavistic about it all.

By the time of the college ball, word had already gotten around college about this discovery, and when he heard me play my lute the Master said: "Frank, how would you like to perform on your lute for the Queen?"

Everyone knew that the Queen was due to visit the college in May as the highlight of the celebrations. I, like most students, was simply hoping for a glimpse of royalty. But now I found myself actually preparing to be presented to Her Majesty in person, along with a musical performance.

When the big day arrived, I had been versed in advance in royal protocol: The first time one is addressed by the Queen, the appropriate response should include "Your Majesty"; after that, it's generally "yes Ma'am" or "no Ma'am," something I could easily remember as a well-bred Southerner. The Master had organized a reception in the Master's Garden for college fellows and various distinguished guests, and he'd asked me to perform appropriately Elizabethan pieces on my lute as the Queen and Prince Philip entered the garden from the Master's Lodgings. (I felt a strange sense of déjà vu too, as this was the same spot where five years earlier I'd greeted President and Mrs. Clinton in May '94.)

As I sat on the garden bench warming up, the thrill I experienced upon first seeing the Queen is indescribable. As the Master and Lady Butler escorted the Queen and Prince Philip into the garden, I continued performing as I heard the Master introducing me. Then on cue I stood up as the Queen came towards me with her outstretched, white-gloved hand. I took her hand gently and then bowed slightly with my lute, feeling in my colorful academic regalia like a medieval minstrel if there ever was one. The Queen was dressed in a bright yellow suit, complemented with a yellow hat to match.

Then the Queen asked: "Is that a real Elizabethan lute?"

"No, Your Majesty," I replied. "This is a replica, as there are no surviving complete Elizabethan lutes."

This had gone well, but then Prince Philip—sporting, as an Honorary Fellow of the college, the official Univ tie and looking curiously at my lute—decided to offer a comment of his own.

"I think they've got some complete Elizabethan lutes at the Victoria and Albert Museum," said the Prince.

I suppose, to be politically correct, I should have simply said "Oh yes, you're right, Your Royal Highness, in fact there are." But instead I waxed academic, and proceeded to explain that there were no, in fact, completely intact Renaissance lutes. Having just contradicted the Prince added an element of tension to the proceedings, but fortunately the Master—a consummate diplomat—stepped in, and I was greatly relieved that his comment appeared to side with me in the matter.

"Surely the wooden frame wouldn't have survived that long," said the Master. Then the Queen tactfully changed the subject to allow me a graceful exit:

"But you *were* playing Elizabethan music then?"

With the Queen, Prince Philip, and the Master of University College, Lord Butler, at University College, Oxford, May 1999.

"Yes, Ma'am," I replied, and with a pleasant laugh the royal couple continued on their way to the garden party. I sat back on the bench with my lute, took a deep breath, and smiled knowing I'd just had yet another extraordinary experience to treasure a lifetime.

Soon afterwards I finally got a job: I was offered a teaching position in Greece, at the American School in Thessaloniki. I accepted in a heartbeat. I'd always wanted to visit Greece but had not had the opportunity to do so. Now, not only would I visit that glorious country, but I would be there on a full three-year contract. This was an adventure I could not refuse, and later that summer I bid farewell to my Oxford friends and headed off on what would prove yet another grand adventure, in a strikingly unique city at the "crossroads of the world"—where, from my balcony, I could see in the distance the majestic silhouette of Mt. Olympus itself.

But thereto hangs another tale altogether.

Afterword: Coming Home

We write to taste life twice, in the moment and in retrospection.

—Anaïs Nin,
The Diary of Anaïs Nin, Vol. 5

Follow your bliss . . . and doors will open up for you. The world will come to help.

—Joseph Campbell, *The Hero's Journey*

Midway through life's journey, I found myself lost
In a dark wood . . .

Midway through life's journey. For the poet, this meant the ripe age of thirty-five, seventy being the presumed life span in medieval Italy (depending largely on one's luck in avoiding the plague). Like the poet, I find myself at similar cross-roads. I began this memoir on the occasion of my 42nd birthday, when the density both of past experience and that of the anticipated but uncertain future weighed as heavily as the shadow-enshrouded boughs of Dante's allegorical forest. Yet it is the past upon which I've found myself dwelling at this juncture in life, and this book is an account of my first 32 years—a time during which I accumulated a number of experiences I've long been encouraged by friends finally to set down in writing. I delayed doing so, however, for reasons perhaps expressed best by Henry Miller in his *Nexus*: "In some deep, forgotten pit were buried all the thoughts and experiences which I might properly call my own, and which were certainly unique, but which I lacked the courage to resuscitate." I finally did find the courage to summon up remembrance of things past, and while the end result may seem at times rather anecdotal in nature, this is in large part a reflection of my life itself.

It must be noted that in the wake of several recent veracity-challenged memoirs, I have as a rule included only material that can be readily documented. I have likewise followed a principle of strict accuracy in my account, only changing the occasional name here and there as necessary for reasons of personal privacy. In the case of dialogue, I have used it only when I'm confident that what I am quoting is as reasonably accurate (if not word for word) as memory will permit. (There will no doubt be occasional discrepancies with the memories of others present during specific events.)

Last, it should be noted that a primary motive for writing this memoir is my hope that the reader may find vicariously, through my own experiences, something that is ultimately inspiring—and, maybe, even cathartic.

I returned one day to Crossett and to the pond where I'd found such magic as a boy. The snakes were gone, but as I stared out into the familiar black water, I wondered if there were still any catfish beneath the dark surface. I wept there with compassion for my mother's suffering—she had been diagnosed with Alzheimer's. Following a period of reflective meditation, I perceived the true essence of my life-long quest for a "Renaissance ideal" in life: Through the steadfast pursuit of knowledge, creative artistic expression, and the celebration of life through love, I could seek to enrich not only my own life but the lives of others as well. I finally realized that true meaning comes from living to help others above devotion to oneself.

It is a simple but powerful philosophy, and one expressed over two millennia ago in the words attributed to King Solomon in *Ecclesiastes*:

> There is nothing better for a man, than that he should eat and drink, and that he should make his soul enjoy good in his labour . . . Whatsoever thy hand findeth to do, do it with thy might; for there is no work, nor device, nor knowledge, nor wisdom, in the grave, whither thou goest.

—*Ecclesiastes* 2:24 and 9:10

Amen.

Little Rock, Arkansas
April 23, 2011

APPENDIX: ORIGINS

My mother was christened Barbara Ann Hancock. According to a history of the family published by my late aunt, Blanche Hancock Turlington, "Hancock" is a medieval English name derived from Flemish *Hann* (Johan or John) in combination with the Middle English suffix "cok" (Old English "cocc"), connoting a "male bird or fowl" and indicative of proud youth. The name eventually became "Handcock" or "Hancock." By the time William the Conqueror created the first census and tax schedules of the Anglo-Saxons some twenty years after subduing England in 1066, the name "Handcock" appeared in his ledgers.

My aunt's research discovered that the progenitor of our Hancock line in America (now confirmed by genetic testing through a national family tree DNA project) was William Hancock, born circa 1580 in Devonshire, England. William Hancock is listed among the "corporators" of the Second Charter of King James I in 1609, as being one of the "adventurers" who helped found the Virginia Company of London. He is recorded as having invested a substantial sum into the treasury for this endeavor. Along with 39 other passengers, Hancock sailed from London for Virginia on September 16, 1619 aboard a ship called *The Margrett of Bristow* (Bristol), and after a rough voyage dropped anchor in Chesapeake Bay on November 30th. The first entry in the record of an old Family Bible provides this report:

> In the year 1620, Wm. Hancock, in search of forest for his building of ships embarked for ye plantations, being one of the company owners thereof, leaving his familie in England. On the 22nd of March 1622, he, with others, was massacred by ye savages at Thor-

pe's House, Berkeley Hundreds, fifty miles from Charles City. In 1630, Augustin, son and heir of William, came to claim the estate, and died, leaving children.

My aunt traced our line through three centuries from these early New World colonial pioneers, documenting the family history over the course of ten generations from their beginnings in Virginia, South Carolina and Georgia to the present, including their participation in the American Revolution and the Civil War. My great grandfather, Jesse Bowden Hancock, wrote an account of his experience in a field hospital following the Civil War Battle of Sharpsburg (Antietam), where he was severely wounded in both legs by shrapnel:

> I was wounded badly at Sharpesburg [sic] in my legs. My sister, Salley, came the day before they were to cut my legs off. I told her where the swords were kept and she went and got two and slipped

Lt. Jesse B. Hancock, CSA

them out. When they came the next morning to amputate my legs, we both drew our swords on them, and today I limp only in one leg slightly.

He returned to Georgia to recuperate, and was cited by General D.H. Hill for bravery on the battlefield and awarded a field commission as first Lieutenant. (He was later awarded the Southern Cross of Honor.) After recovering, Jesse returned to his unit to participate in the bloody three-day battle at Gettysburg, in which General Robert E. Lee was forced to retreat to Virginia. Although the wounds he received at Antietam were the most serious, he was inflicted with further wounds at Gettysburg and other battles. (His wife later said there was hardly an unscarred spot on his body.) At the end of the war, Jesse Hancock was on special assignments by General Lee for the Confederacy, and was at home again on wounded furlough when the war ended in 1865.

He later became involved with work for the local Democratic Party in Henry County, Alabama, during the period leading up to the 1872 election. Around this time, some "outrageous" acts committed by Union soldiers (part of a campaign of voter intimidation) at the homes of various local citizens during nighttime hours, including—according to the October 25 *Henry County Register*—having "violated with their ruffian presence the sleeping chamber of two young ladies"—led to Jesse and some comrades taking matters into their own hands. He later described the incident as "some trouble in town one night," in which following an exchange of gunfire with Union soldiers he and other Confederate veterans were forced to flee the territory on horseback with Federal troops in pursuit. He spent the next few years as an outlaw, constantly alert and on the move, occasionally getting work as a cowboy. This eventually led him into Indian Territory (Oklahoma), where one night he had a close call: While sitting around the campfire with fellow cowboys, a group of Indians attempted to steal their horses, resulting in the near loss of all their possessions.

During that time, Jesse avoided living on main roads or ever having his name on a mailbox, lest he be recognized by a Federal lawman or bounty hunter. Finally, however, the U.S. Government issued a blanket pardon to Confederate veterans, and he returned to Alabama to see his mother, sisters and other family. Jesse eventually married Bettie Richardson, who as a child had lost her father, also a Civil War soldier, during the war. They met while Jesse worked as an overseer on a plantation in Arkansas, and settled near Bettie's home in Ashley County. He died in Wilmar, Arkansas, on September 3, 1912.

His son (and my grandfather), Frank Askew Hancock, was born in Milo, Arkansas, on October 2, 1896. He relished the opportunity to learn at school, and could still in his late nineties recite poetry—especially that of Longfellow— memorized as a boy. And as a member of the Crossett High School track team, he would be the first local athlete to win a state track gold medal after winning first place in the 880-yard run. He left school prematurely in 1917 at the outbreak of World War I to enlist (along with his twin brother Fred) in the U.S. Army. His regiment was posted in France and participated in heavy fighting when the Allied Forces broke through the fortified Hindenburg line, for which he later received medals for the battles of St. Mihiel, Meuse-Argonne, and the Defensive Sector after fighting to prevent German forces from mounting another offensive. After the Armistice took effect at 11:00 A.M. on the 11th day of the 11th month of 1918, my grandfather shipped back to the United States and finally returned home to Arkansas in February 1919. He would spend the rest of his days as a farmer, but at the end of his life became obsessed with recalling his war experiences, giving me as a child the opportunity (and the honor) of hearing a WWI veteran's stories firsthand. (He also shared with me his old handwritten journal he'd written in the trenches.)

Frank A. Hancock, United States Army, World War I

After returning from the war, my grandfather bought the 160 acre farm near Crossett in 1922. He had, as my aunt describes in her book, "the inborn ability to make things grow and prosper, as well as the absolute joy he derived from plowing the ground and seeing his crops in their wonderful green luster." She points out that the generations of farming men before him had all likewise had land near a river, thus providing the most fertile soil available in whichever region of the South they lived—despite the constant threat of treacherous (and sometimes disastrous) flooding. (Mark Twain describes in *Life on the Mississippi* floating over the eerie remains of an entire Arkansas community that had been completely inundated by a notorious flood.) When asked why he settled on such difficult and precarious terrain, my grandfather explained that here he had "good bottom land, the best for farming." (During Prohibition he apparently also made a bit of bootleg moonshine on the side.)

In 1923 he married my grandmother Doris Katherine Noble, whose paternal grandfather Mark Noble had likewise fought for

Mark Noble, Second Arkansas Cavalry
Photo Courtesy of Barbara Thurmond

the Confederacy before moving to Ashley County—and whose own grandfather was in turn a Revolutionary War soldier from North Carolina. Mark's wife Sarah Brewer's lineage would provide me with my fascinating discovery years later in Oxford (see pp. 218-219). Her maternal grandfather, Captain John Francis Gomellon, was a steamboat captain who transported goods and passengers by boat between New Orleans and Monroe, Louisiana upon his steamship *Belle D'Arbonne* (see p. 33).

References

Title Page
Elliot, T. S. *Four Quartets*. Boston: Harcourt, 1943.

Part I: Rites of Passage
Larkin, Philip. "This Be The Verse." First published in *New Humanist*, 1971.

1 Beginnings
Angelou, Maya. *I Know Why The Caged Bird Sings*. New York: Random, 1969.
Keats, John. "To Autumn." First published 1819.
Shakespeare, William. *As You Like It*, 2.7.142-43.
Switzer, Barry. *Bootlegger's Boy*. Morrow, 1990.

2 *La Petite Roche*
Twain, Mark. *The Innocents Abroad*. New York: Harper & Brothers, 1869.

3 Innocence Lost
Cash, Jon David. *Before They Were Cardinals: Major League Baseball In Nineteenth-Century St. Louis*. Columbia: U of Missouri P 2002.
Shakespeare, William. *As You Like It*, 2.7.144-46.

4 Poetry & Music
Arkansas Online, June 2006.
Shakespeare, William. *Julius Caesar*, 4.2.270-76.
Thoreau, Henry David. *Walden*. Boston: Tickner and Fields, 1865.
Wain, John. *Sprightly Running*. New York: St. Martin's, 1963.

Part II: Spires And Aspirations

7 Big D
Ginsberg, Allen. "Howl." *Howl and other Poems*. San Francisco: City Lights, 1956.

8 From Russia With Love
Chekov, Anton. "Concerning Love." Trans. Ronald Hingley. Oxford: Oxford UP, 1990.

9 City of Dreaming Spires
Arnold, Matthew. "Thyrsis." First published 1866.

10 An Unearthly Encounter
Blake, William. *The Marriage of Heaven and Hell*. Oxford: Oxford UP, 1975.
Campbell, Joseph. *The Inner Reaches of Outer Space*. Novato, CA: New World Library, 2002.

Chuang-tzu. *Three Ways of Thought in Ancient China.* Trans. Arthur Waley. New York: Macmillan 1939.

Einstein, Albert. *Cosmic Religion: With Other Opinions and Aphorisms.* New York: Covici-Friede, 1931.

Hawking, Stephen. *Black Holes and Baby Universes and Other Essays.* New York: Bantam, 1994.

Hitchens, Christopher quoting Sir Martin Rees. *The Atlantic,* January/February 2010.

Tao Te Ching. Trans. Dwight Goddard. Seattle: CreateSpace, 2009.

11 Interlude
Hemingway, Ernest. *The Sun Also Rises.* New York: Scribner's, 1926.
Shakespeare, William. *Othello,* 3.3.169-71.

12 An Inaugural and a Commencement
International Herald Tribune, December 16, 1992.

Part III: Full Circle
Dickinson, Emily. Poem #1741, "That it will never come again."
Rilke, Rainer Maria. *Letters to a Young Poet.* New York: W.W. Norton, 1993.

13 Homeward Bound
Shakespeare, William. *As You Like It,* 2.4.12-14.

15 Atonement
Chaucer, Geoffrey. *The General Prologue* from *The Canterbury Tales.*
Frost, Robert. "Stopping by Woods on a Snowy Evening." First published 1923.
Shakespeare, William. Sonnet 18.

16 A Royal Celebration
Darwall-Smith, Robin. *A History of University College, Oxford.* Oxford: Oxford UP, 2008.

Afterward: Coming Home
Campbell, Joseph. *The Hero's Journey* (documentary video). PublicMedia Video, 1989.
Ecclesiastes. King James Version of the Holy Bible.
Nin, Anaïs. *The Diary of Anaïs Nin, Vol. 5.* New York: Marine, 1975.

Appendix: Origins
Turlington, Blanche Hancock. *Cow Pens and Plantations: Backtracking a Southern Hancock Family.* 2008.

* 9 7 8 0 9 8 2 8 1 8 4 1 1 *